Compu-M.E.C.H.

Mechanically Engineered and Computerized Hero ®

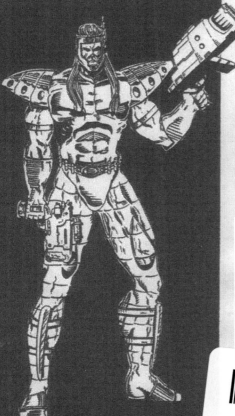

TM

MONOLITH COMICS PRESENTS
Compu-M.E.C.H. ®

Welcome to the exciting adventures of Dr. Green, the inventor of the Compu-M.E.C.H. Program and Tommy Chase, the controller of the M.E.C.H. unit.

They unite there skills to combat the evils in the world with truth and justice. They are our protecters.

Together They are:
The Compu-M.E.C.H. Program!

SPECIAL THANKS TO:

My loving wife, Melissa Jane Riddle, Marian Hillsdon, plus all the people who believed in me and gave me a chance.

Technical Production:

...GENE
...ve Design
...eensboro, NC 27403
...132

D1501875

ALSO SPECIAL THANKS TO MY GOOD FRIEND AND MENTOR JOE KUBERT FOR HIS GUIDANCE IN MY LONG JOURNEY!

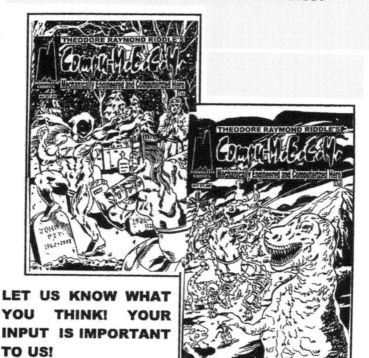

2

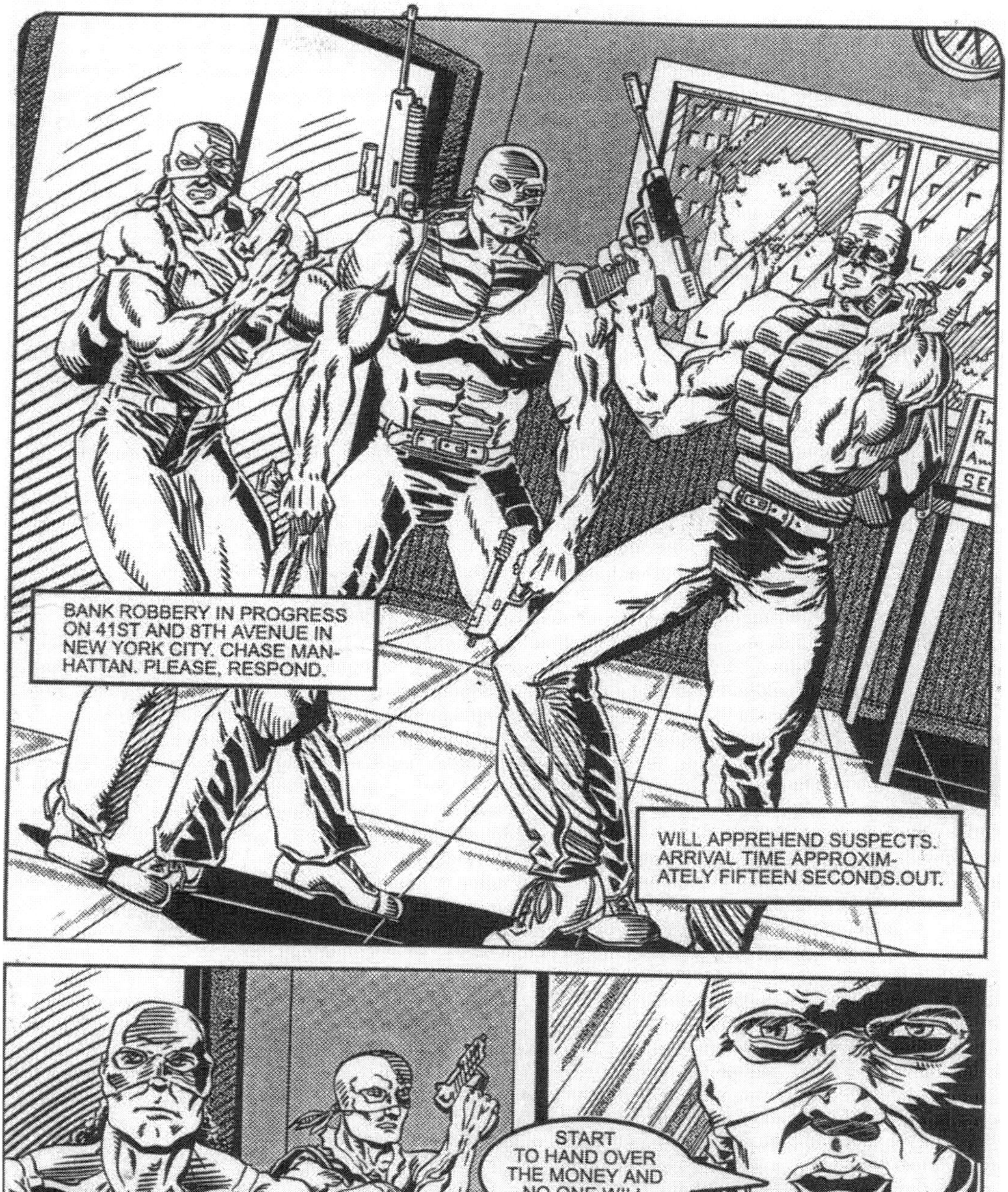
BANK ROBBERY IN PROGRESS ON 41ST AND 8TH AVENUE IN NEW YORK CITY. CHASE MAN-HATTAN. PLEASE, RESPOND.
WILL APPREHEND SUSPECTS. ARRIVAL TIME APPROXIM-ATELY FIFTEEN SECONDS.OUT.
START TO HAND OVER THE MONEY AND NO ONE WILL DIE!

Compu-M.E.C.H. Volume 2, Issue 1. 2009 First Printing. Monolith Comics Office of Publication: 78 Possum Hollow Drive, Hackettstown, NJ 07840-1617. E-mail Address: monolithcomics@earthlink.net. Web site: monolithcomics.com. $12.95. Compu-M.E.C.H. The Mechanically Engineered and Computerized Hero is a Registered. Trademark and C. Copyright Theodore Raymond Riddle. Any similarities to persons living or dead is purely coincidental. This is a work of fiction and any events which occur are also fictitious. Some of the stories use past historical events and persons. They are then changed into a work of fiction to make for a dramatic fictional story. With the exception of artwork used for review purposes, none of this publication may be used without the permission of Theodore Raymond Riddle or Monolith Comics. Printed in USA.

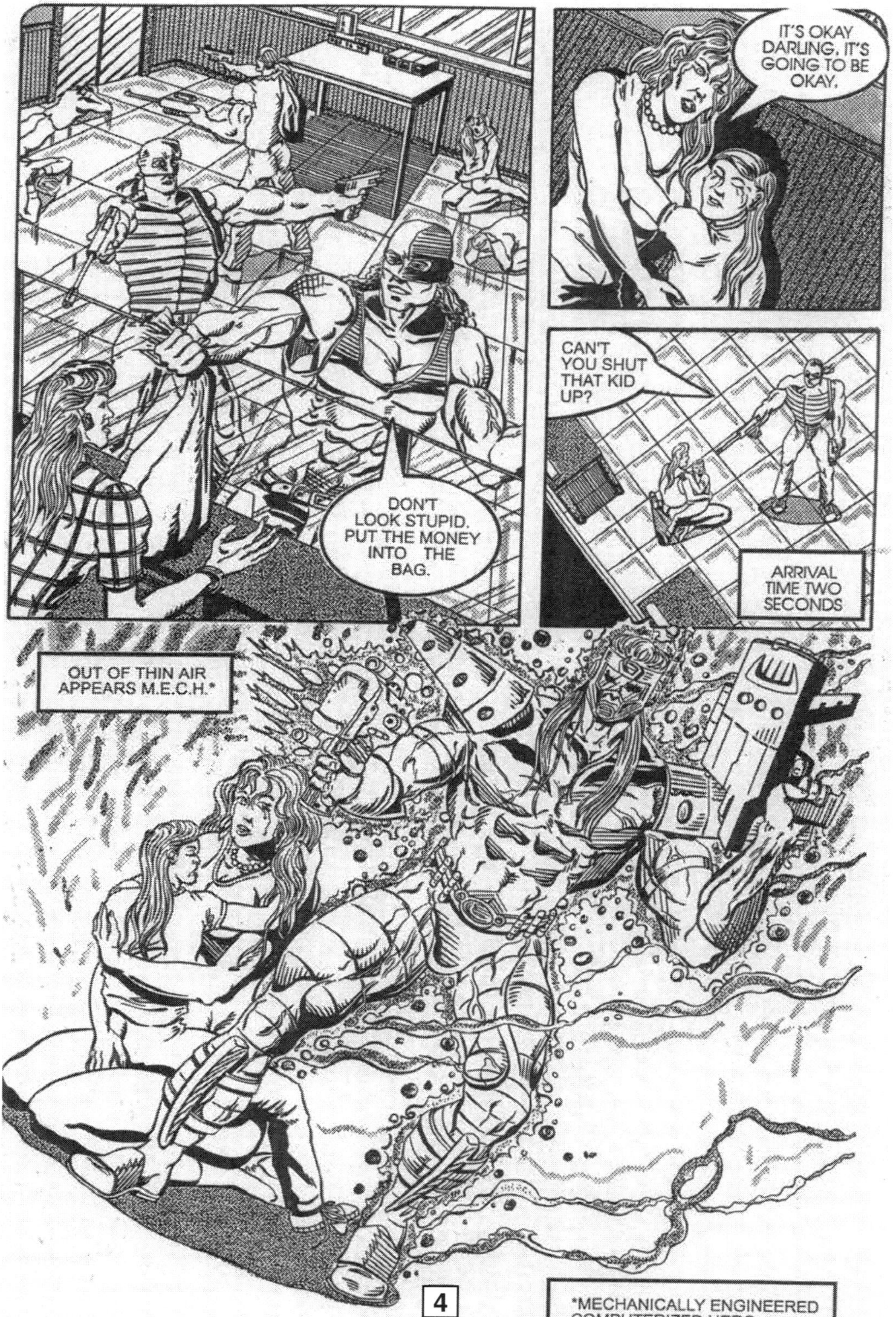
DON'T LOOK STUPID. PUT THE MONEY INTO THE BAG.
IT'S OKAY DARLING, IT'S GOING TO BE OKAY.
CAN'T YOU SHUT THAT KID UP?
ARRIVAL TIME TWO SECONDS
OUT OF THIN AIR APPEARS M.E.C.H.*
*MECHANICALLY ENGINEERED COMPUTERIZED HERO.

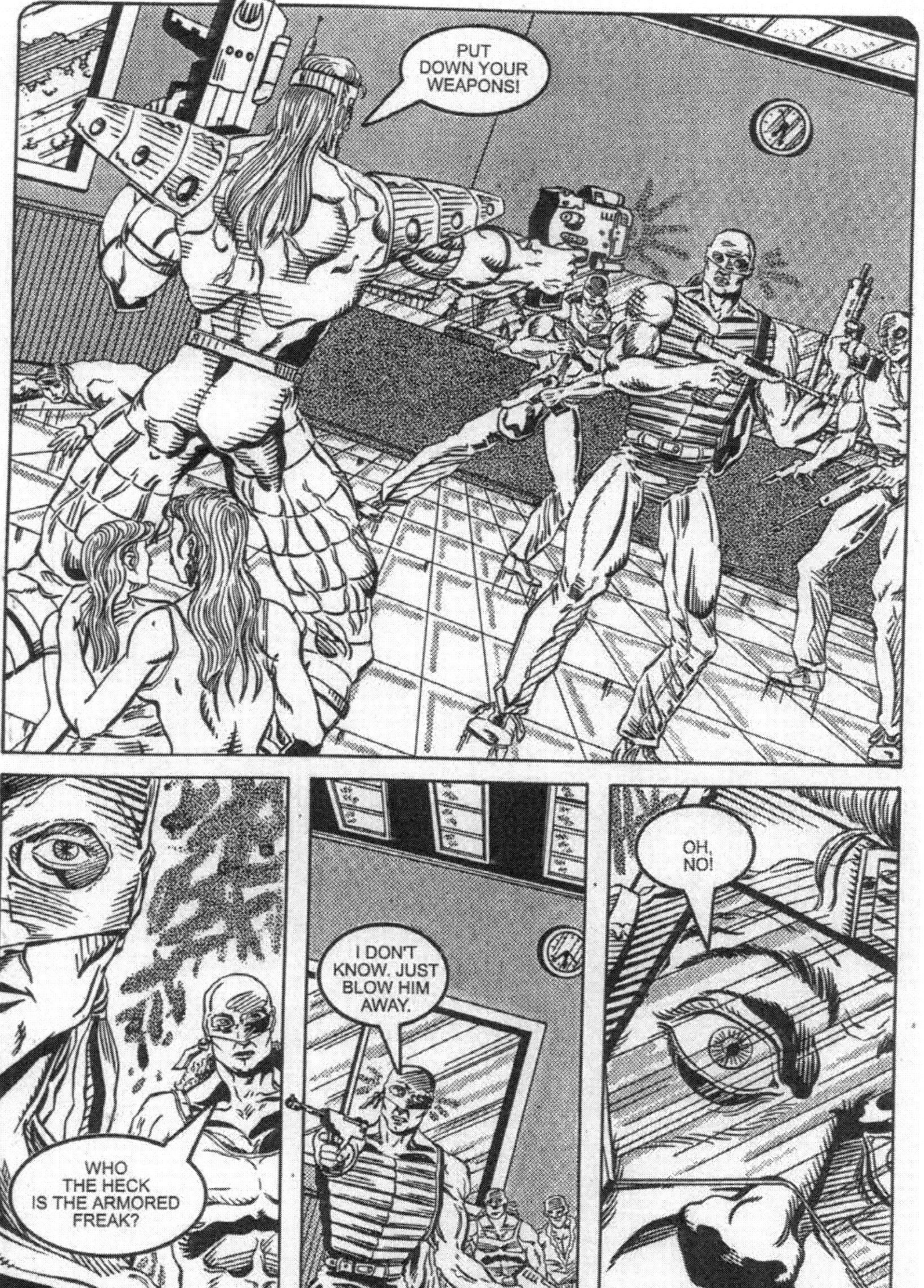
PUT DOWN YOUR WEAPONS!
WHO THE HECK IS THE ARMORED FREAK?
I DON'T KNOW. JUST BLOW HIM AWAY.
OH, NO!

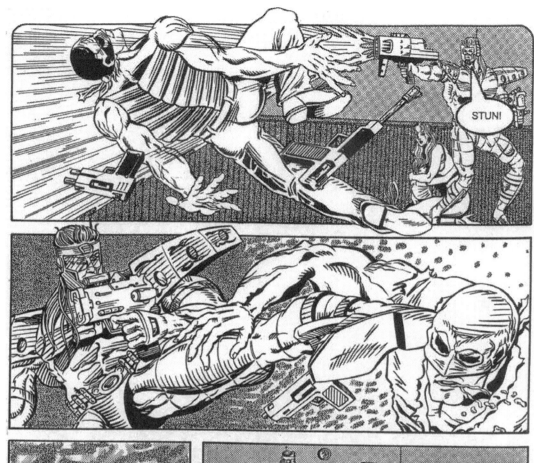

STUN!

NOW IT'S ONLY YOU AND ME!

SORRY BUD, BUT YOU'VE GOT THE CROWD TO WORRY ABOUT...

...AND, THIS ONES GOING TO DIE!

6

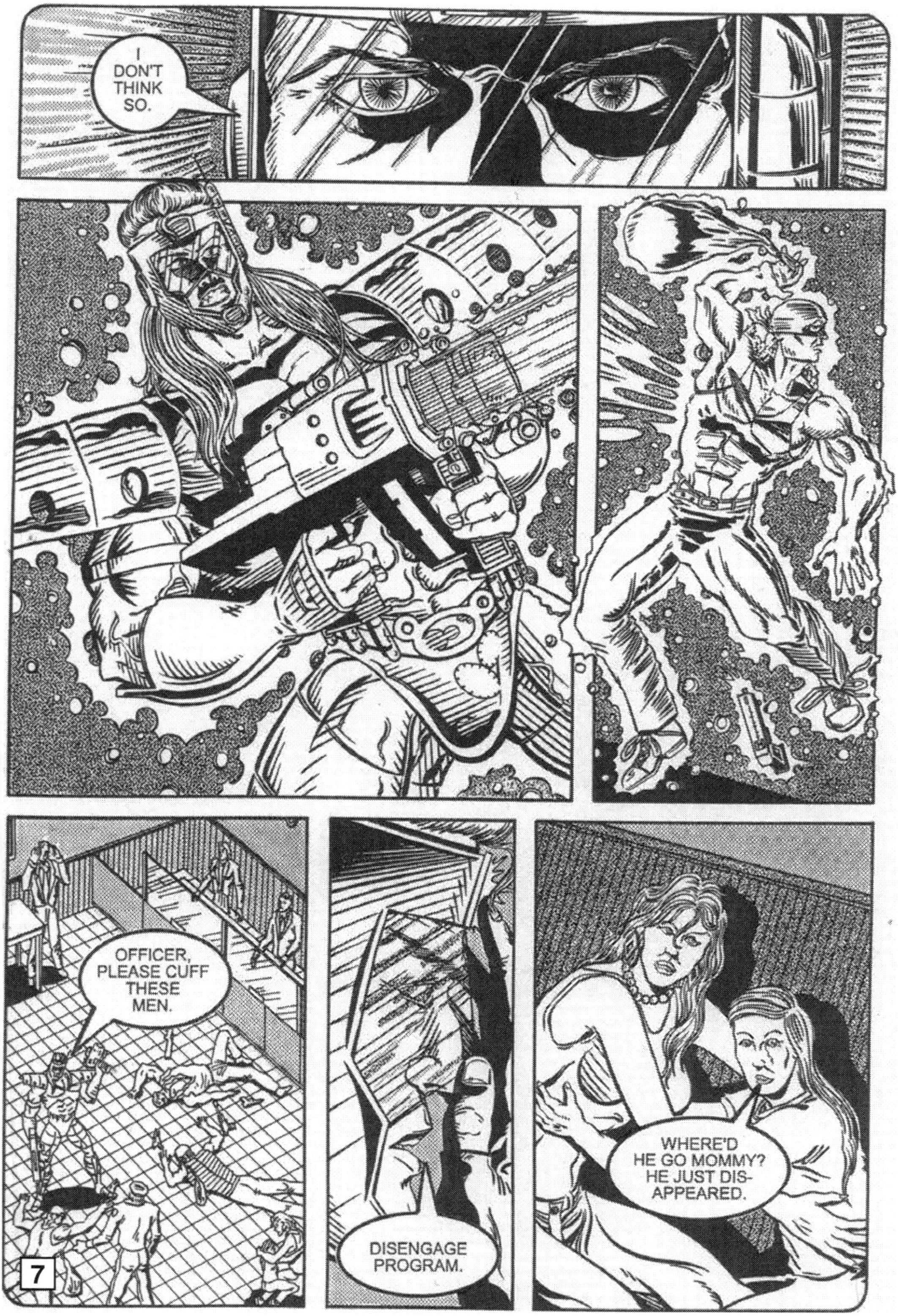
I DON'T THINK SO.
OFFICER, PLEASE CUFF THESE MEN.
DISENGAGE PROGRAM.
WHERE'D HE GO MOMMY? HE JUST DIS-APPEARED.
7

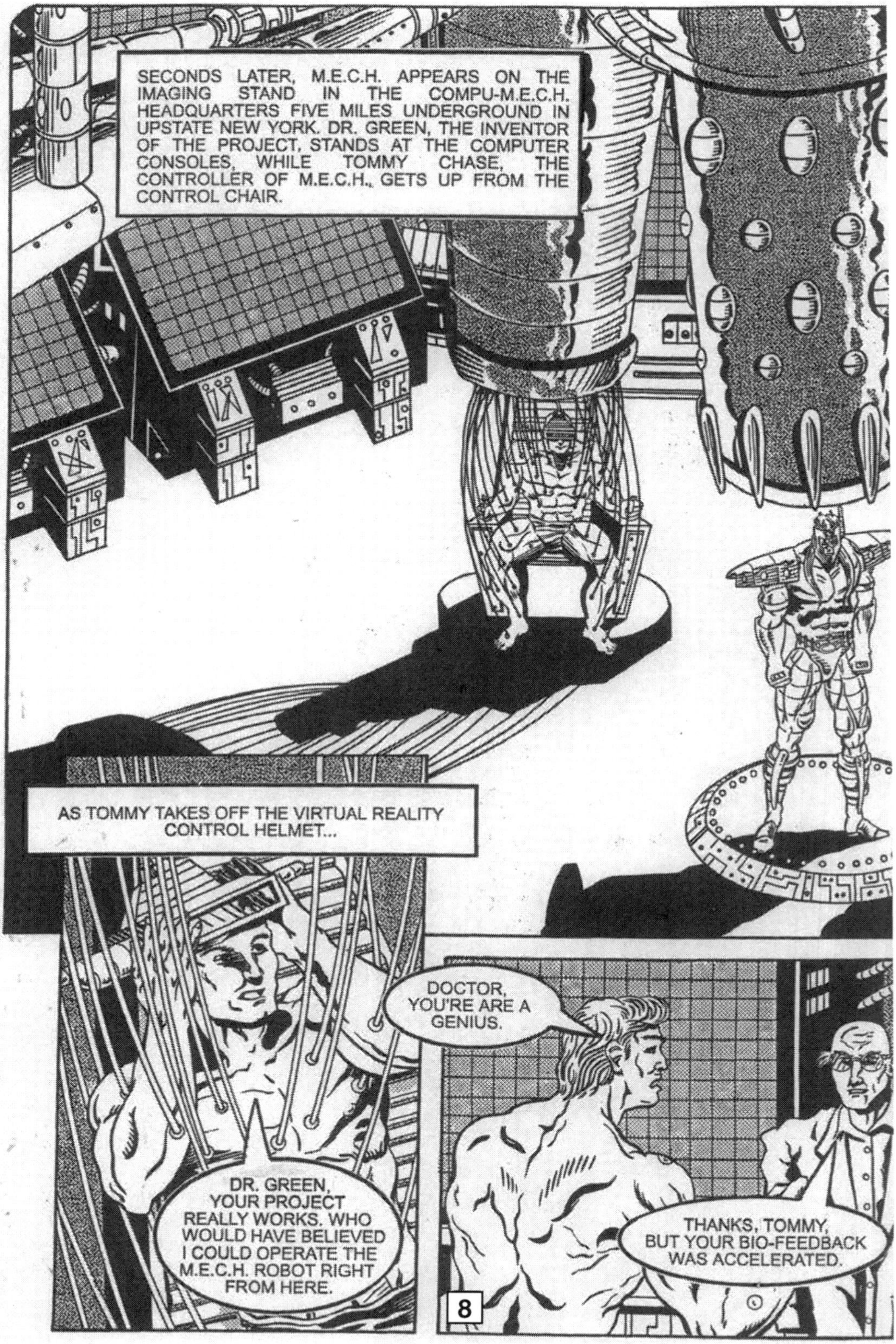
SECONDS LATER, M.E.C.H. APPEARS ON THE IMAGING STAND IN THE COMPU-M.E.C.H. HEADQUARTERS FIVE MILES UNDERGROUND IN UPSTATE NEW YORK. DR. GREEN, THE INVENTOR OF THE PROJECT, STANDS AT THE COMPUTER CONSOLES, WHILE TOMMY CHASE, THE CONTROLLER OF M.E.C.H., GETS UP FROM THE CONTROL CHAIR.
AS TOMMY TAKES OFF THE VIRTUAL REALITY CONTROL HELMET...
DR. GREEN, YOUR PROJECT REALLY WORKS. WHO WOULD HAVE BELIEVED I COULD OPERATE THE M.E.C.H. ROBOT RIGHT FROM HERE.
DOCTOR, YOU'RE ARE A GENIUS.
THANKS, TOMMY, BUT YOUR BIO-FEEDBACK WAS ACCELERATED.

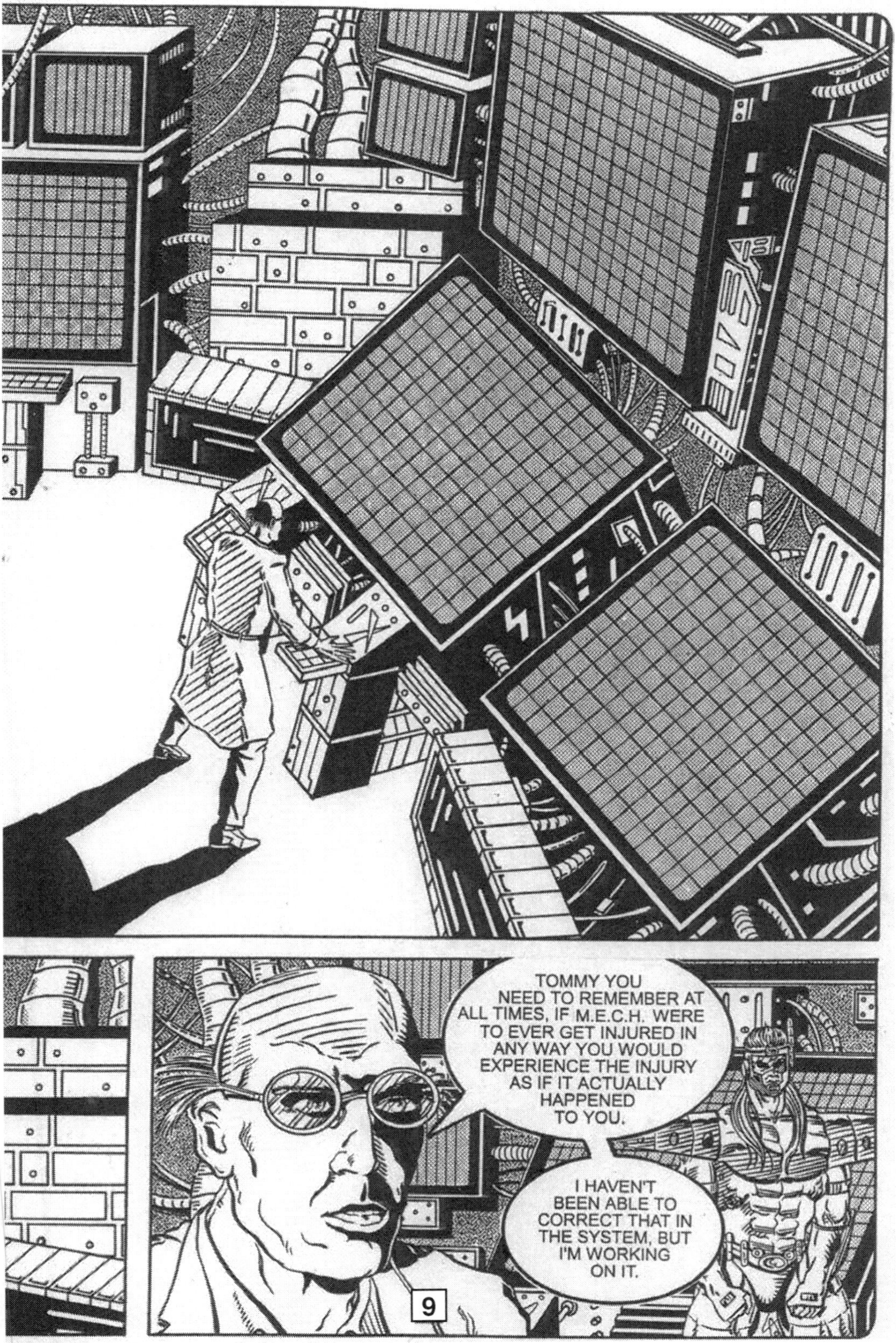
TOMMY YOU NEED TO REMEMBER AT ALL TIMES, IF M.E.C.H. WERE TO EVER GET INJURED IN ANY WAY YOU WOULD EXPERIENCE THE INJURY AS IF IT ACTUALLY HAPPENED TO YOU.
I HAVEN'T BEEN ABLE TO CORRECT THAT IN THE SYSTEM, BUT I'M WORKING ON IT.

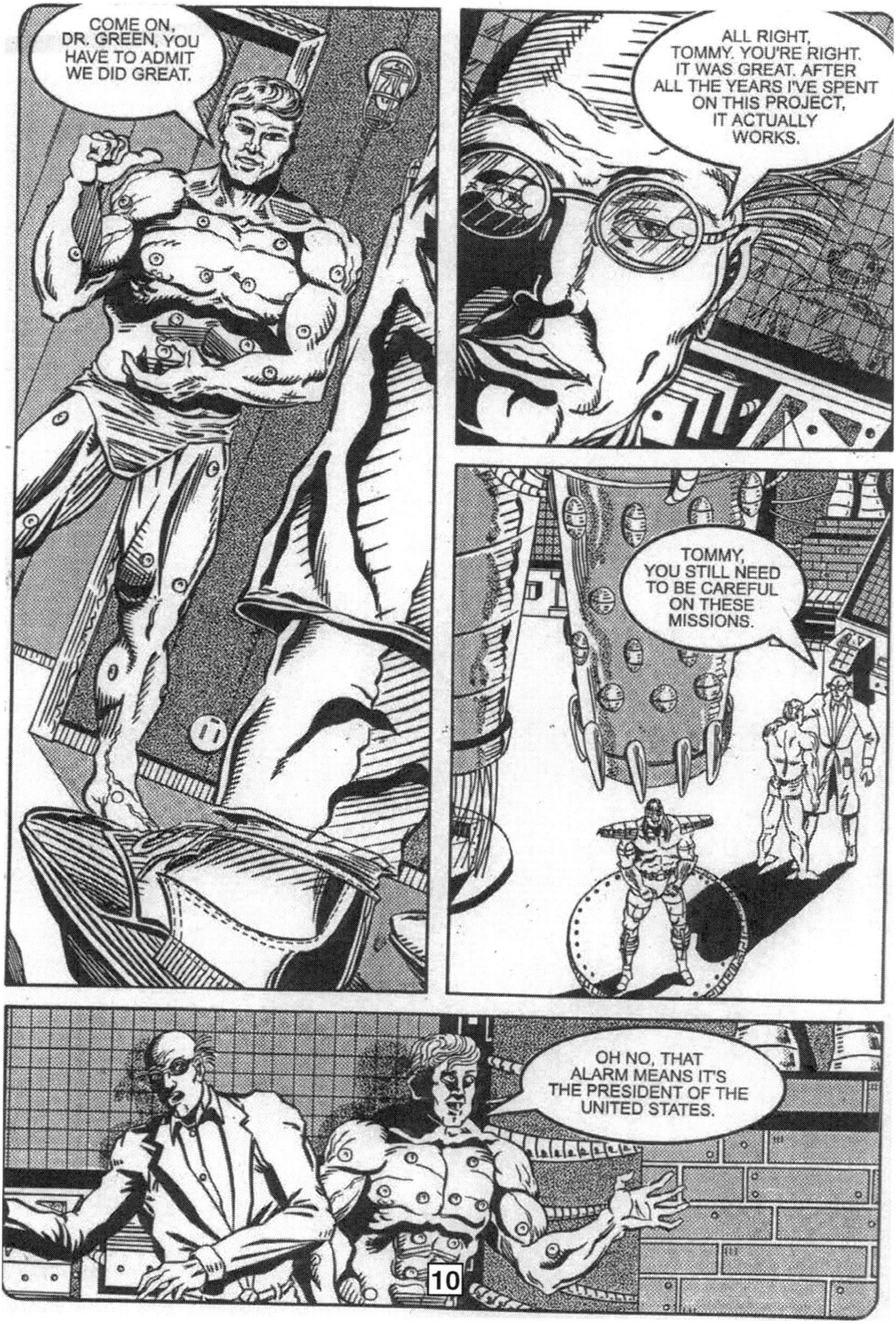
COME ON, DR. GREEN, YOU HAVE TO ADMIT WE DID GREAT.
ALL RIGHT, TOMMY. YOU'RE RIGHT. IT WAS GREAT. AFTER ALL THE YEARS I'VE SPENT ON THIS PROJECT, IT ACTUALLY WORKS.
TOMMY, YOU STILL NEED TO BE CAREFUL ON THESE MISSIONS.
OH NO, THAT ALARM MEANS IT'S THE PRESIDENT OF THE UNITED STATES.

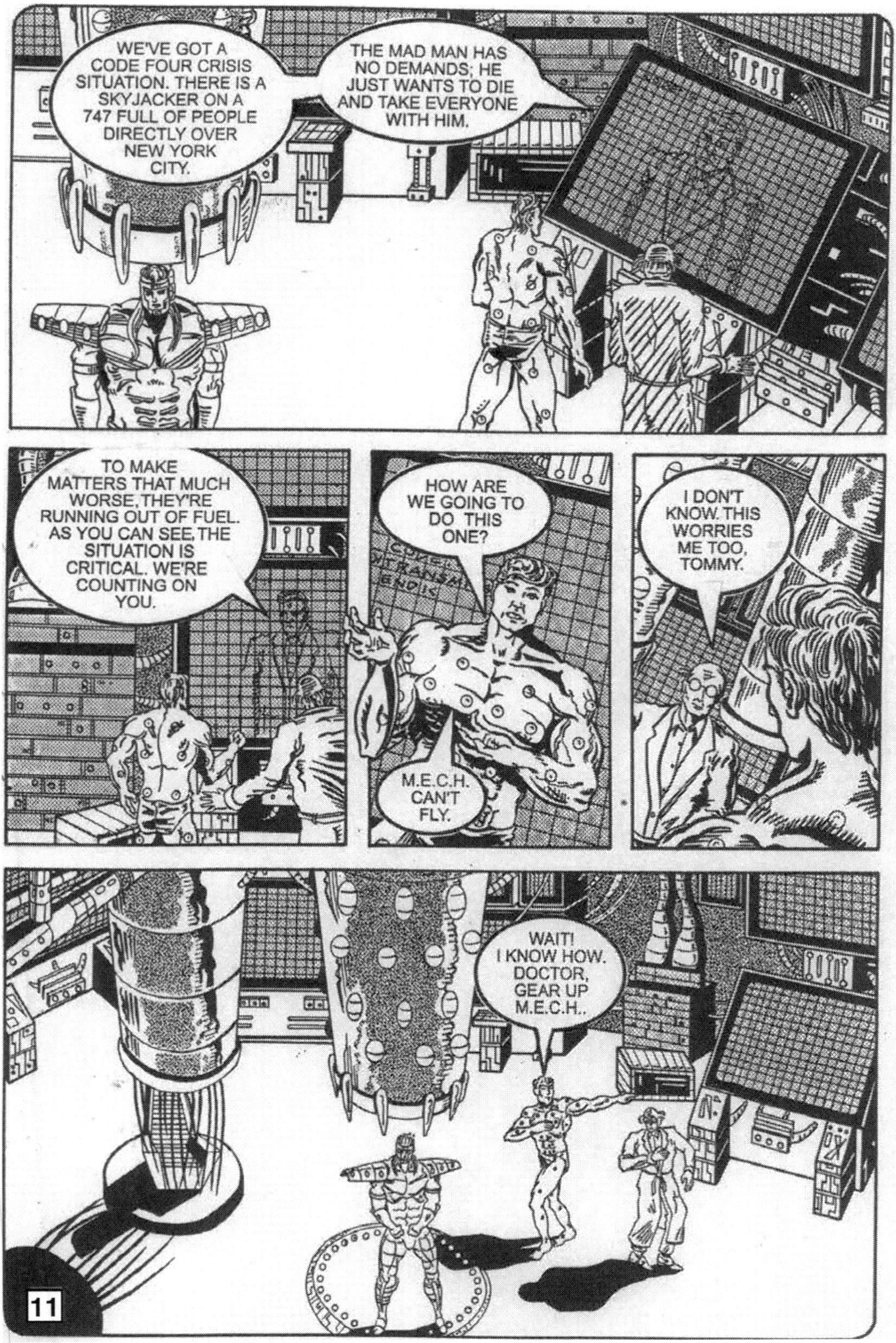
WE'VE GOT A CODE FOUR CRISIS SITUATION. THERE IS A SKYJACKER ON A 747 FULL OF PEOPLE DIRECTLY OVER NEW YORK CITY.
THE MAD MAN HAS NO DEMANDS; HE JUST WANTS TO DIE AND TAKE EVERYONE WITH HIM.
TO MAKE MATTERS THAT MUCH WORSE,THEY'RE RUNNING OUT OF FUEL. AS YOU CAN SEE,THE SITUATION IS CRITICAL. WE'RE COUNTING ON YOU.
HOW ARE WE GOING TO DO THIS ONE?
M.E.C.H. CAN'T FLY.
I DON'T KNOW. THIS WORRIES ME TOO, TOMMY.
WAIT! I KNOW HOW. DOCTOR, GEAR UP M.E.C.H..

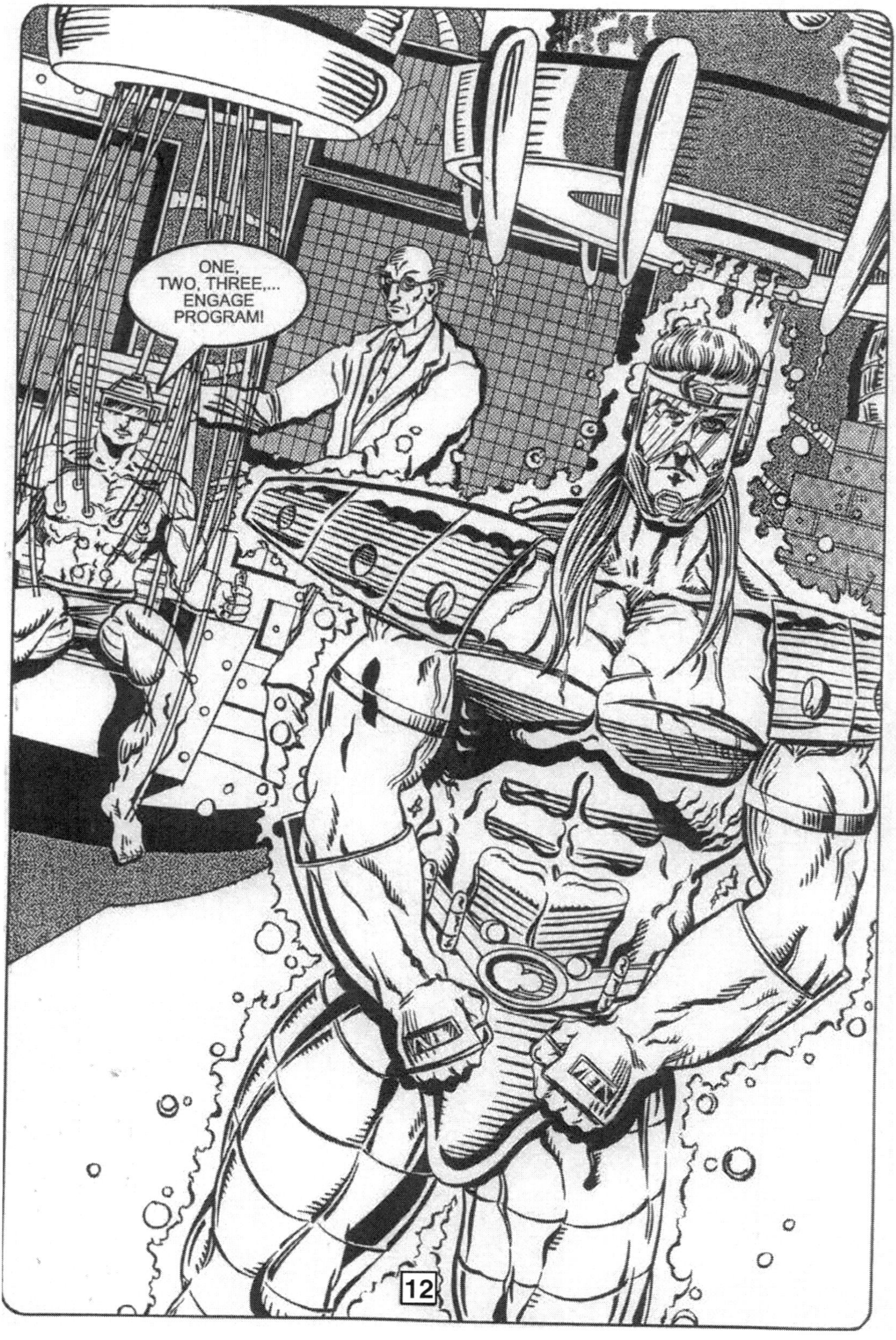
ONE, TWO, THREE,... ENGAGE PROGRAM!

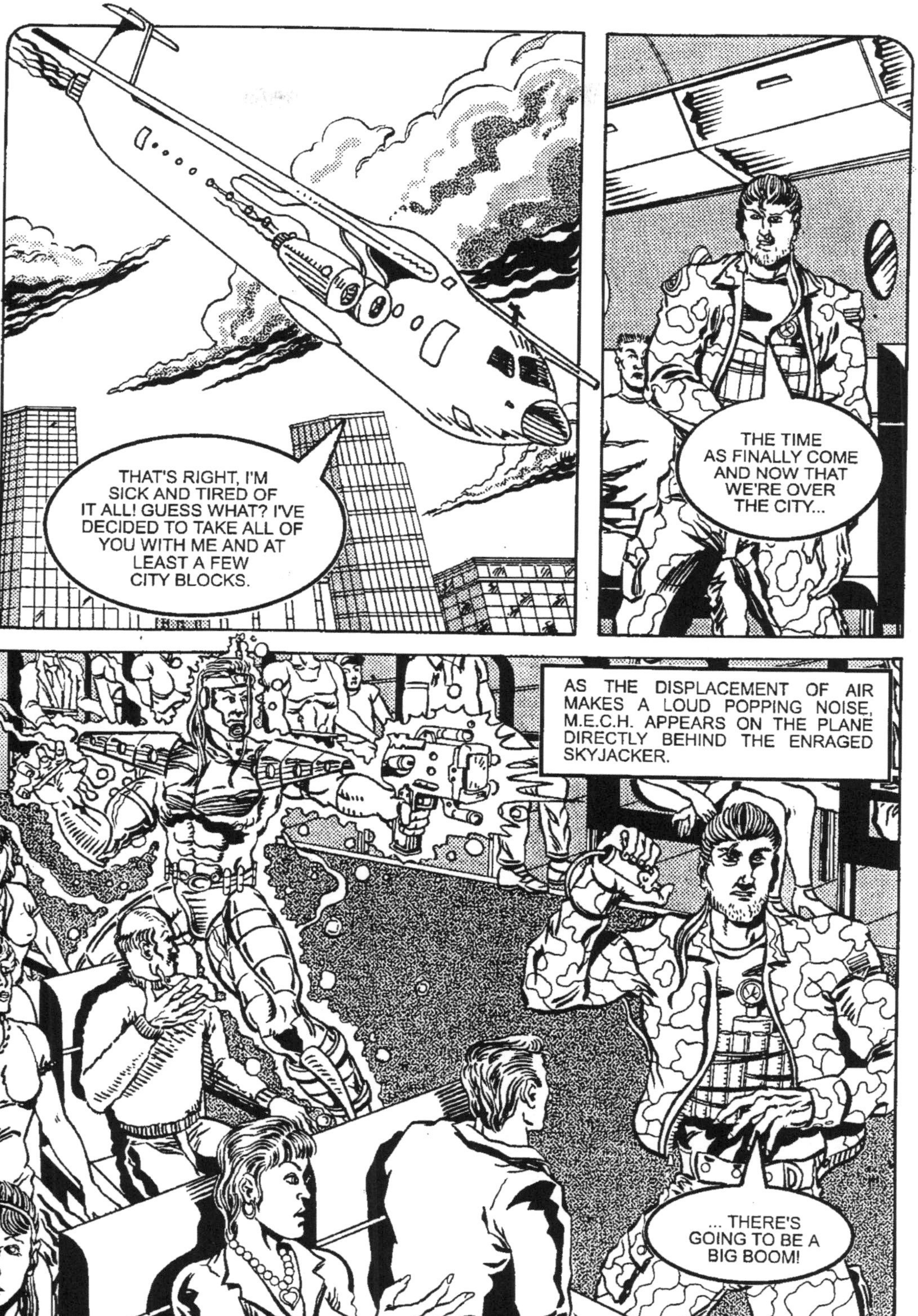
THAT'S RIGHT, I'M SICK AND TIRED OF IT ALL! GUESS WHAT? I'VE DECIDED TO TAKE ALL OF YOU WITH ME AND AT LEAST A FEW CITY BLOCKS.
THE TIME AS FINALLY COME AND NOW THAT WE'RE OVER THE CITY...
AS THE DISPLACEMENT OF AIR MAKES A LOUD POPPING NOISE, M.E.C.H. APPEARS ON THE PLANE DIRECTLY BEHIND THE ENRAGED SKYJACKER.
... THERE'S GOING TO BE A BIG BOOM!

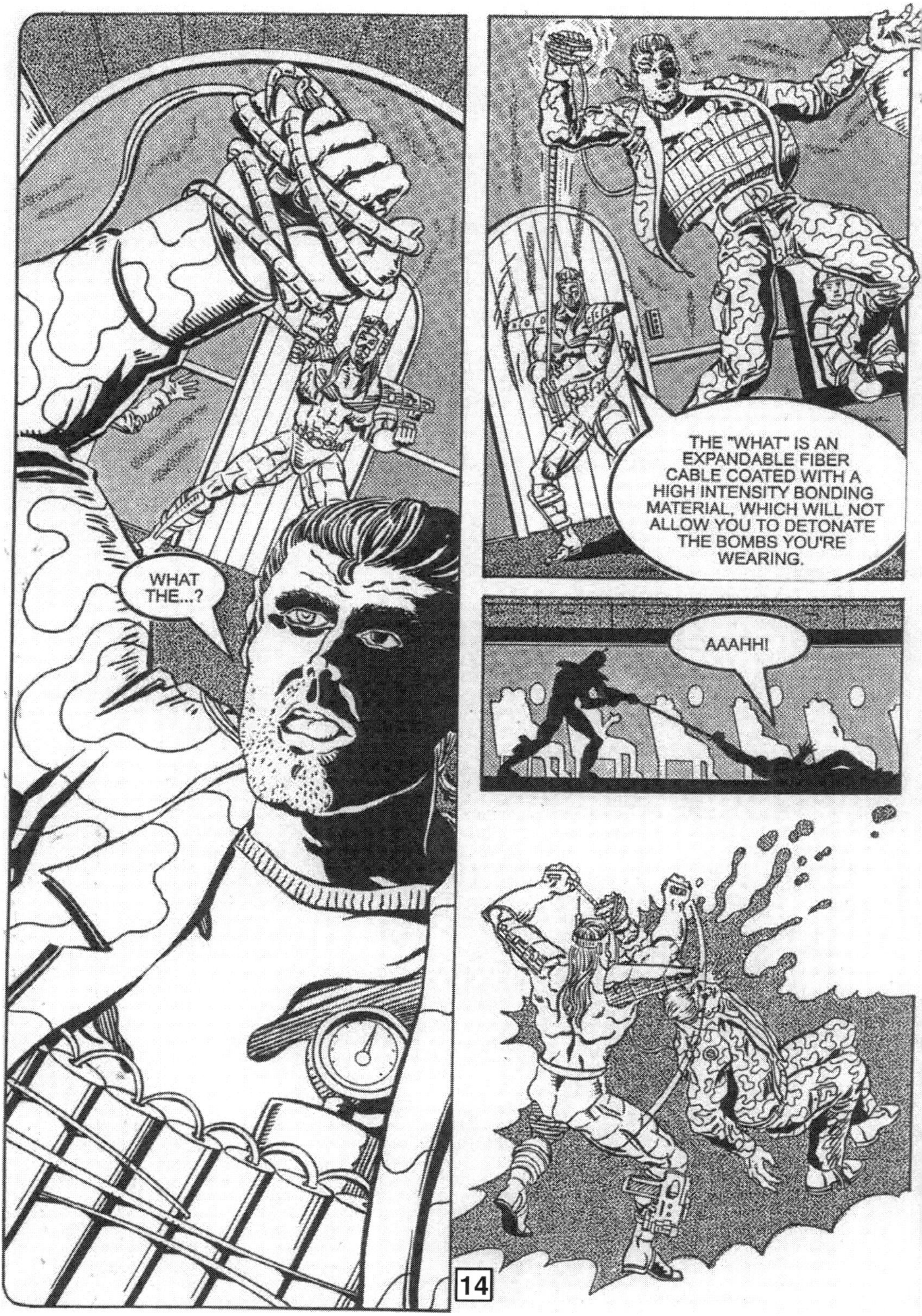
WHAT THE...?
THE "WHAT" IS AN EXPANDABLE FIBER CABLE COATED WITH A HIGH INTENSITY BONDING MATERIAL, WHICH WILL NOT ALLOW YOU TO DETONATE THE BOMBS YOU'RE WEARING.
AAAHH!

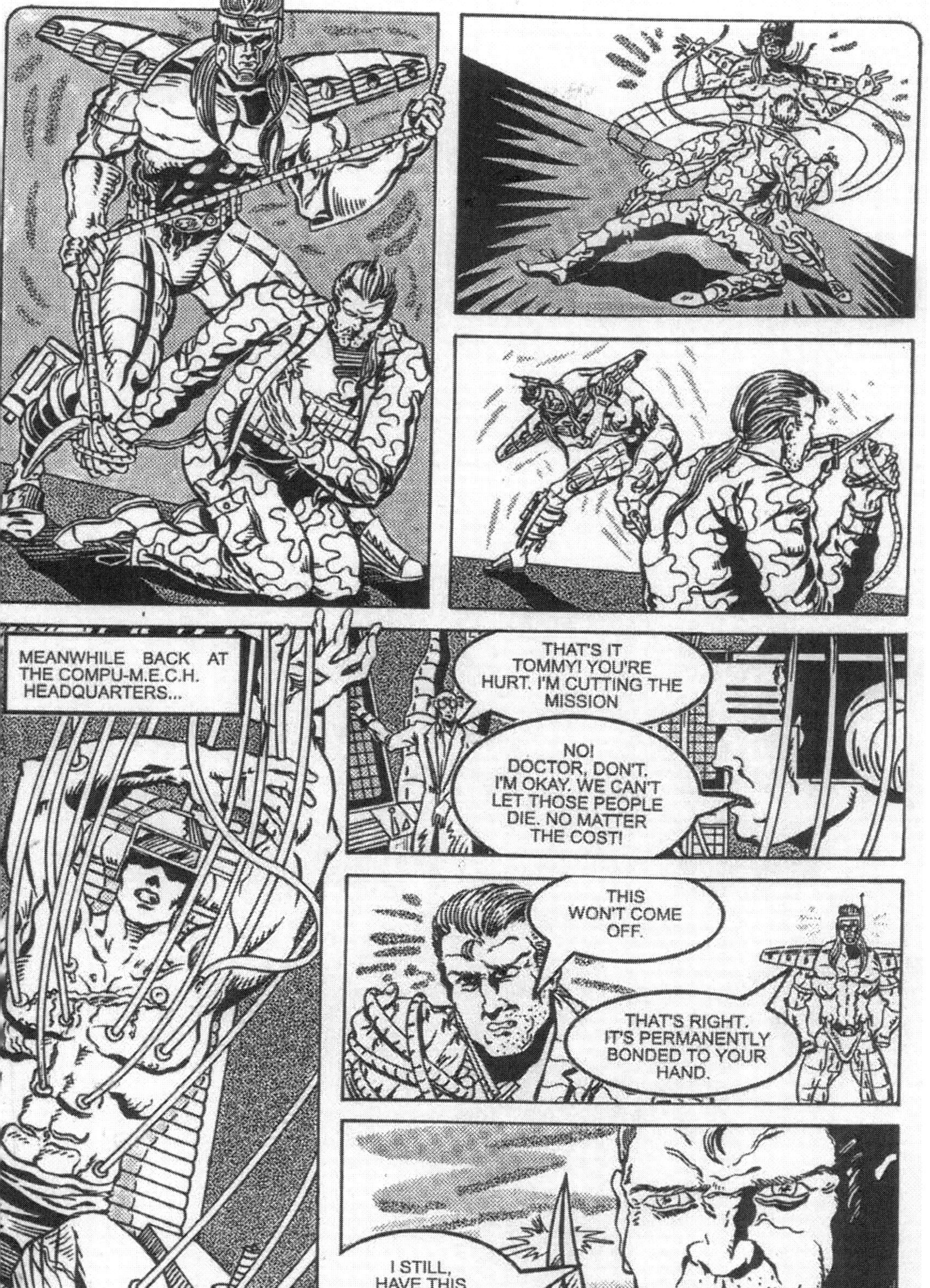

MEANWHILE BACK AT THE COMPU-M.E.C.H. HEADQUARTERS...
THAT'S IT TOMMY! YOU'RE HURT. I'M CUTTING THE MISSION
NO! DOCTOR, DON'T. I'M OKAY. WE CAN'T LET THOSE PEOPLE DIE. NO MATTER THE COST!
THIS WON'T COME OFF.
THAT'S RIGHT. IT'S PERMANENTLY BONDED TO YOUR HAND.
I STILL, HAVE THIS AND I CUT YOU ONCE BEFORE.

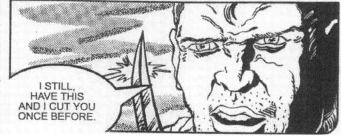

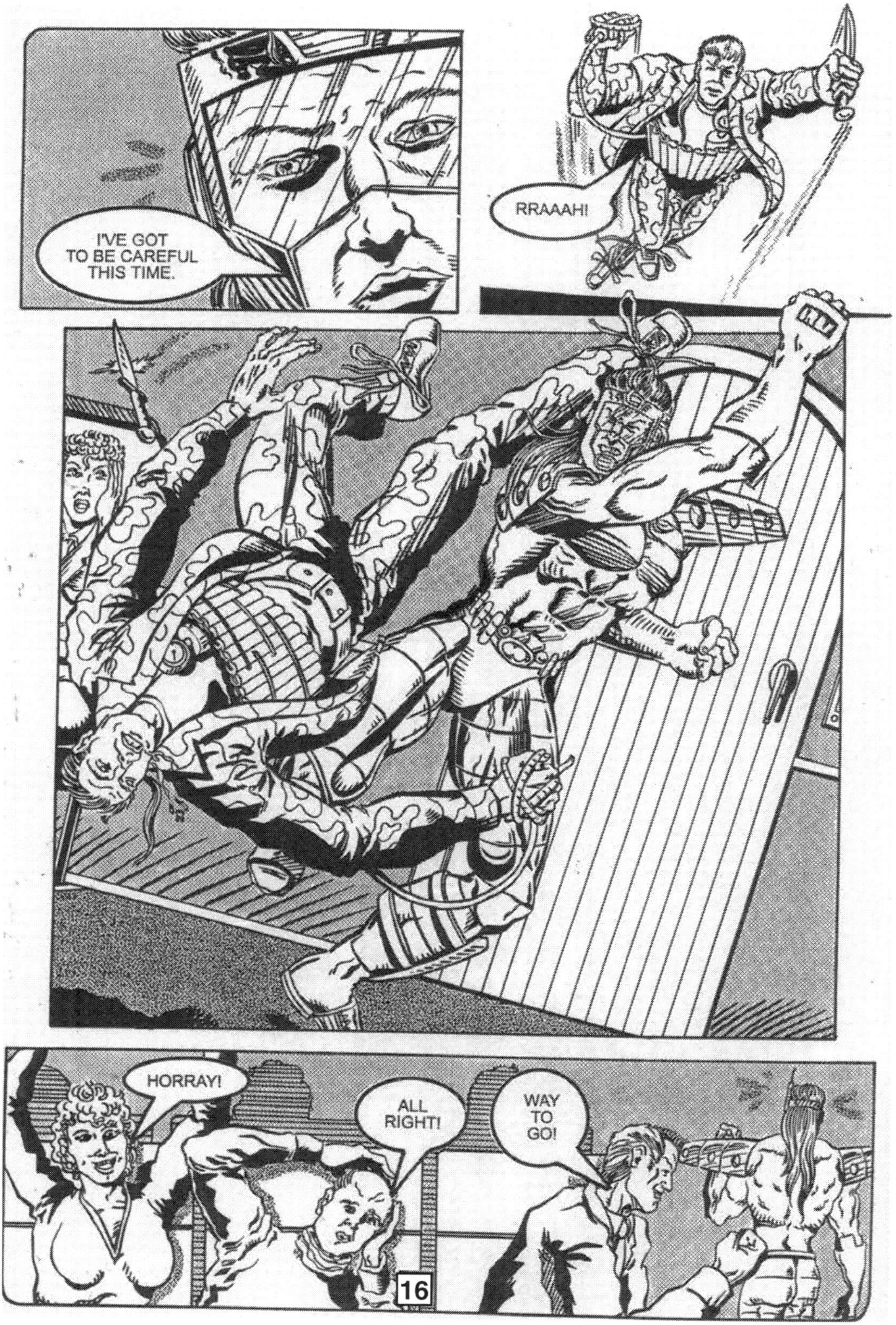
I'VE GOT TO BE CAREFUL THIS TIME.
RRAAAH!
HORRAY!
ALL RIGHT!
WAY TO GO!

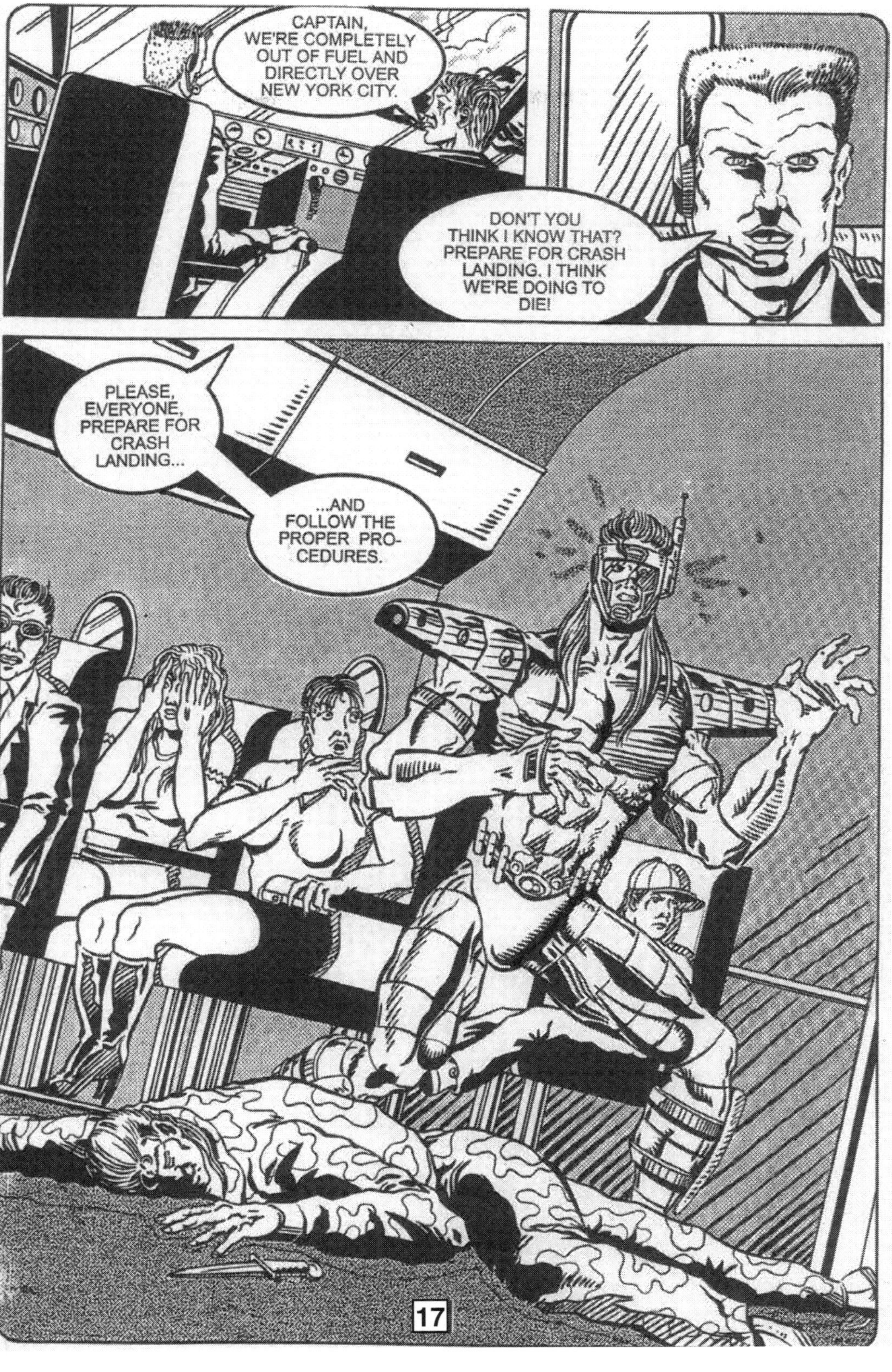
CAPTAIN, WE'RE COMPLETELY OUT OF FUEL AND DIRECTLY OVER NEW YORK CITY.
DON'T YOU THINK I KNOW THAT? PREPARE FOR CRASH LANDING. I THINK WE'RE DOING TO DIE!
PLEASE, EVERYONE, PREPARE FOR CRASH LANDING...
...AND FOLLOW THE PROPER PRO-CEDURES.

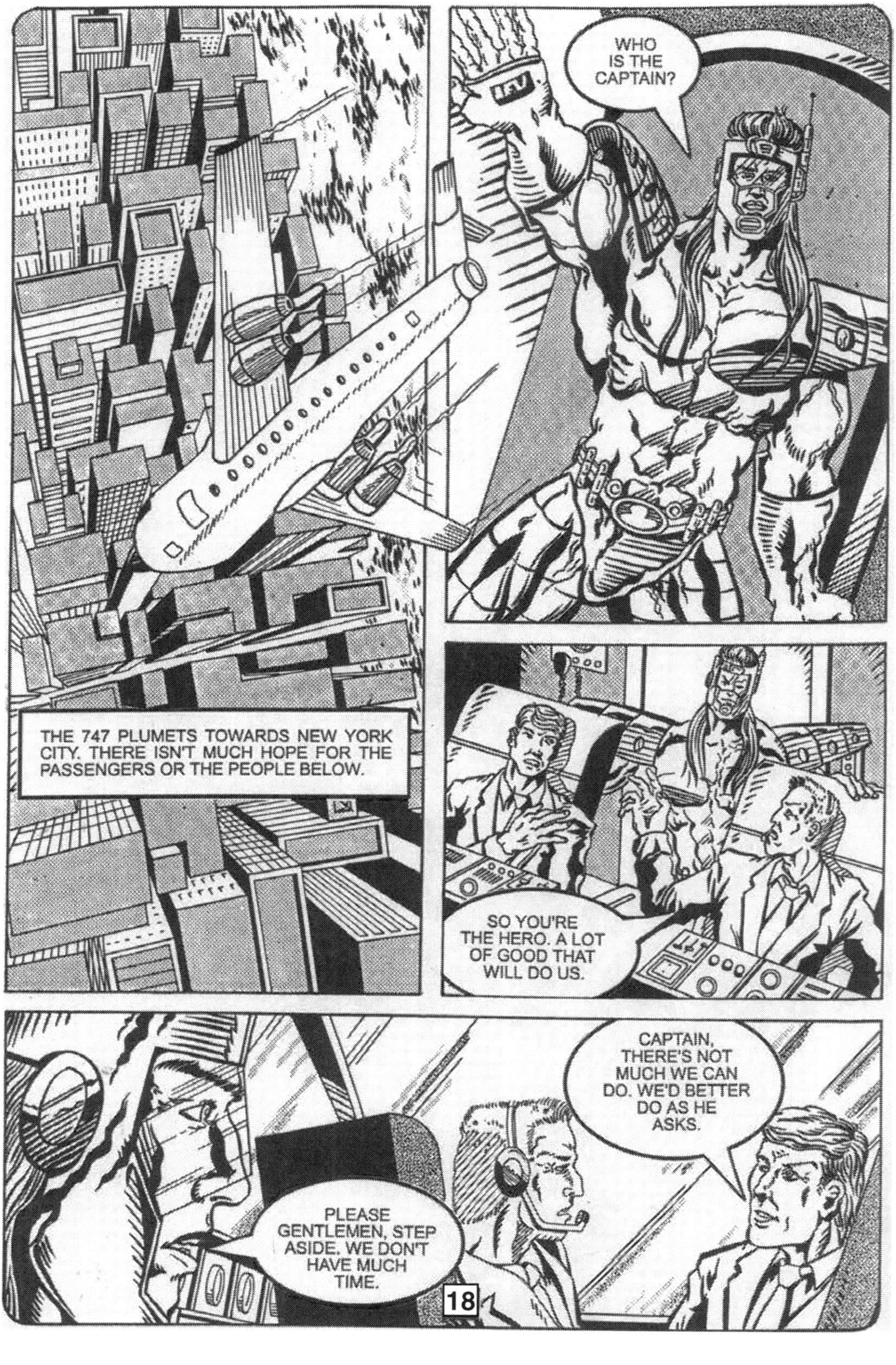
THE 747 PLUMETS TOWARDS NEW YORK CITY. THERE ISN'T MUCH HOPE FOR THE PASSENGERS OR THE PEOPLE BELOW.
WHO IS THE CAPTAIN?
SO YOU'RE THE HERO. A LOT OF GOOD THAT WILL DO US.
PLEASE GENTLEMEN, STEP ASIDE. WE DON'T HAVE MUCH TIME.
CAPTAIN, THERE'S NOT MUCH WE CAN DO. WE'D BETTER DO AS HE ASKS.

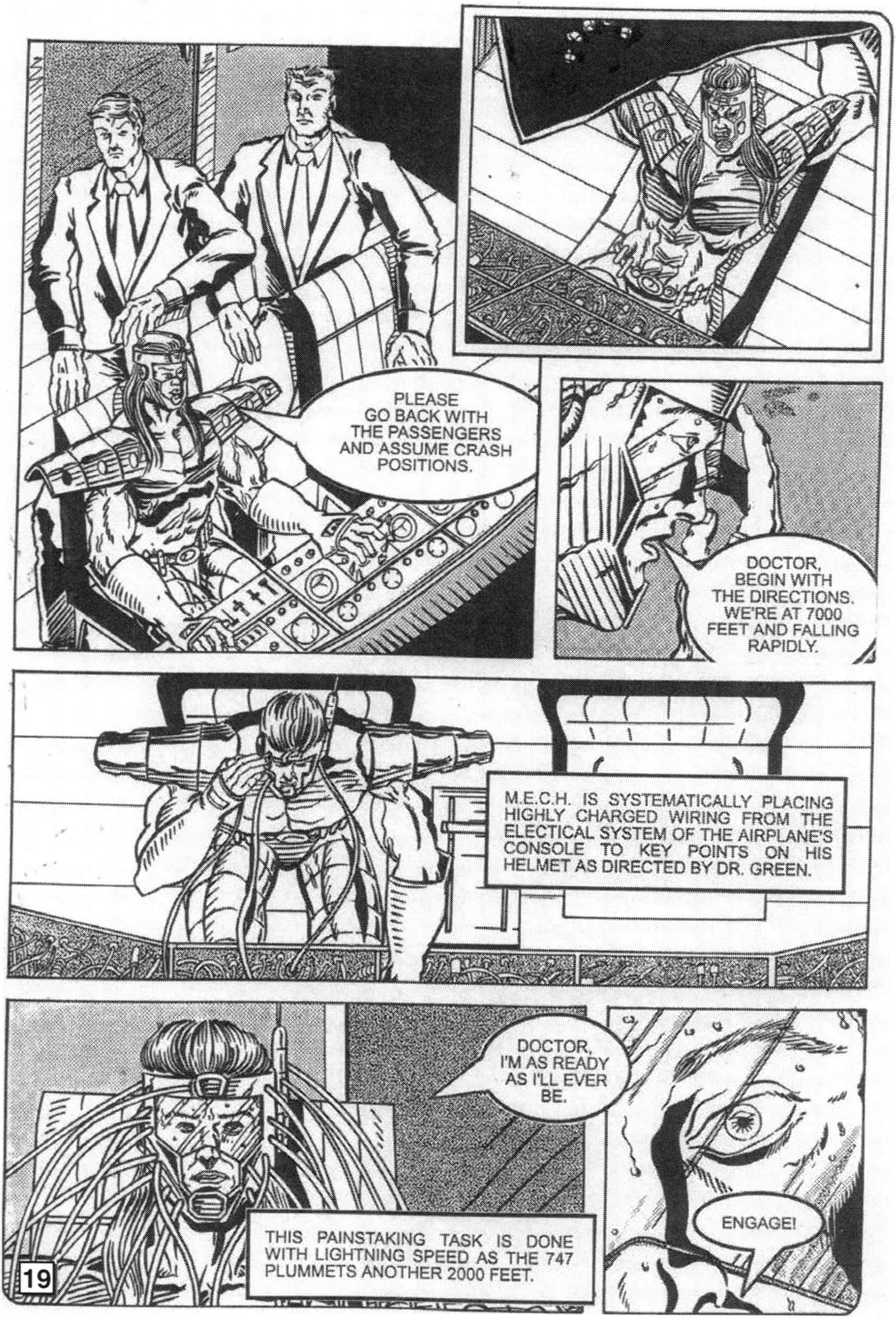
PLEASE GO BACK WITH THE PASSENGERS AND ASSUME CRASH POSITIONS.
DOCTOR, BEGIN WITH THE DIRECTIONS. WE'RE AT 7000 FEET AND FALLING RAPIDLY.
M.E.C.H. IS SYSTEMATICALLY PLACING HIGHLY CHARGED WIRING FROM THE ELECTICAL SYSTEM OF THE AIRPLANE'S CONSOLE TO KEY POINTS ON HIS HELMET AS DIRECTED BY DR. GREEN.
DOCTOR, I'M AS READY AS I'LL EVER BE.
THIS PAINSTAKING TASK IS DONE WITH LIGHTNING SPEED AS THE 747 PLUMMETS ANOTHER 2000 FEET.
ENGAGE!

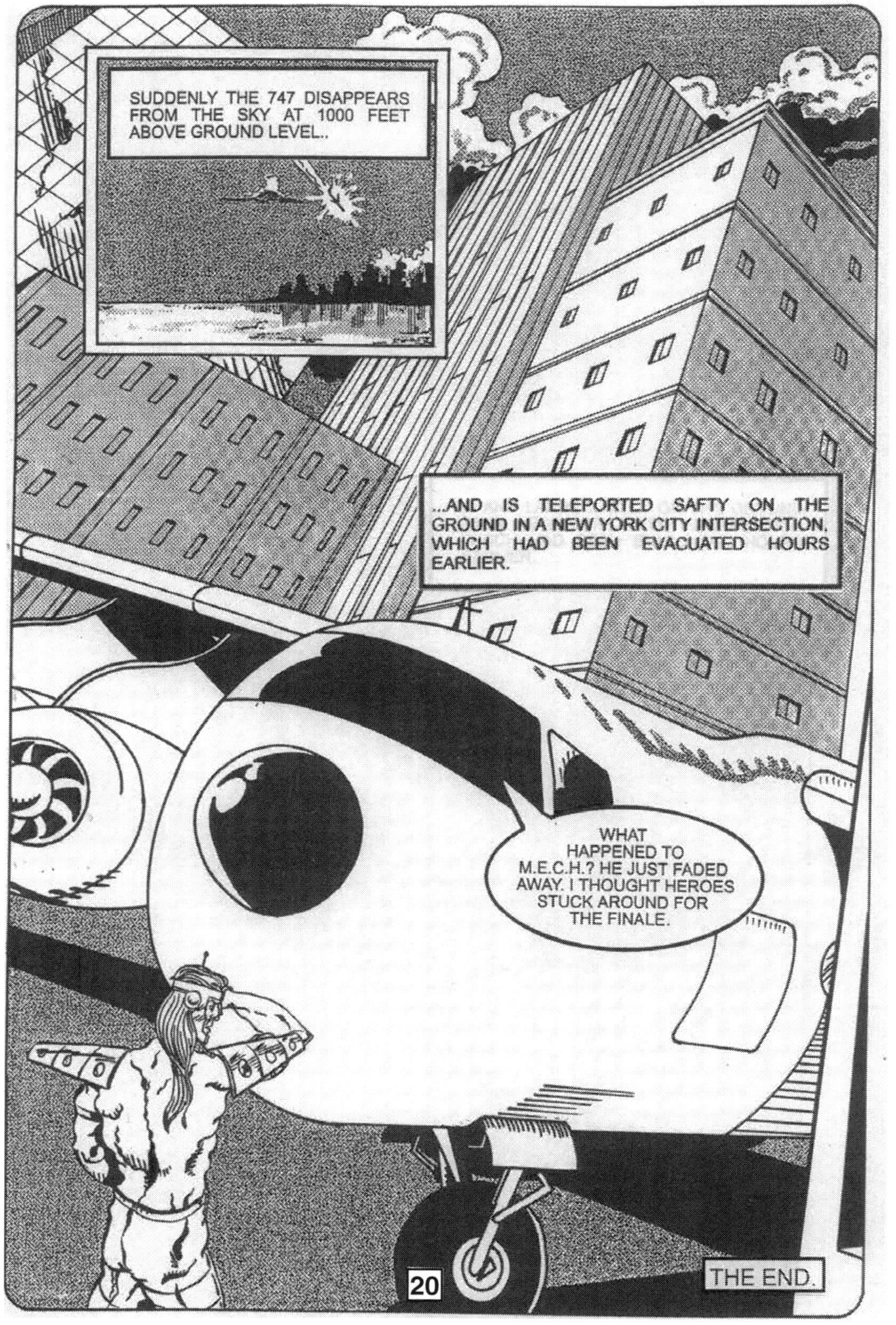
SUDDENLY THE 747 DISAPPEARS FROM THE SKY AT 1000 FEET ABOVE GROUND LEVEL..
...AND IS TELEPORTED SAFTY ON THE GROUND IN A NEW YORK CITY INTERSECTION, WHICH HAD BEEN EVACUATED HOURS EARLIER.
WHAT HAPPENED TO M.E.C.H.? HE JUST FADED AWAY. I THOUGHT HEROES STUCK AROUND FOR THE FINALE.
THE END.

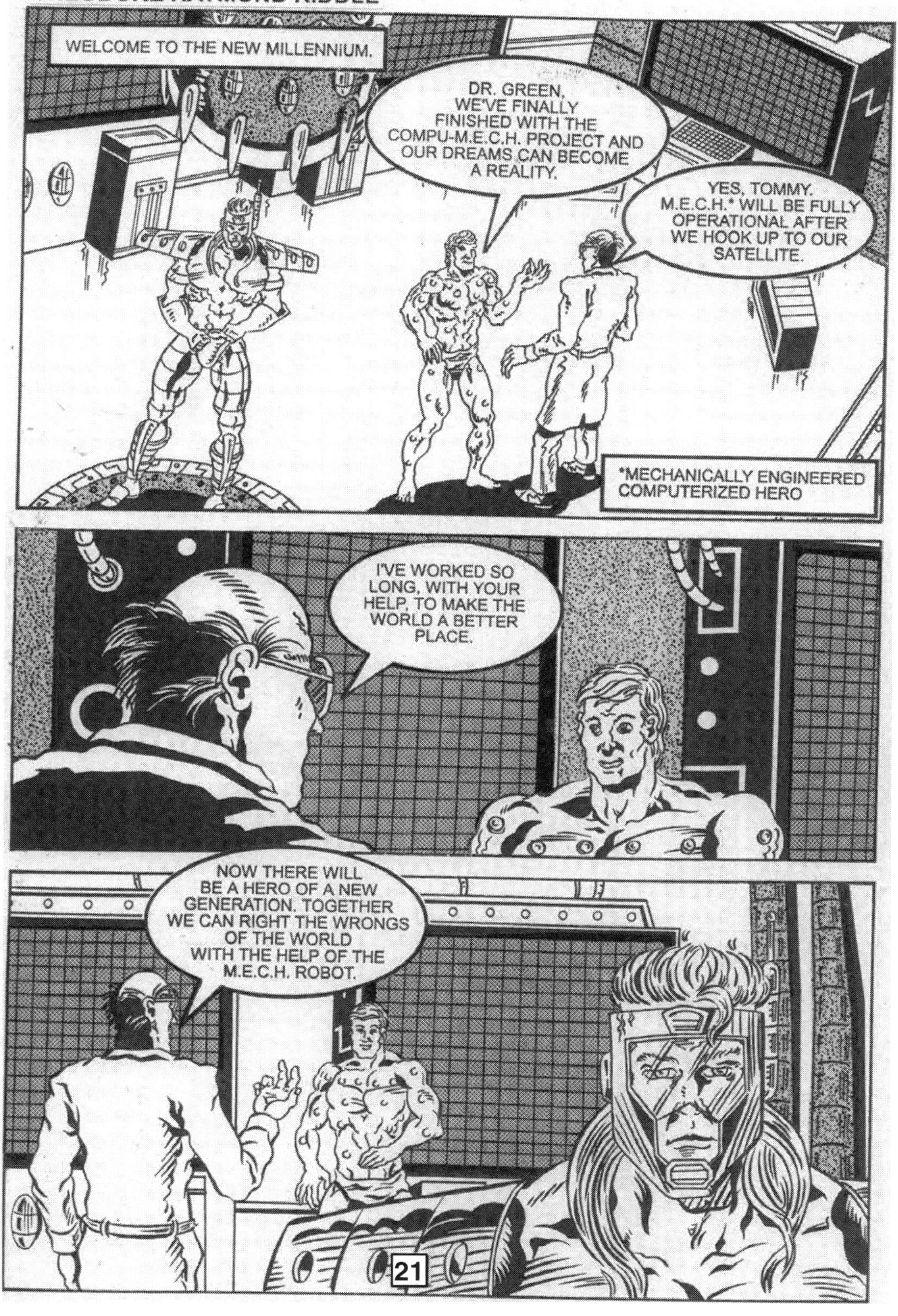
WELCOME TO THE NEW MILLENNIUM.
DR. GREEN, WE'VE FINALLY FINISHED WITH THE COMPU-M.E.C.H. PROJECT AND OUR DREAMS CAN BECOME A REALITY.
YES, TOMMY. M.E.C.H.* WILL BE FULLY OPERATIONAL AFTER WE HOOK UP TO OUR SATELLITE.
*MECHANICALLY ENGINEERED COMPUTERIZED HERO
I'VE WORKED SO LONG, WITH YOUR HELP, TO MAKE THE WORLD A BETTER PLACE.
NOW THERE WILL BE A HERO OF A NEW GENERATION. TOGETHER WE CAN RIGHT THE WRONGS OF THE WORLD WITH THE HELP OF THE M.E.C.H. ROBOT.

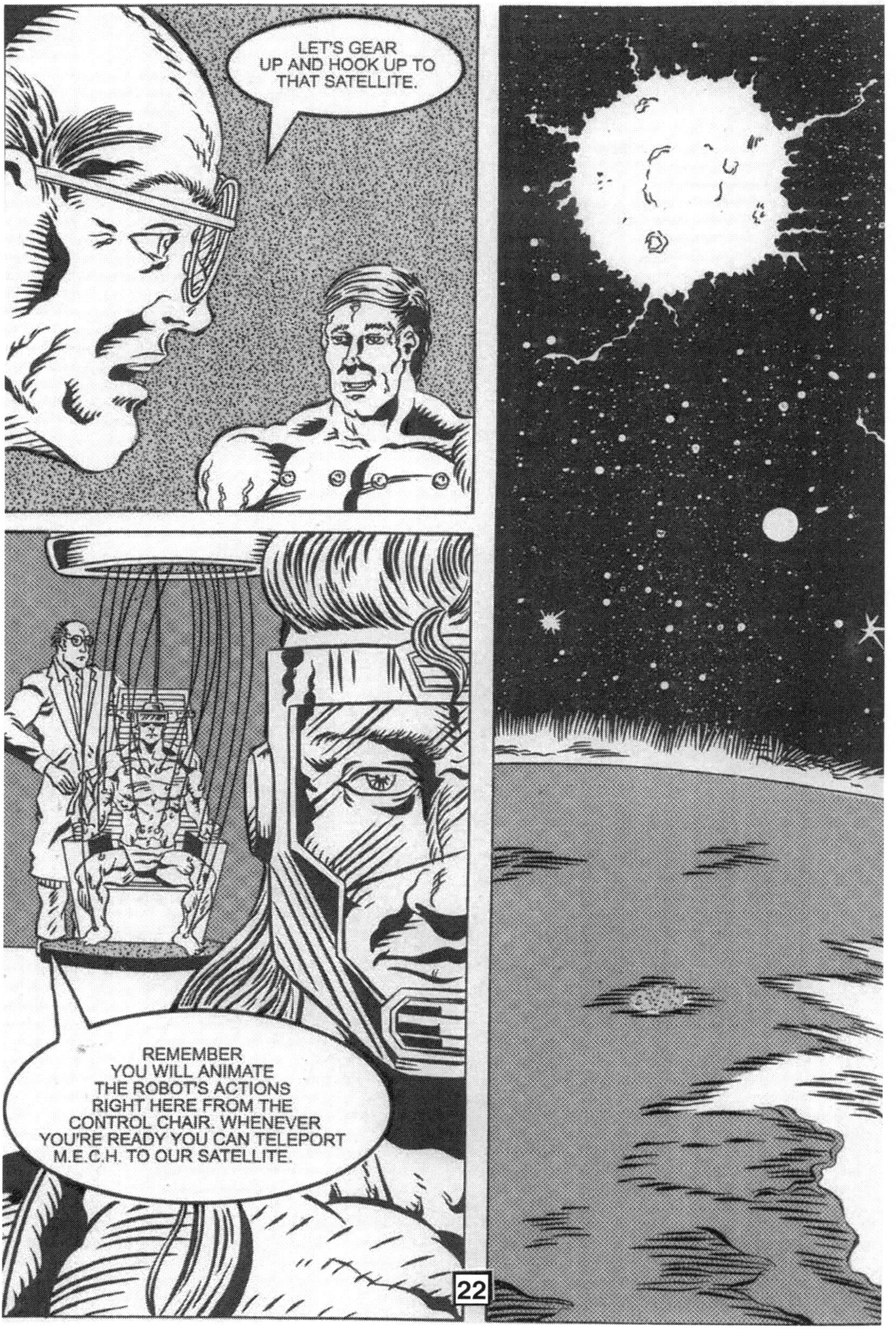
LET'S GEAR UP AND HOOK UP TO THAT SATELLITE.
REMEMBER YOU WILL ANIMATE THE ROBOT'S ACTIONS RIGHT HERE FROM THE CONTROL CHAIR. WHENEVER YOU'RE READY YOU CAN TELEPORT M.E.C.H. TO OUR SATELLITE.

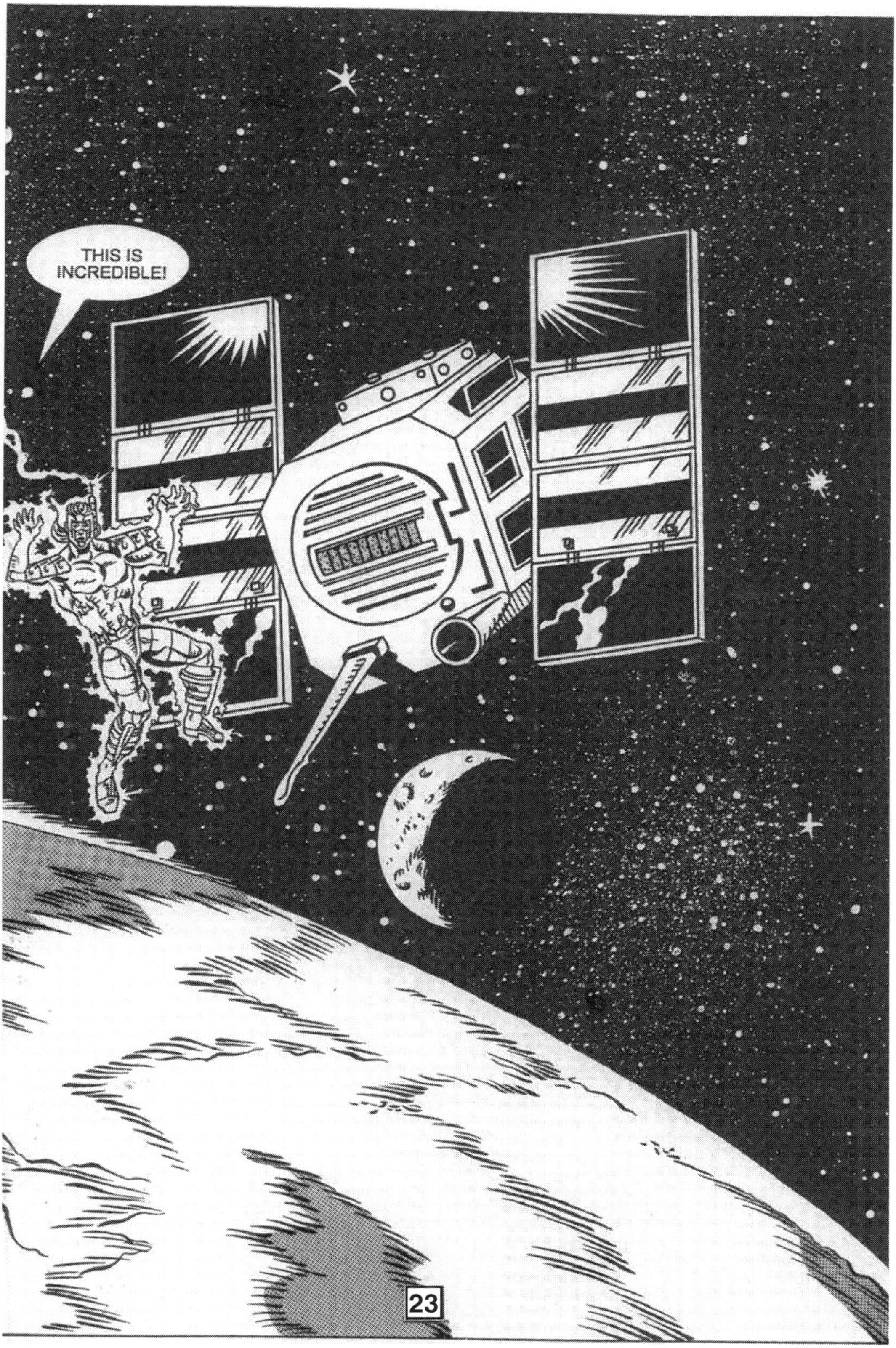
THIS IS INCREDIBLE!

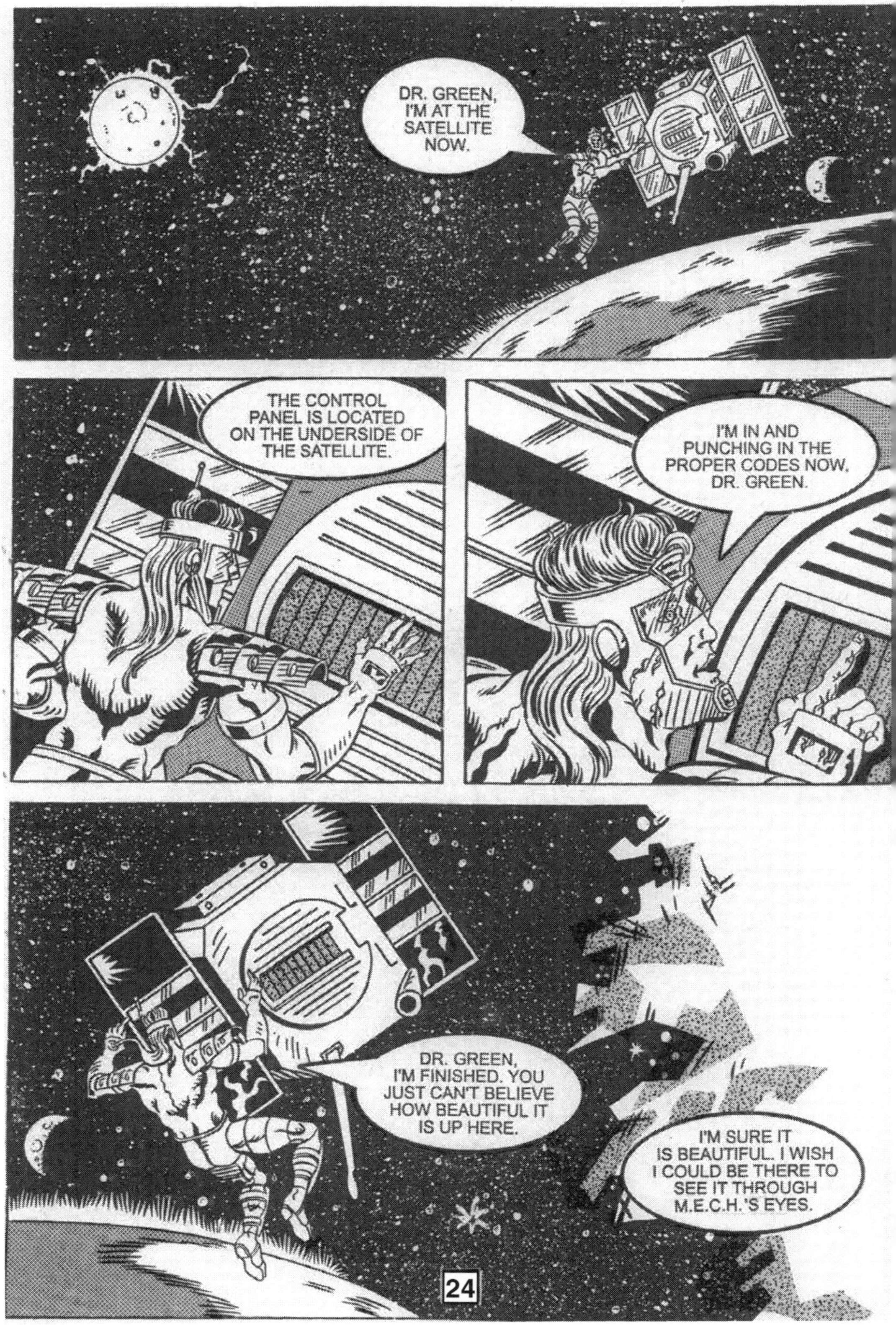
DR. GREEN, I'M AT THE SATELLITE NOW.
THE CONTROL PANEL IS LOCATED ON THE UNDERSIDE OF THE SATELLITE.
I'M IN AND PUNCHING IN THE PROPER CODES NOW, DR. GREEN.
DR. GREEN, I'M FINISHED. YOU JUST CAN'T BELIEVE HOW BEAUTIFUL IT IS UP HERE.
I'M SURE IT IS BEAUTIFUL. I WISH I COULD BE THERE TO SEE IT THROUGH M.E.C.H.'S EYES.

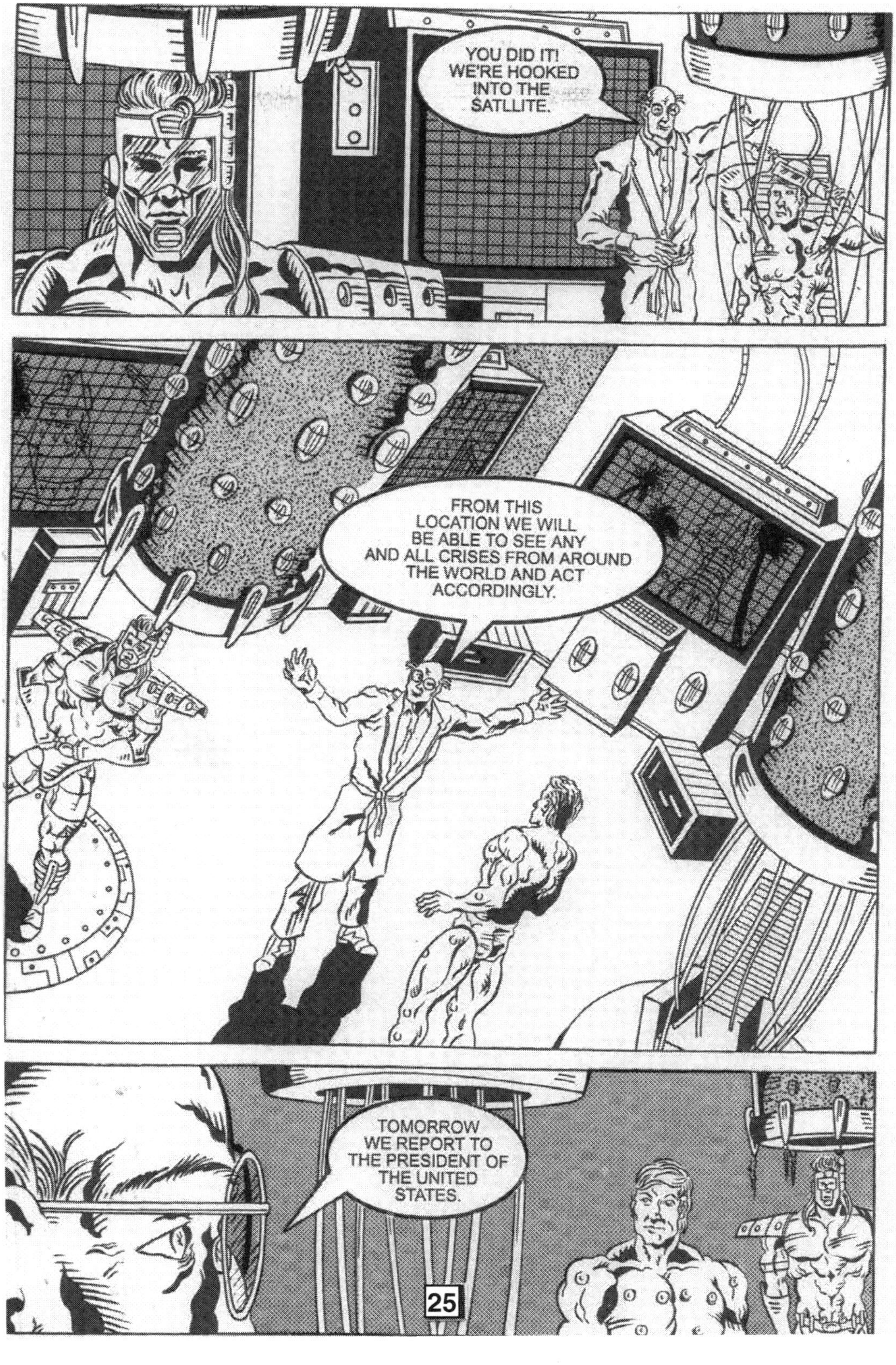
YOU DID IT! WE'RE HOOKED INTO THE SATLLITE.
FROM THIS LOCATION WE WILL BE ABLE TO SEE ANY AND ALL CRISES FROM AROUND THE WORLD AND ACT ACCORDINGLY.
TOMORROW WE REPORT TO THE PRESIDENT OF THE UNITED STATES.

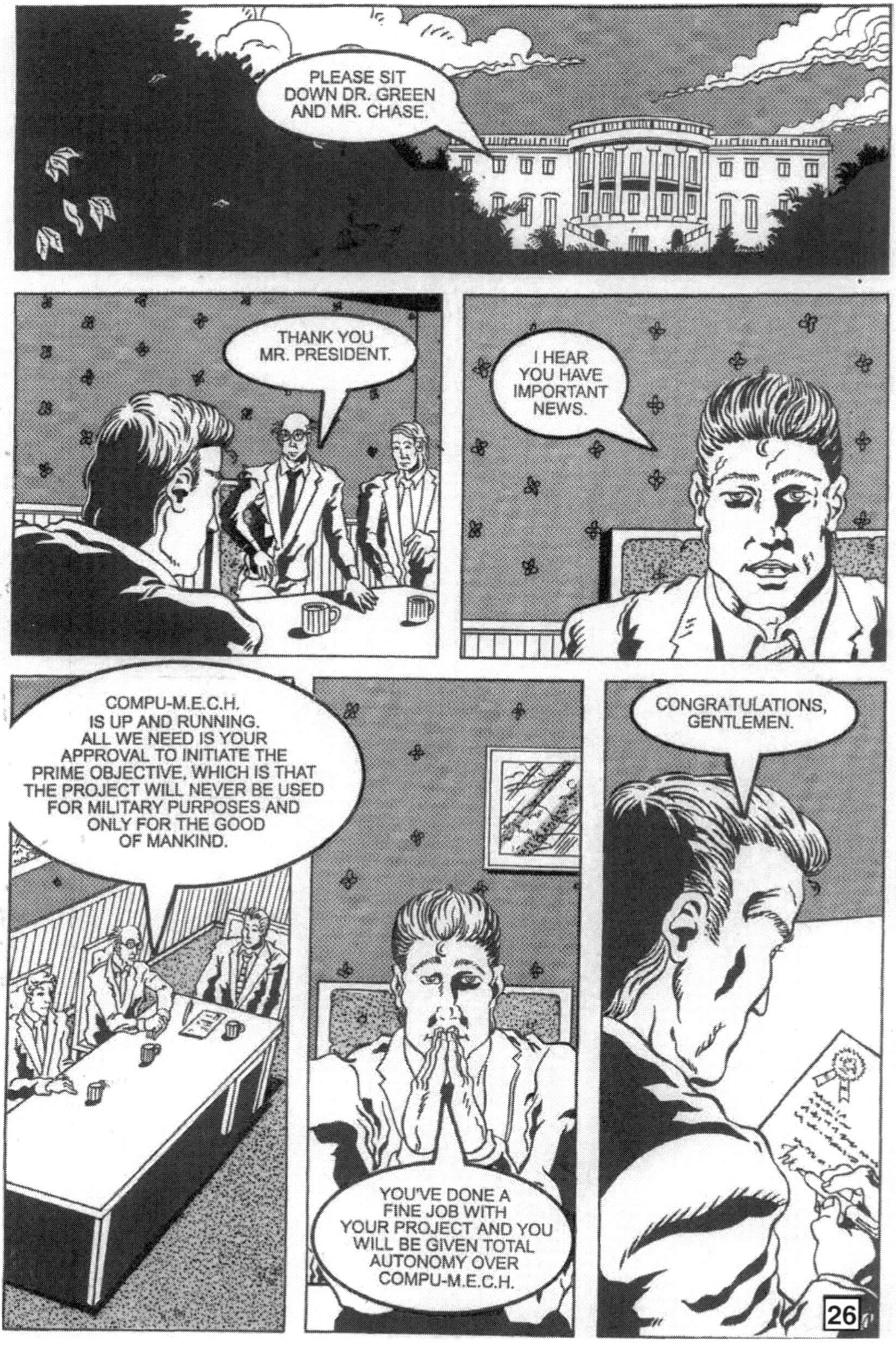
PLEASE SIT DOWN DR. GREEN AND MR. CHASE.
THANK YOU MR. PRESIDENT.
I HEAR YOU HAVE IMPORTANT NEWS.
COMPU-M.E.C.H. IS UP AND RUNNING. ALL WE NEED IS YOUR APPROVAL TO INITIATE THE PRIME OBJECTIVE, WHICH IS THAT THE PROJECT WILL NEVER BE USED FOR MILITARY PURPOSES AND ONLY FOR THE GOOD OF MANKIND.
YOU'VE DONE A FINE JOB WITH YOUR PROJECT AND YOU WILL BE GIVEN TOTAL AUTONOMY OVER COMPU-M.E.C.H.
CONGRATULATIONS, GENTLEMEN.

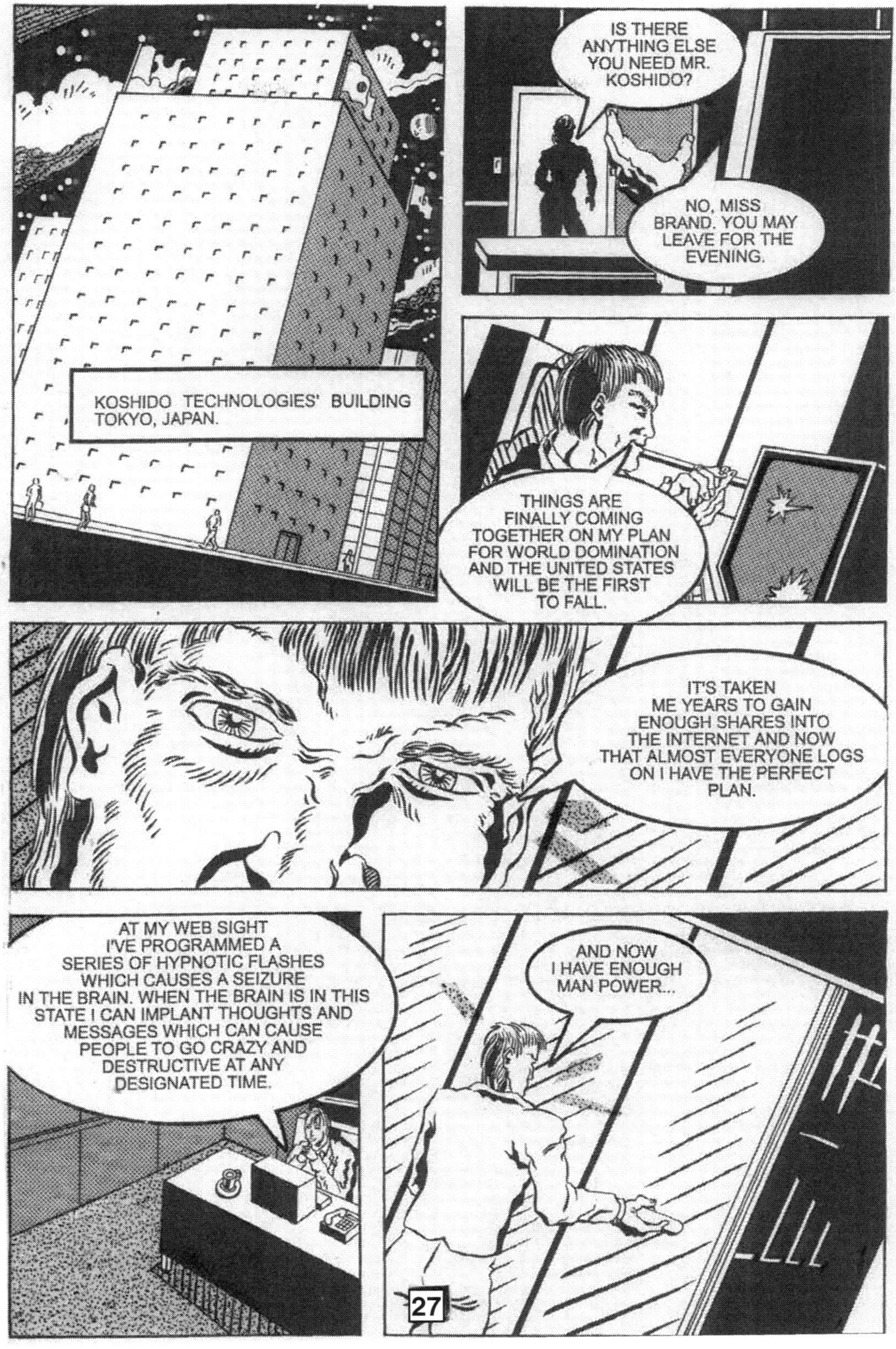

KOSHIDO TECHNOLOGIES' BUILDING TOKYO, JAPAN.
IS THERE ANYTHING ELSE YOU NEED MR. KOSHIDO?
NO, MISS BRAND. YOU MAY LEAVE FOR THE EVENING.
THINGS ARE FINALLY COMING TOGETHER ON MY PLAN FOR WORLD DOMINATION AND THE UNITED STATES WILL BE THE FIRST TO FALL.
IT'S TAKEN ME YEARS TO GAIN ENOUGH SHARES INTO THE INTERNET AND NOW THAT ALMOST EVERYONE LOGS ON I HAVE THE PERFECT PLAN.
AT MY WEB SIGHT I'VE PROGRAMMED A SERIES OF HYPNOTIC FLASHES WHICH CAUSES A SEIZURE IN THE BRAIN. WHEN THE BRAIN IS IN THIS STATE I CAN IMPLANT THOUGHTS AND MESSAGES WHICH CAN CAUSE PEOPLE TO GO CRAZY AND DESTRUCTIVE AT ANY DESIGNATED TIME.
AND NOW I HAVE ENOUGH MAN POWER...

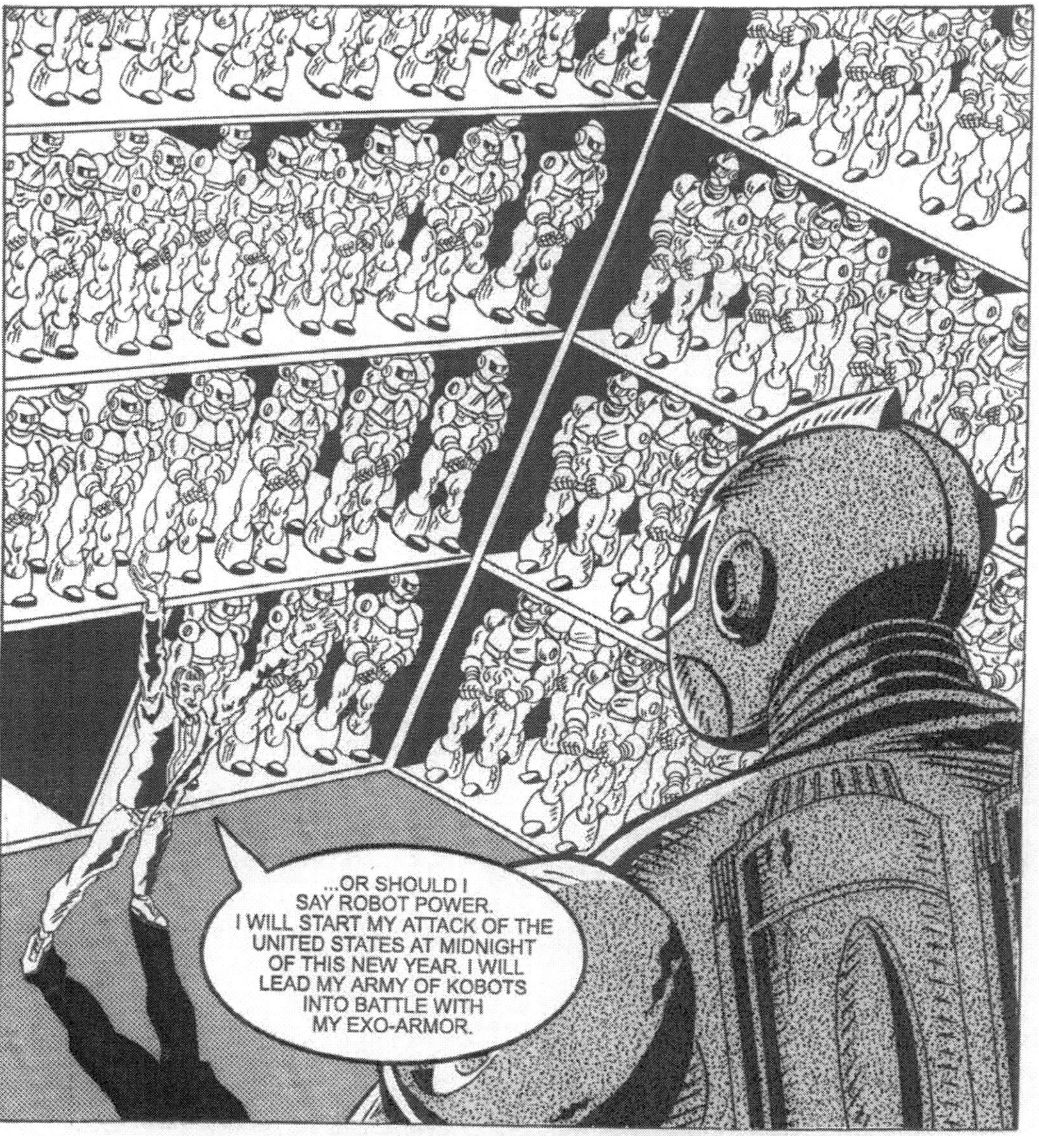
...OR SHOULD I SAY ROBOT POWER. I WILL START MY ATTACK OF THE UNITED STATES AT MIDNIGHT OF THIS NEW YEAR. I WILL LEAD MY ARMY OF KOBOTS INTO BATTLE WITH MY EXO-ARMOR.
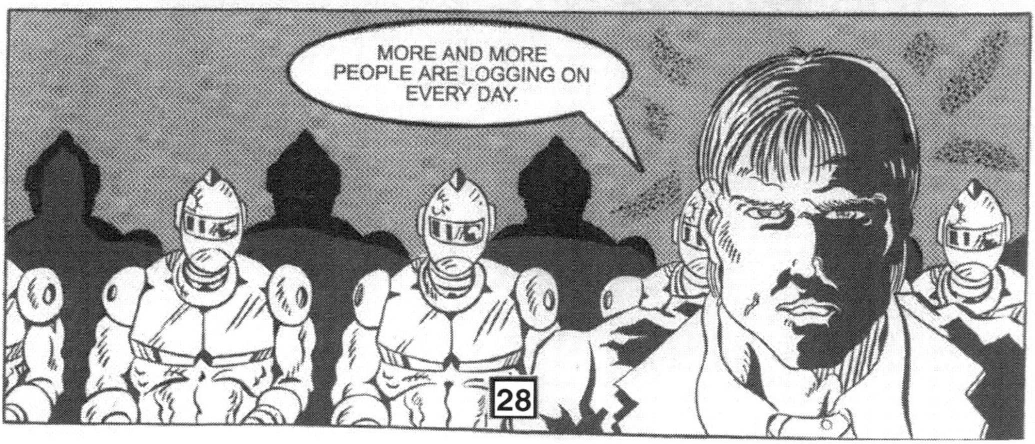
MORE AND MORE PEOPLE ARE LOGGING ON EVERY DAY.

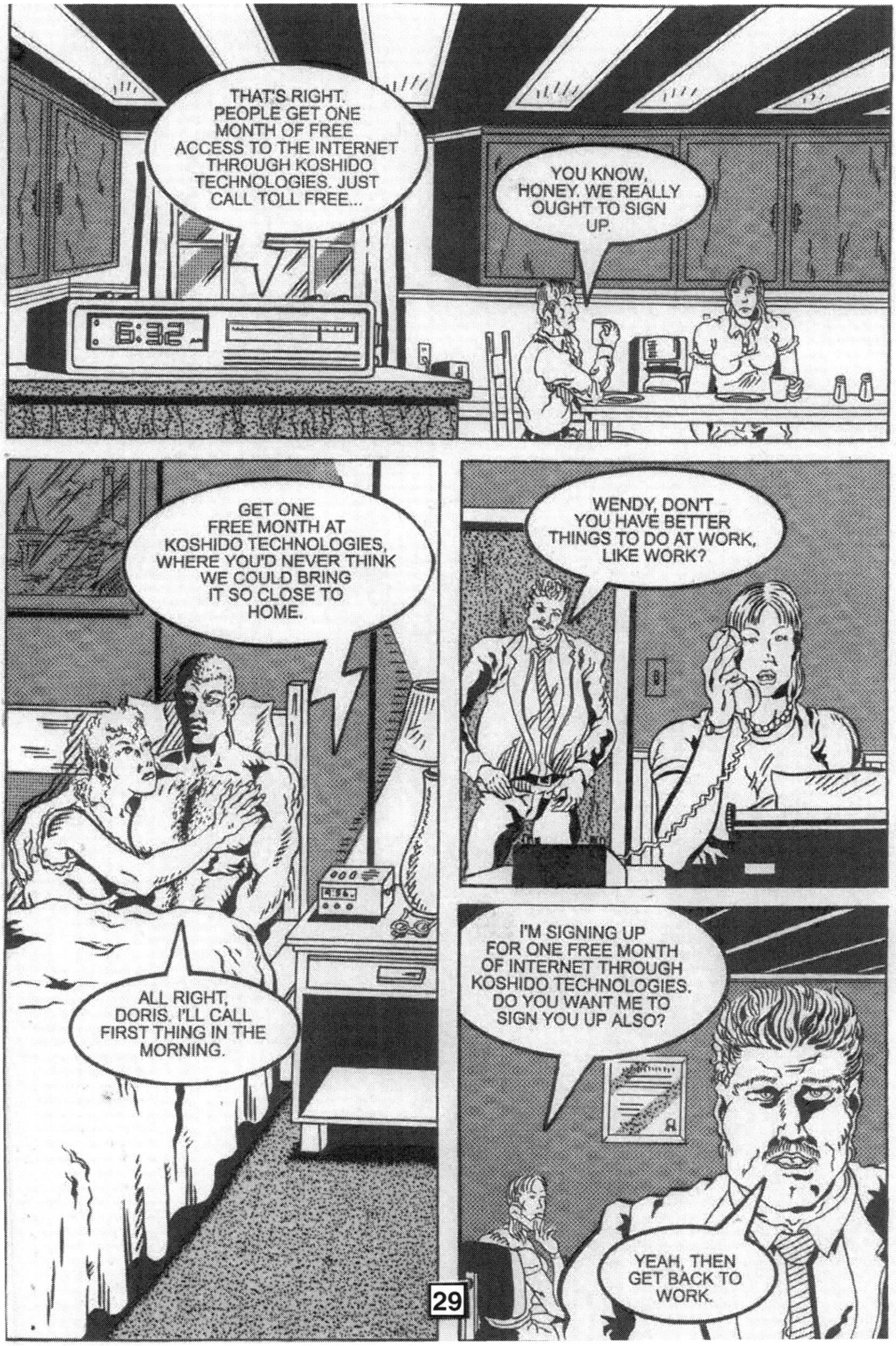
THAT'S RIGHT. PEOPLE GET ONE MONTH OF FREE ACCESS TO THE INTERNET THROUGH KOSHIDO TECHNOLOGIES. JUST CALL TOLL FREE...
YOU KNOW, HONEY. WE REALLY OUGHT TO SIGN UP.
GET ONE FREE MONTH AT KOSHIDO TECHNOLOGIES, WHERE YOU'D NEVER THINK WE COULD BRING IT SO CLOSE TO HOME.
ALL RIGHT, DORIS. I'LL CALL FIRST THING IN THE MORNING.
WENDY, DON'T YOU HAVE BETTER THINGS TO DO AT WORK, LIKE WORK?
I'M SIGNING UP FOR ONE FREE MONTH OF INTERNET THROUGH KOSHIDO TECHNOLOGIES. DO YOU WANT ME TO SIGN YOU UP ALSO?
YEAH, THEN GET BACK TO WORK.

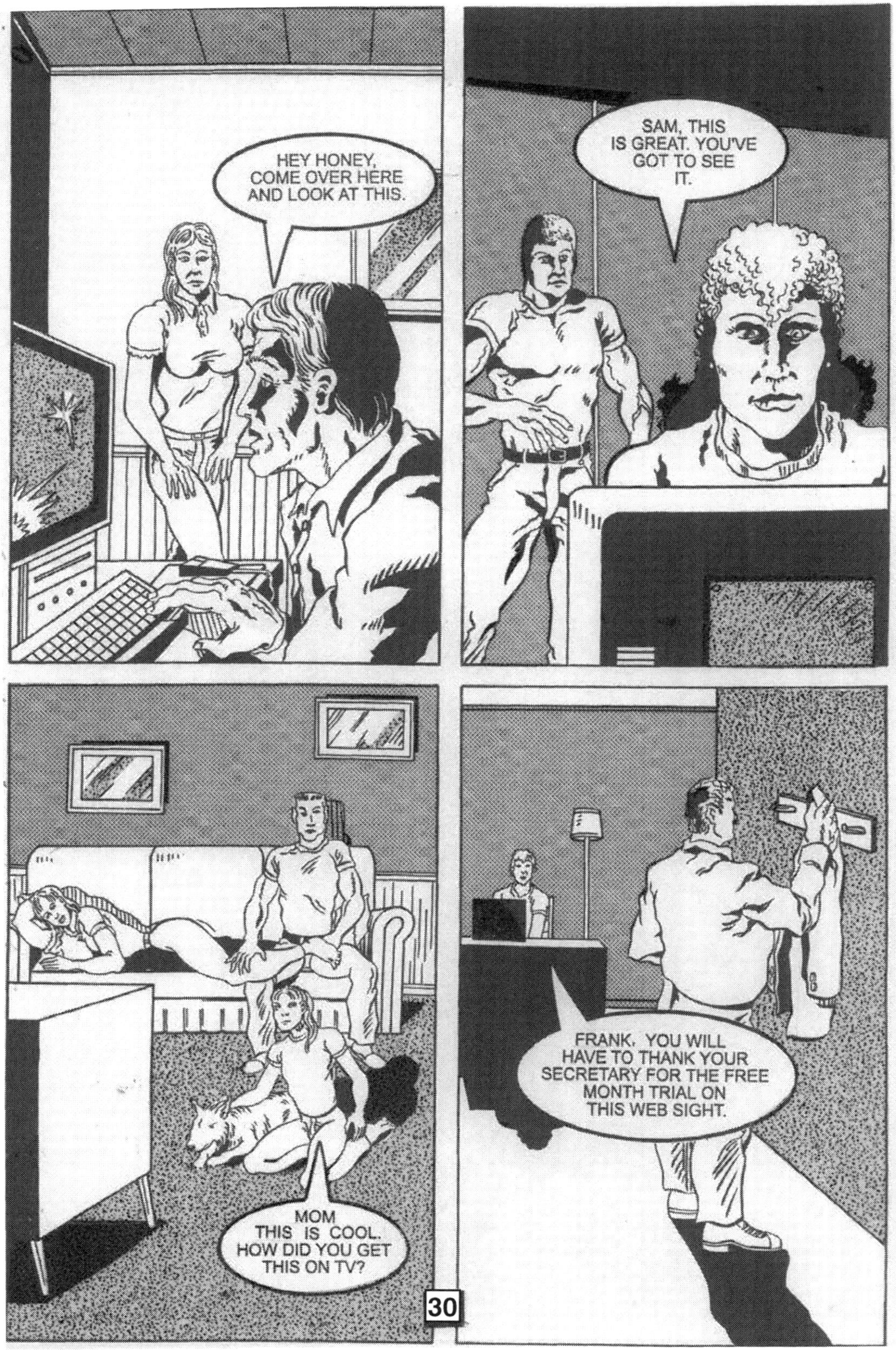
HEY HONEY, COME OVER HERE AND LOOK AT THIS.
SAM, THIS IS GREAT. YOU'VE GOT TO SEE IT.
MOM THIS IS COOL. HOW DID YOU GET THIS ON TV?
FRANK. YOU WILL HAVE TO THANK YOUR SECRETARY FOR THE FREE MONTH TRIAL ON THIS WEB SIGHT.

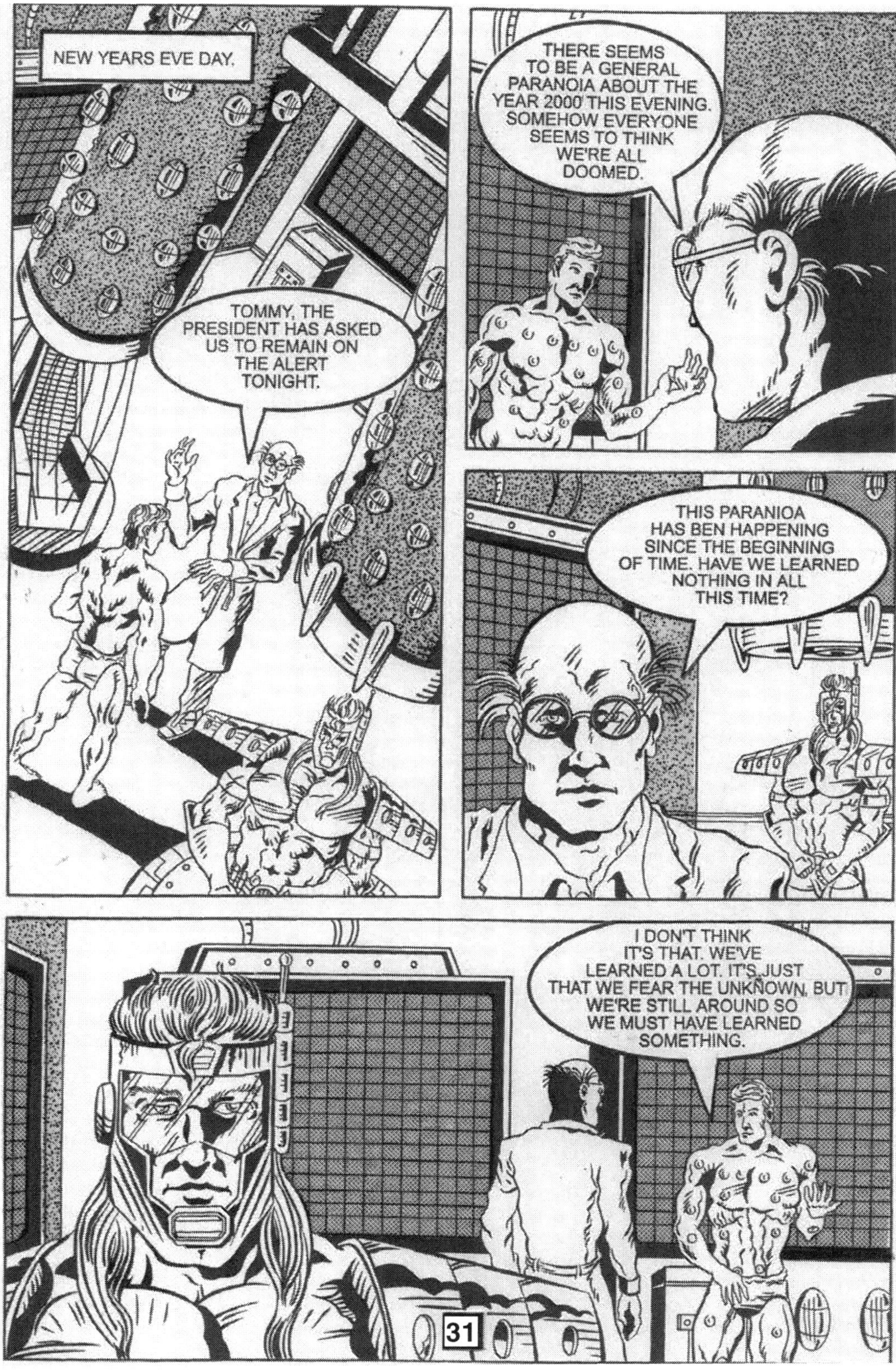
NEW YEARS EVE DAY.
TOMMY, THE PRESIDENT HAS ASKED US TO REMAIN ON THE ALERT TONIGHT.
THERE SEEMS TO BE A GENERAL PARANOIA ABOUT THE YEAR 2000 THIS EVENING. SOMEHOW EVERYONE SEEMS TO THINK WE'RE ALL DOOMED.
THIS PARANIOA HAS BEN HAPPENING SINCE THE BEGINNING OF TIME. HAVE WE LEARNED NOTHING IN ALL THIS TIME?
I DON'T THINK IT'S THAT. WE'VE LEARNED A LOT. IT'S JUST THAT WE FEAR THE UNKNOWN, BUT WE'RE STILL AROUND SO WE MUST HAVE LEARNED SOMETHING.

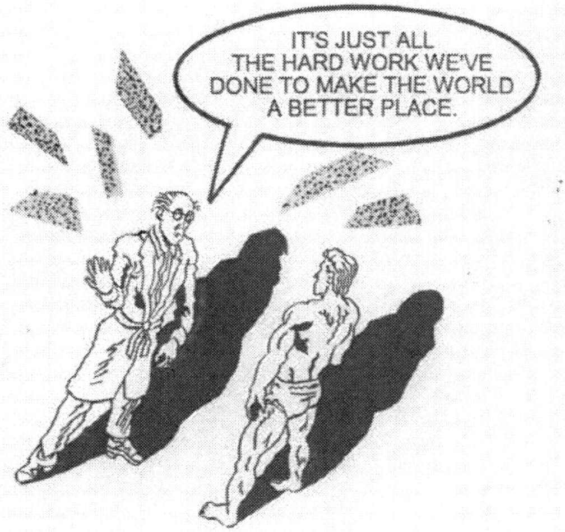
IT'S JUST ALL THE HARD WORK WE'VE DONE TO MAKE THE WORLD A BETTER PLACE.

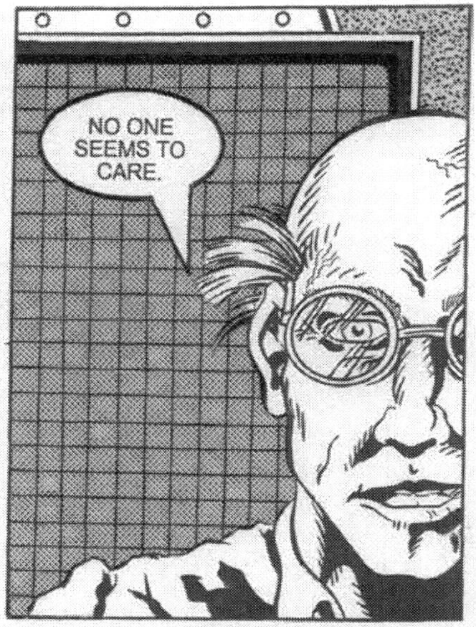
NO ONE SEEMS TO CARE.

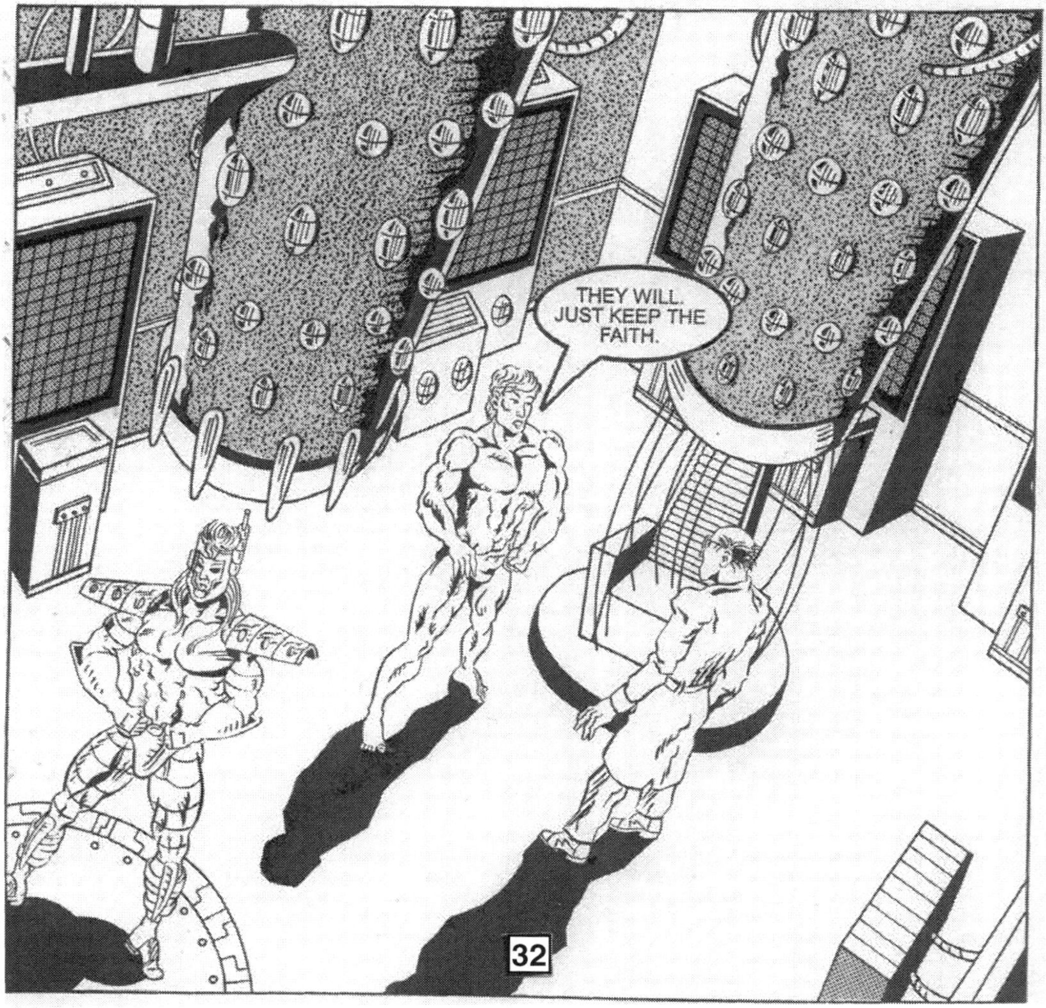
THEY WILL. JUST KEEP THE FAITH.

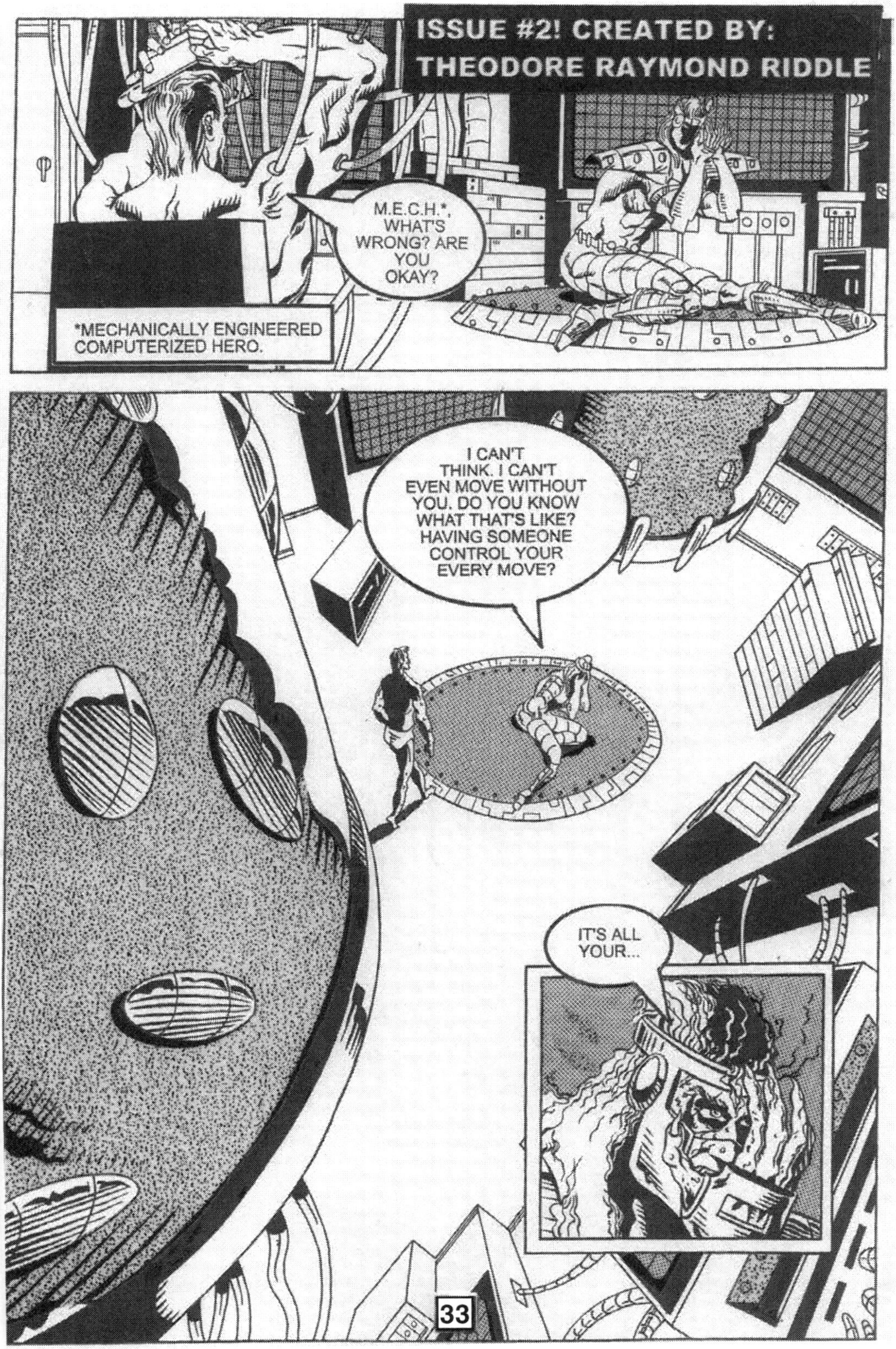
ISSUE #2! CREATED BY: THEODORE RAYMOND RIDDLE
M.E.C.H.*, WHAT'S WRONG? ARE YOU OKAY?
*MECHANICALLY ENGINEERED COMPUTERIZED HERO.
I CAN'T THINK. I CAN'T EVEN MOVE WITHOUT YOU. DO YOU KNOW WHAT THAT'S LIKE? HAVING SOMEONE CONTROL YOUR EVERY MOVE?
IT'S ALL YOUR...

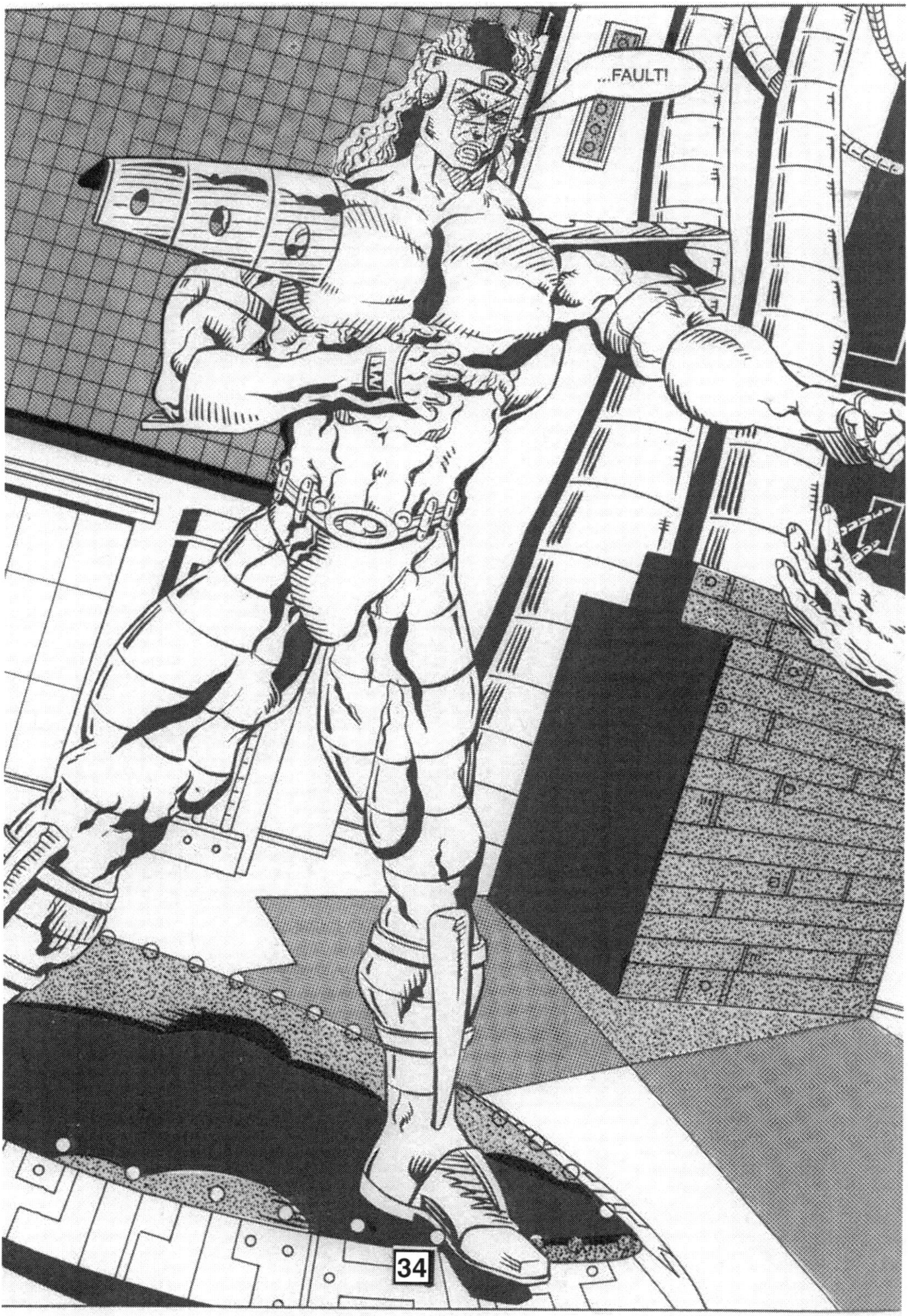
...FAULT!

NOW YOU'RE GOING TO DIE!

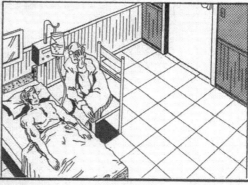

WHILE TOMMY'S SUBCONSCIOUS TRIES TO SURVIVE THE HORRIBLE TRAUMA HIS BODY HAS UNDERGONE WHEN HE SAVED THE SKYJACKED PLANE, HIS PHYSICAL BODY LIES IN A COMA AT RIVERSIDE HOSPITAL.

35

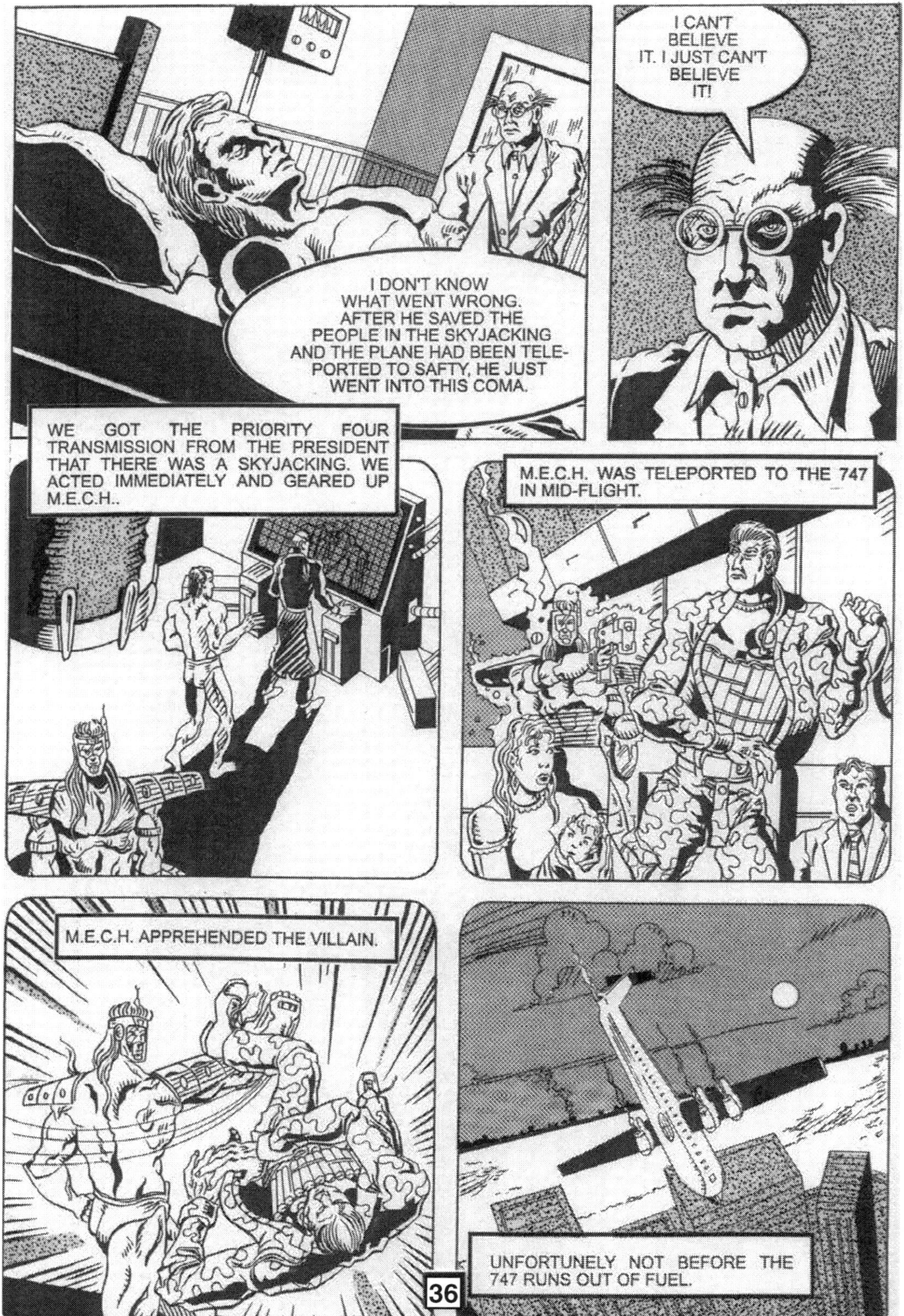

I DON'T KNOW WHAT WENT WRONG. AFTER HE SAVED THE PEOPLE IN THE SKYJACKING AND THE PLANE HAD BEEN TELE-PORTED TO SAFTY, HE JUST WENT INTO THIS COMA.
I CAN'T BELIEVE IT. I JUST CAN'T BELIEVE IT!
WE GOT THE PRIORITY FOUR TRANSMISSION FROM THE PRESIDENT THAT THERE WAS A SKYJACKING. WE ACTED IMMEDIATELY AND GEARED UP M.E.C.H..
M.E.C.H. WAS TELEPORTED TO THE 747 IN MID-FLIGHT.
M.E.C.H. APPREHENDED THE VILLAIN.
UNFORTUNELY NOT BEFORE THE 747 RUNS OUT OF FUEL.

THINKING QUICKLY, M.E.C.H. TRIES TO TELEPORT THE ENTIRE PLANE TO SAFTY BY GROUNDING IT TO HIS HELMET'S TRANSMITTERS.

MIRACULOUSLY HIS PLAN WORKED AND THE 747 RESTED SAFELY ON THE GROUND.

WHEN WE DISENGAGED THE PROGRAM, TOMMY'S BLOOD PRESSURE WENT TOO LOW AND HE PASSED OUT.

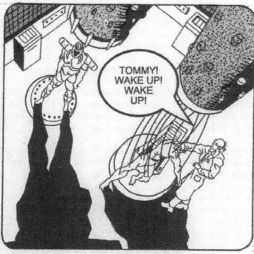

TOMMY! WAKE UP! WAKE UP!

APPARENTLY WHAT HAPPENED WAS THE WEIGHT OF THE 747 WAS TOO MUCH FOR M.E.C.H., MAKING IT TOO MUCH FOR TOMMY TO HANDLE AS WELL.

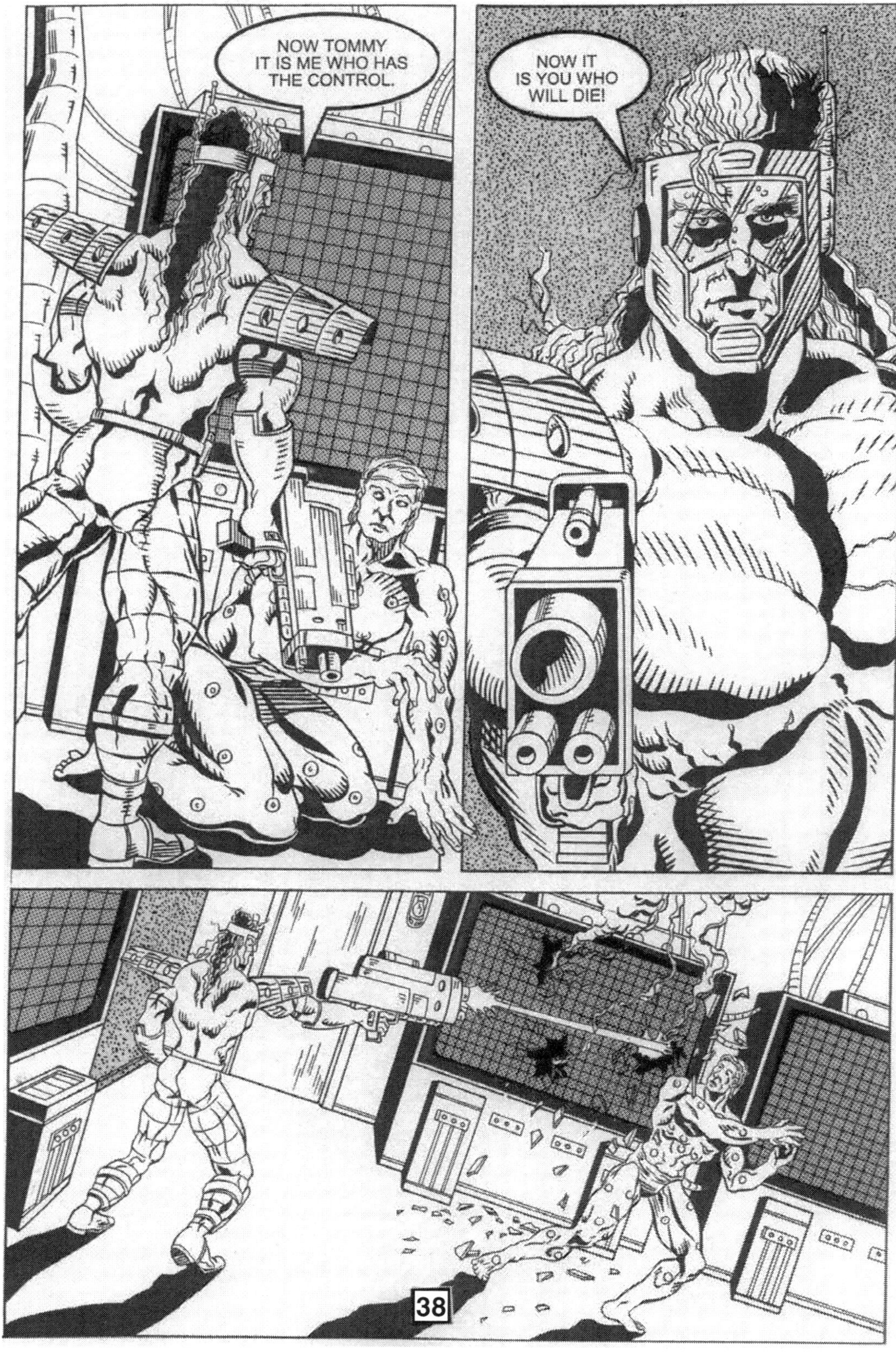
NOW TOMMY
IT IS ME WHO HAS
THE CONTROL.
NOW IT
IS YOU WHO
WILL DIE!

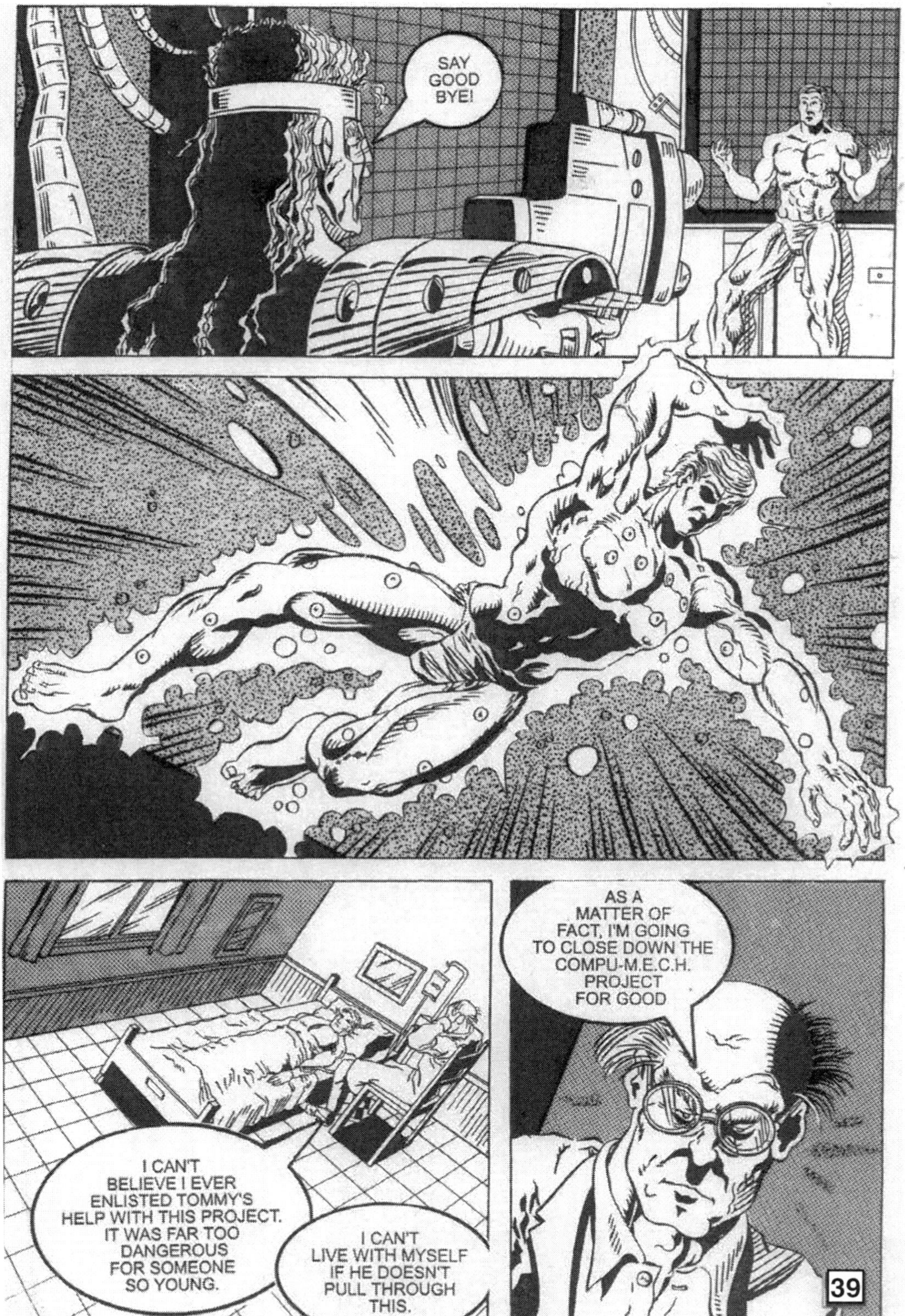

SAY GOOD BYE!
AS A MATTER OF FACT, I'M GOING TO CLOSE DOWN THE COMPU-M.E.C.H. PROJECT FOR GOOD.
I CAN'T BELIEVE I EVER ENLISTED TOMMY'S HELP WITH THIS PROJECT. IT WAS FAR TOO DANGEROUS FOR SOMEONE SO YOUNG.
I CAN'T LIVE WITH MYSELF IF HE DOESN'T PULL THROUGH THIS.

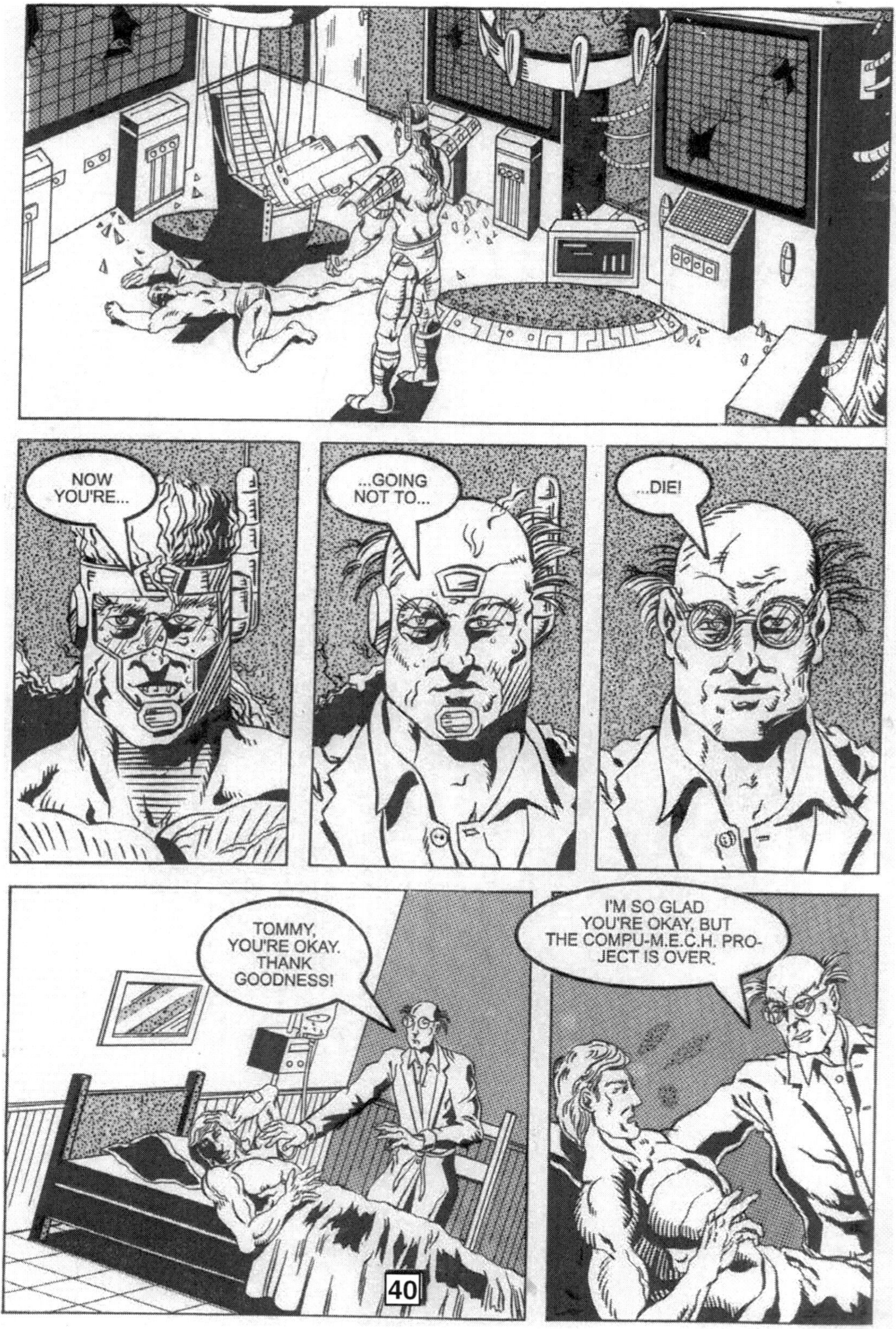
NOW YOU'RE...
...GOING NOT TO...
...DIE!
TOMMY, YOU'RE OKAY. THANK GOODNESS!
I'M SO GLAD YOU'RE OKAY, BUT THE COMPU-M.E.C.H. PROJECT IS OVER.

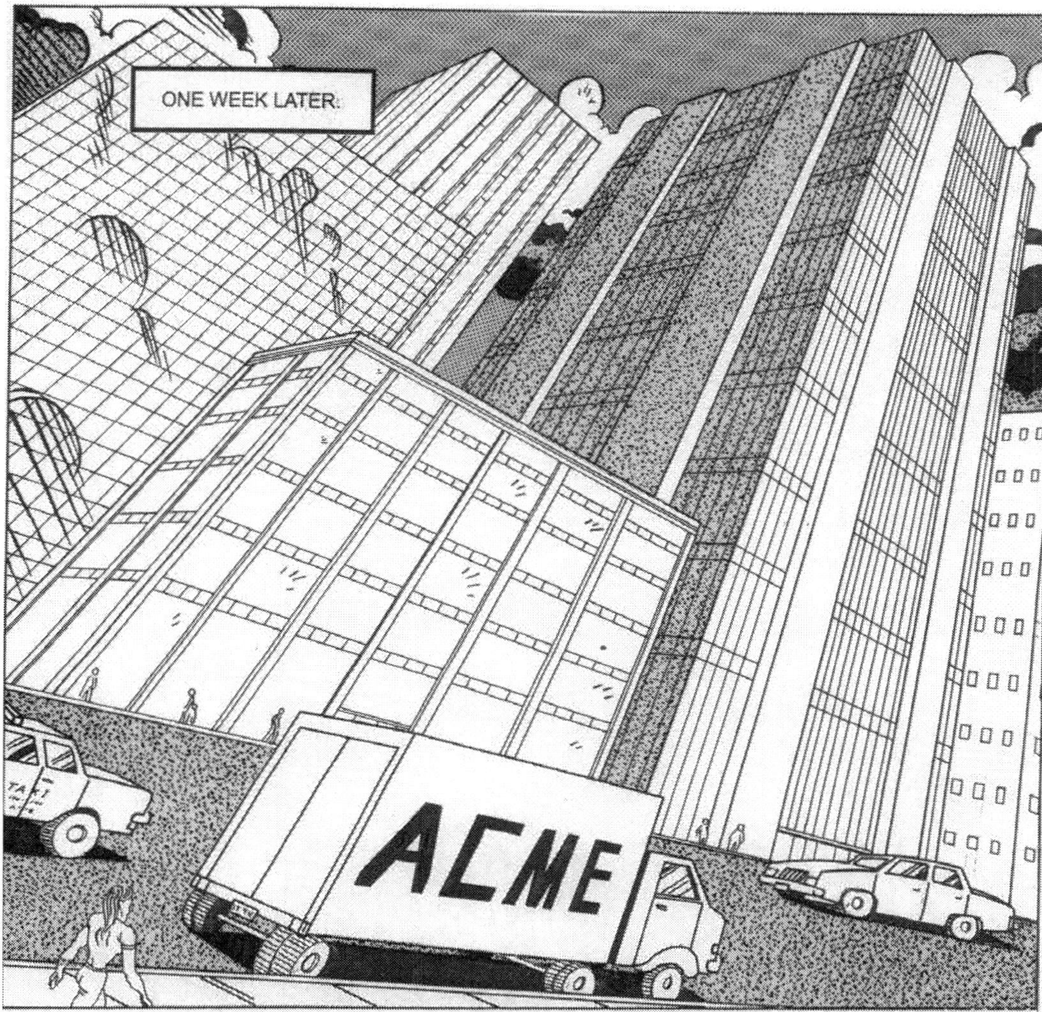
ONE WEEK LATER:
ACME

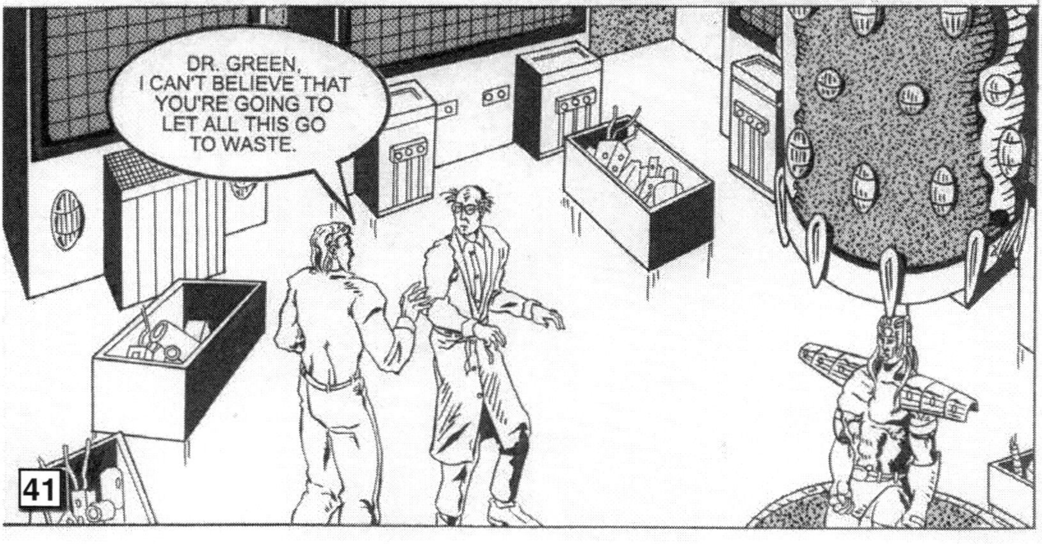
DR. GREEN, I CAN'T BELIEVE THAT YOU'RE GOING TO LET ALL THIS GO TO WASTE.

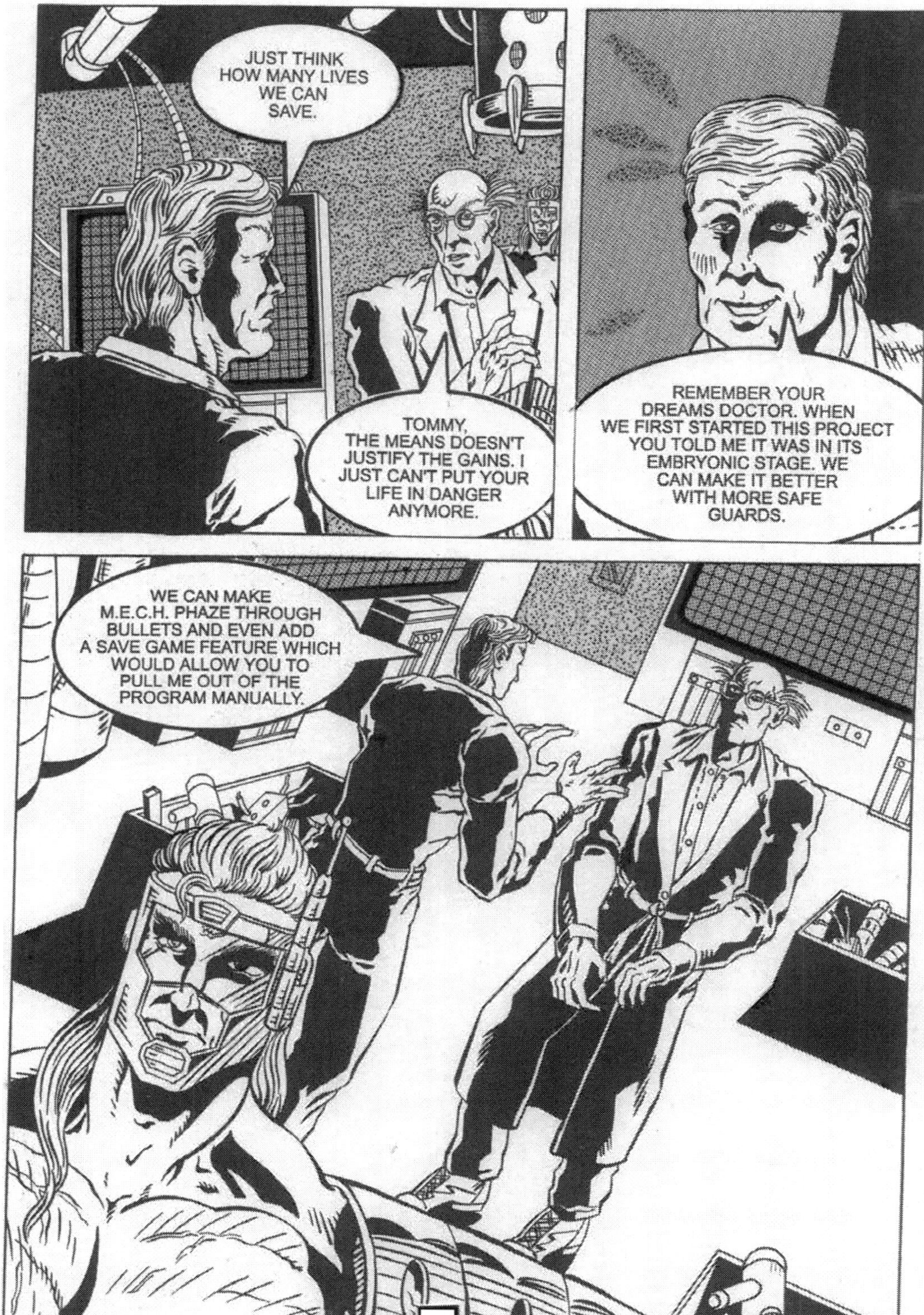
JUST THINK HOW MANY LIVES WE CAN SAVE.
TOMMY, THE MEANS DOESN'T JUSTIFY THE GAINS. I JUST CAN'T PUT YOUR LIFE IN DANGER ANYMORE.
REMEMBER YOUR DREAMS DOCTOR. WHEN WE FIRST STARTED THIS PROJECT YOU TOLD ME IT WAS IN ITS EMBRYONIC STAGE. WE CAN MAKE IT BETTER WITH MORE SAFE GUARDS.
WE CAN MAKE M.E.C.H. PHAZE THROUGH BULLETS AND EVEN ADD A SAVE GAME FEATURE WHICH WOULD ALLOW YOU TO PULL ME OUT OF THE PROGRAM MANUALLY.

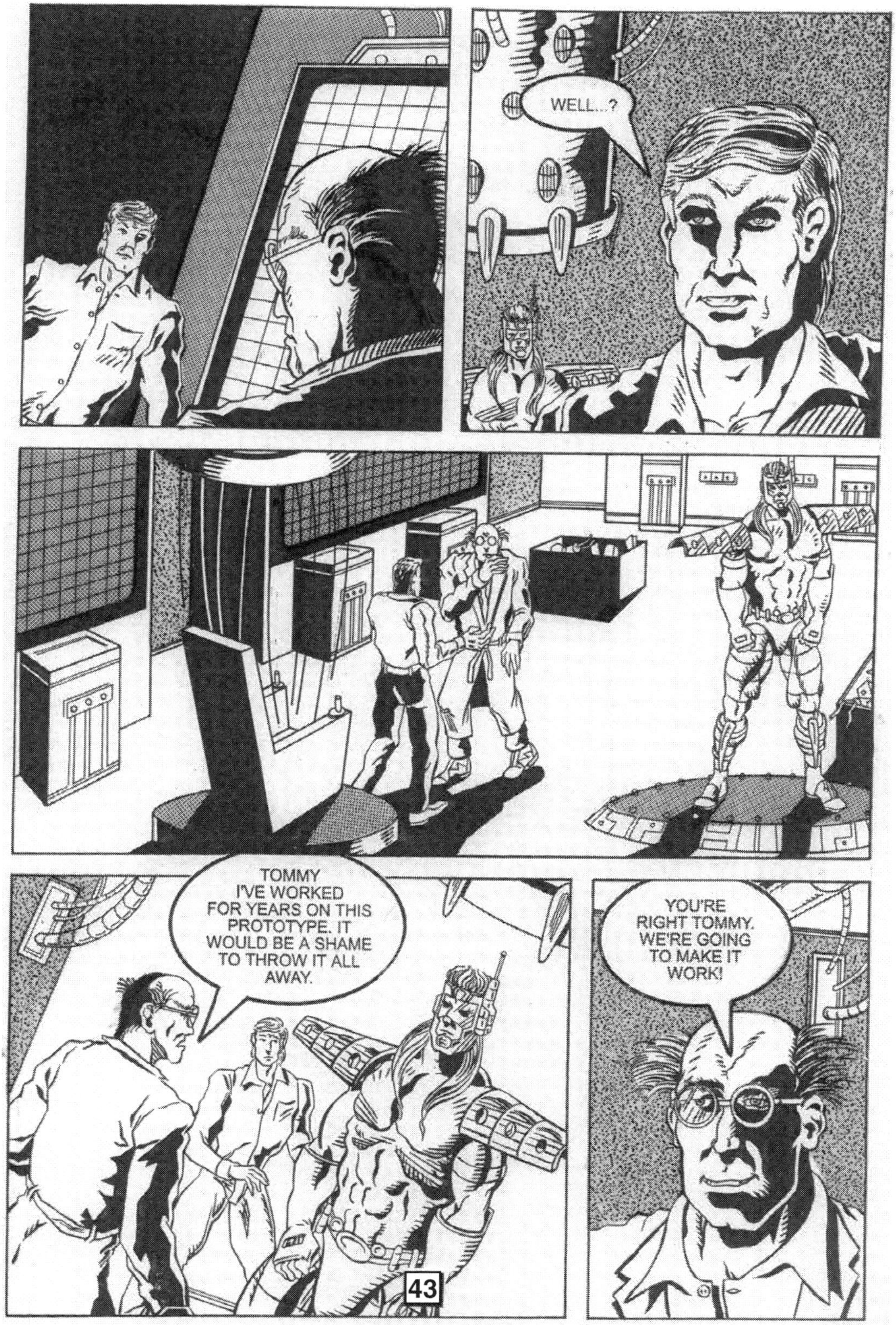
WELL...?
TOMMY I'VE WORKED FOR YEARS ON THIS PROTOTYPE. IT WOULD BE A SHAME TO THROW IT ALL AWAY.
YOU'RE RIGHT TOMMY. WE'RE GOING TO MAKE IT WORK!

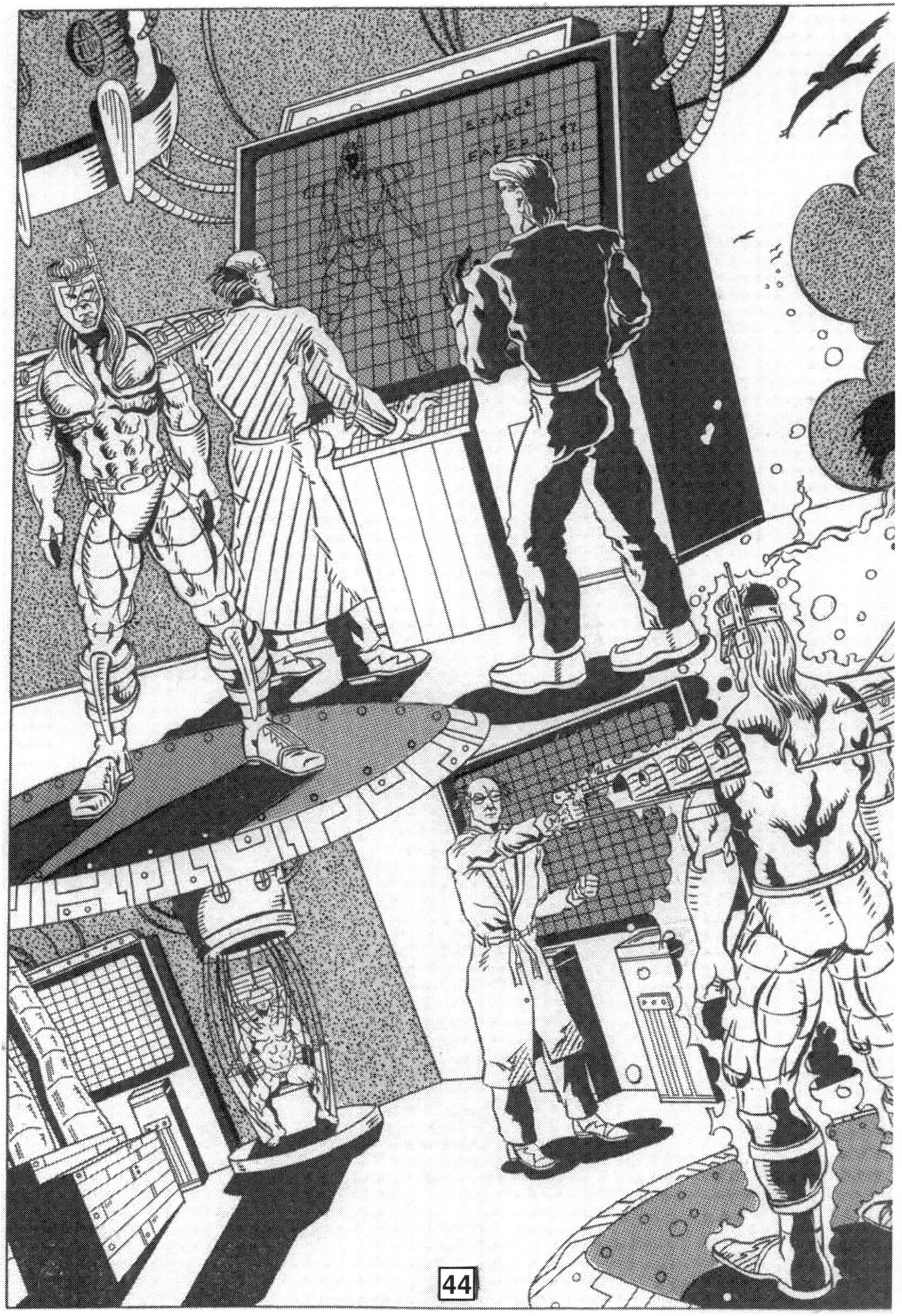

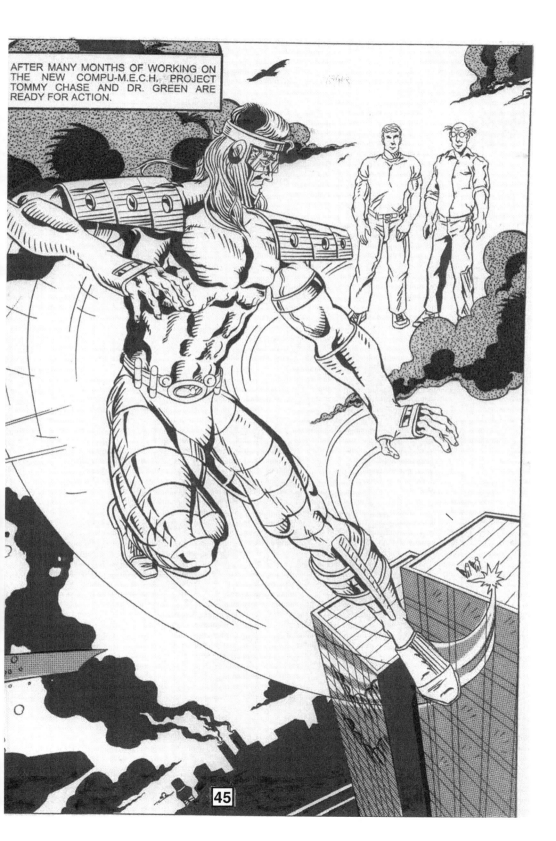

AFTER MANY MONTHS OF WORKING ON THE NEW COMPU-M.E.C.H. PROJECT TOMMY CHASE AND DR. GREEN ARE READY FOR ACTION.

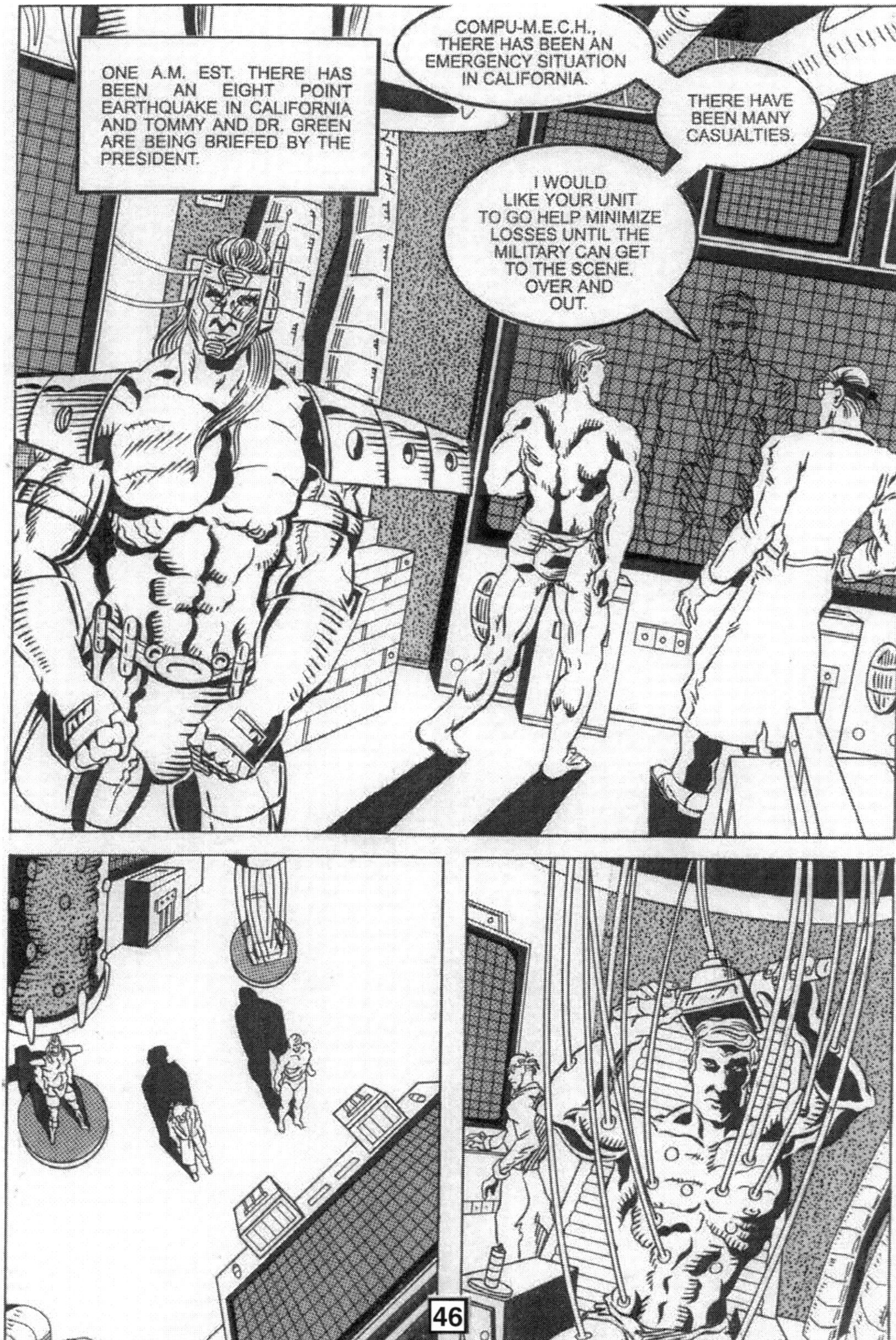
ONE A.M. EST. THERE HAS BEEN AN EIGHT POINT EARTHQUAKE IN CALIFORNIA AND TOMMY AND DR. GREEN ARE BEING BRIEFED BY THE PRESIDENT.
COMPU-M.E.C.H., THERE HAS BEEN AN EMERGENCY SITUATION IN CALIFORNIA.
THERE HAVE BEEN MANY CASUALTIES.
I WOULD LIKE YOUR UNIT TO GO HELP MINIMIZE LOSSES UNTIL THE MILITARY CAN GET TO THE SCENE. OVER AND OUT.

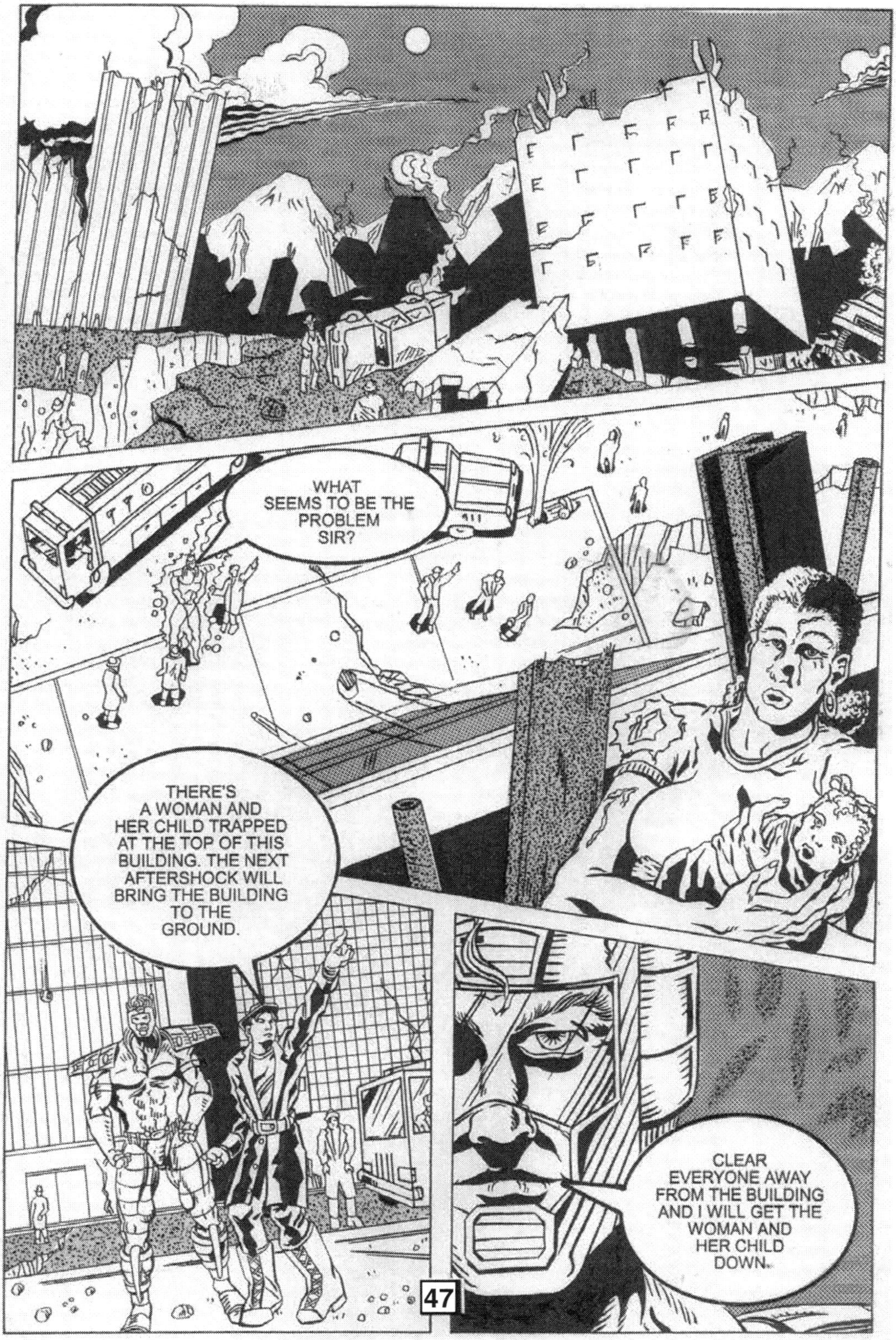
WHAT SEEMS TO BE THE PROBLEM SIR?
THERE'S A WOMAN AND HER CHILD TRAPPED AT THE TOP OF THIS BUILDING. THE NEXT AFTERSHOCK WILL BRING THE BUILDING TO THE GROUND.
CLEAR EVERYONE AWAY FROM THE BUILDING AND I WILL GET THE WOMAN AND HER CHILD DOWN.

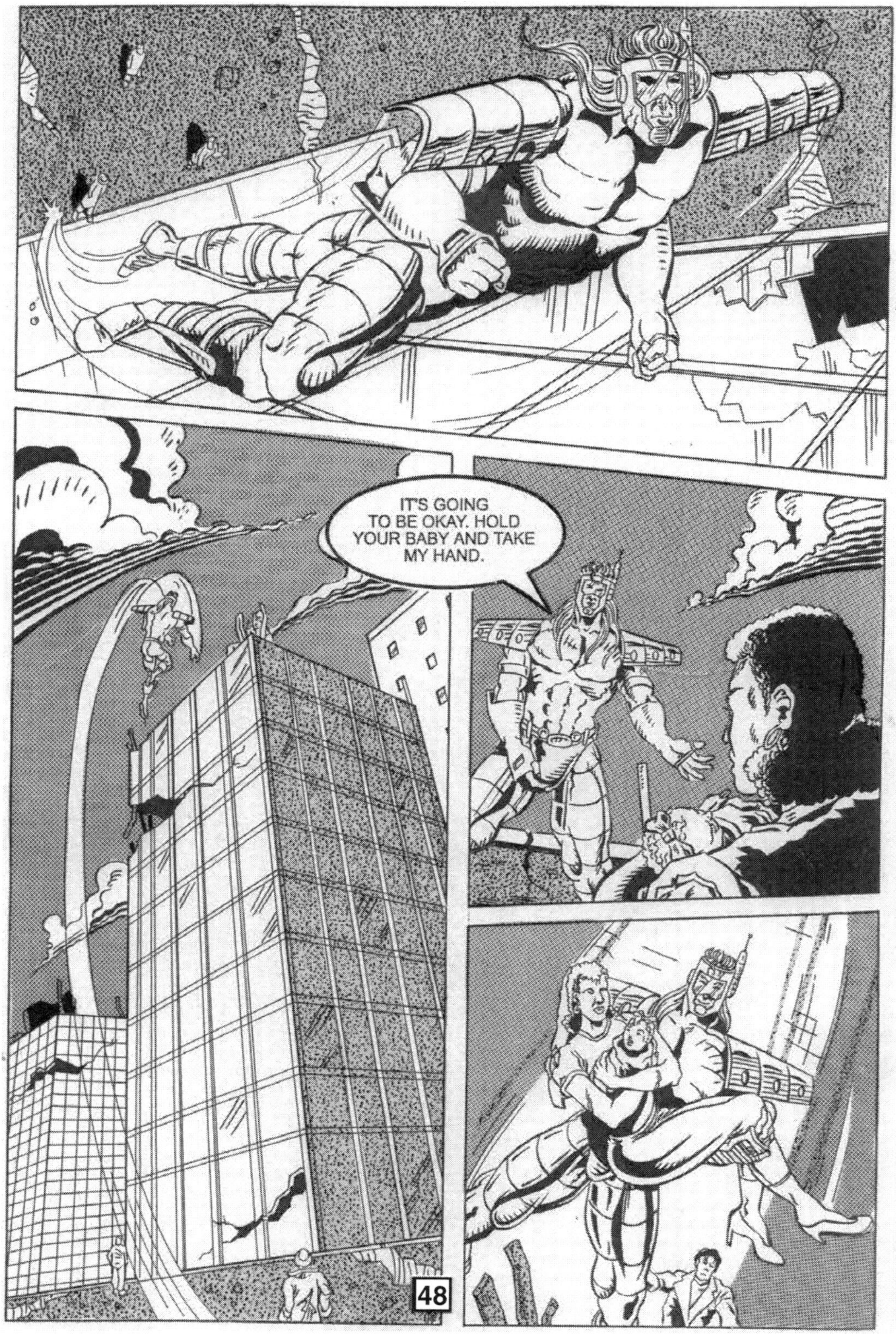
IT'S GOING TO BE OKAY. HOLD YOUR BABY AND TAKE MY HAND.

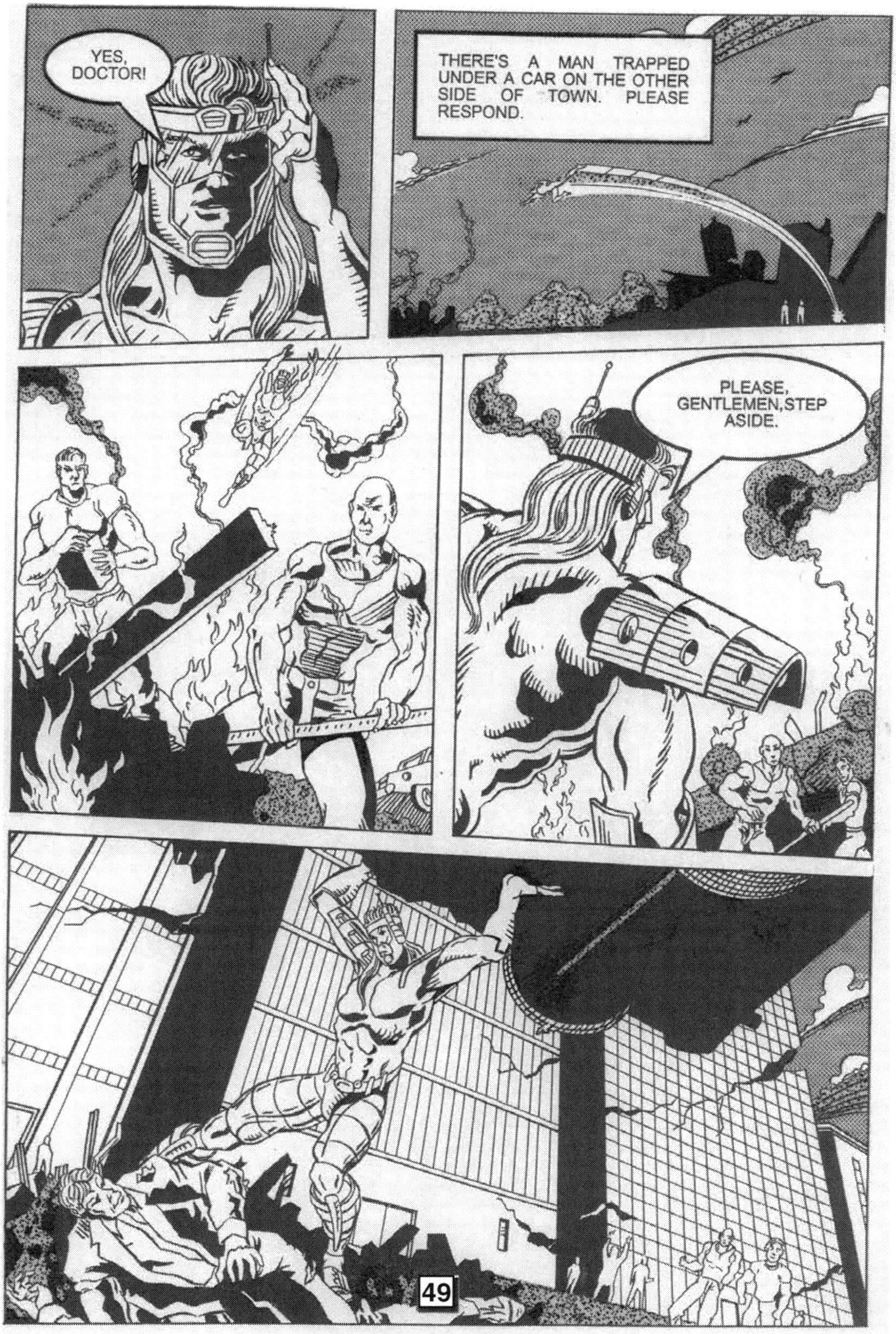
YES, DOCTOR!
THERE'S A MAN TRAPPED UNDER A CAR ON THE OTHER SIDE OF TOWN. PLEASE RESPOND.
PLEASE, GENTLEMEN,STEP ASIDE.

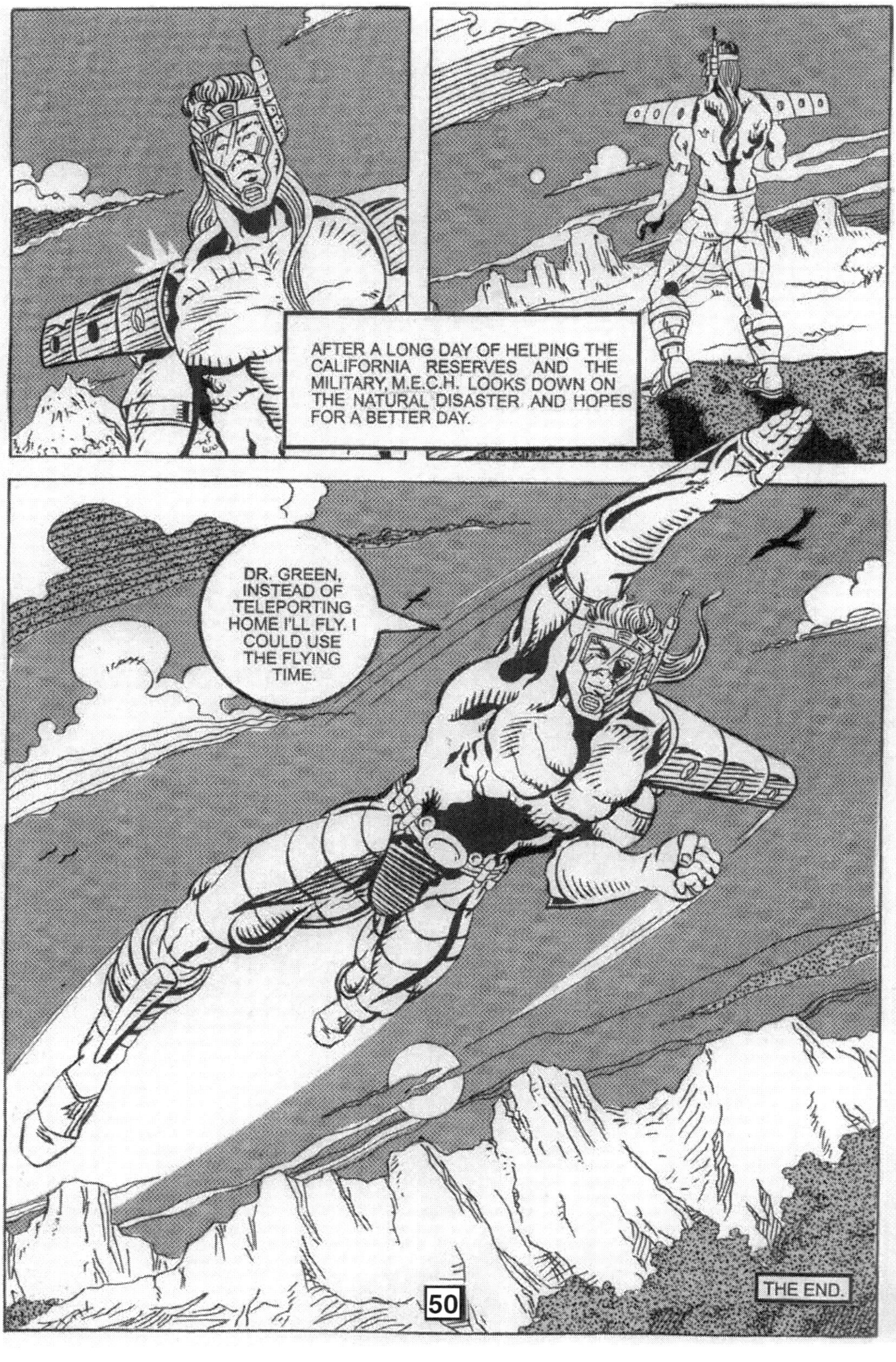
AFTER A LONG DAY OF HELPING THE CALIFORNIA RESERVES AND THE MILITARY, M.E.C.H. LOOKS DOWN ON THE NATURAL DISASTER AND HOPES FOR A BETTER DAY.
DR. GREEN, INSTEAD OF TELEPORTING HOME I'LL FLY. I COULD USE THE FLYING TIME.
THE END.

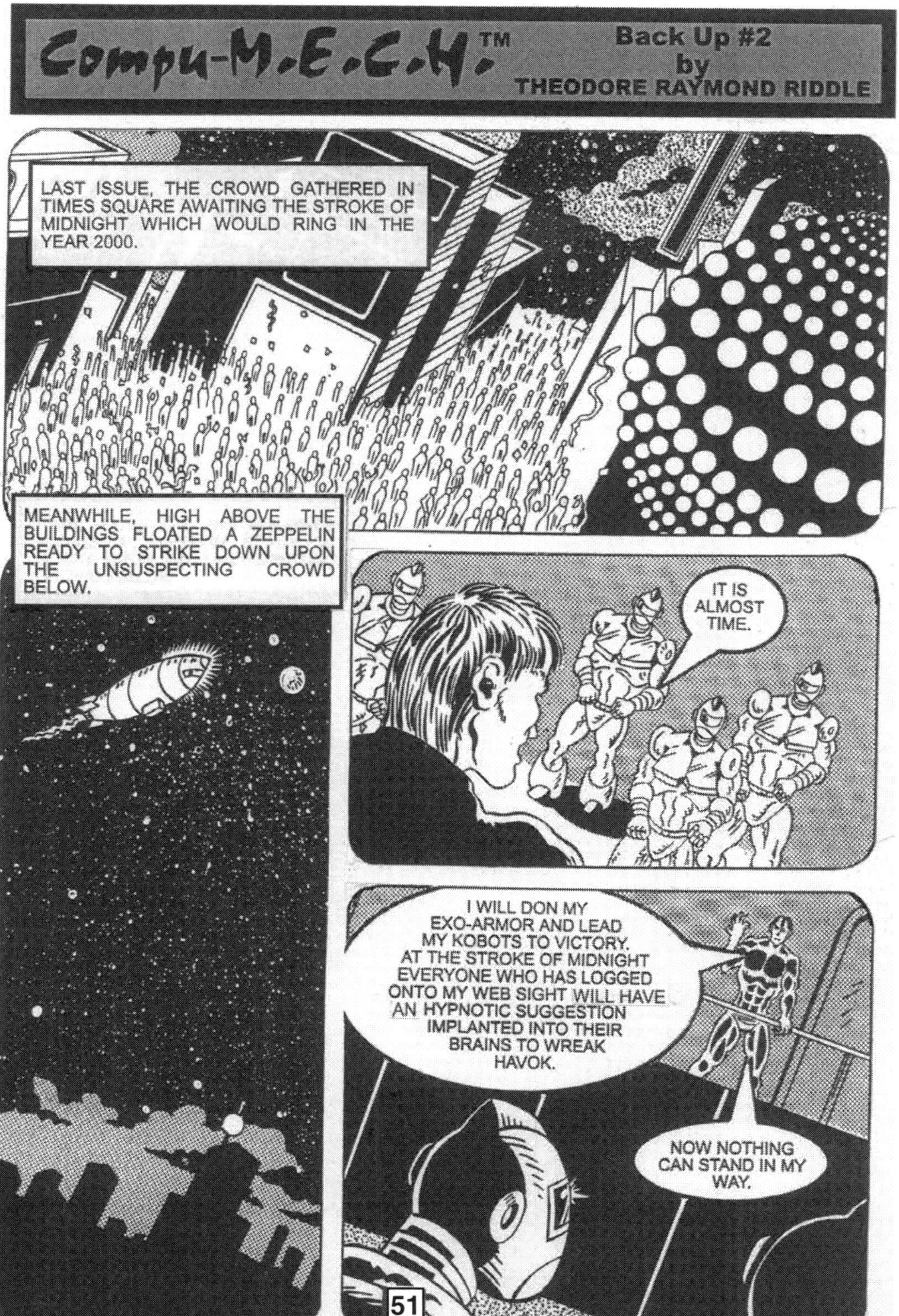
Compu-M.E.C.H.™
Back Up #2
by
THEODORE RAYMOND RIDDLE
LAST ISSUE, THE CROWD GATHERED IN TIMES SQUARE AWAITING THE STROKE OF MIDNIGHT WHICH WOULD RING IN THE YEAR 2000.
MEANWHILE, HIGH ABOVE THE BUILDINGS FLOATED A ZEPPELIN READY TO STRIKE DOWN UPON THE UNSUSPECTING CROWD BELOW.
IT IS ALMOST TIME.
I WILL DON MY EXO-ARMOR AND LEAD MY KOBOTS TO VICTORY. AT THE STROKE OF MIDNIGHT EVERYONE WHO HAS LOGGED ONTO MY WEB SIGHT WILL HAVE AN HYPNOTIC SUGGESTION IMPLANTED INTO THEIR BRAINS TO WREAK HAVOK.
NOW NOTHING CAN STAND IN MY WAY.

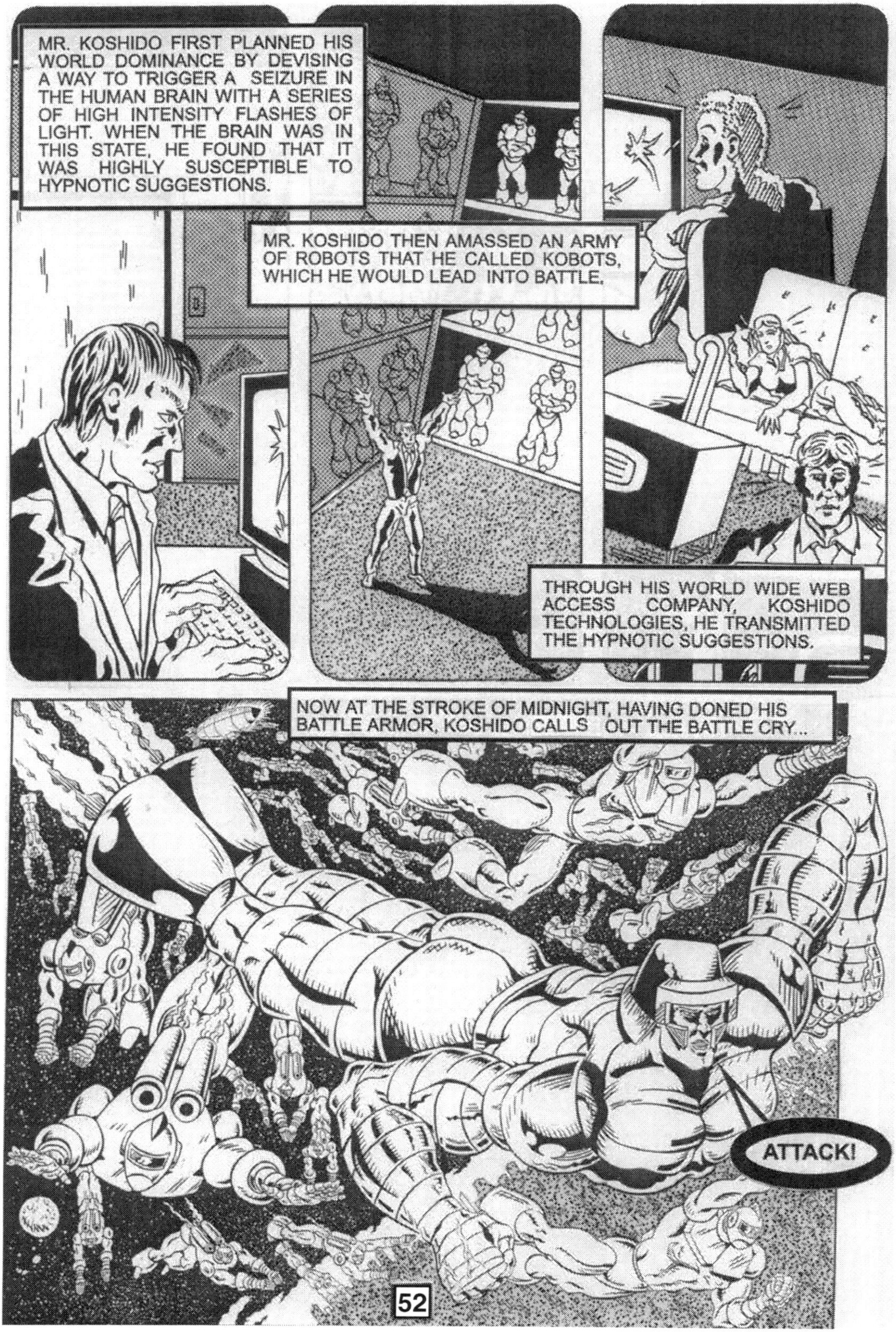
MR. KOSHIDO FIRST PLANNED HIS WORLD DOMINANCE BY DEVISING A WAY TO TRIGGER A SEIZURE IN THE HUMAN BRAIN WITH A SERIES OF HIGH INTENSITY FLASHES OF LIGHT. WHEN THE BRAIN WAS IN THIS STATE, HE FOUND THAT IT WAS HIGHLY SUSCEPTIBLE TO HYPNOTIC SUGGESTIONS.
MR. KOSHIDO THEN AMASSED AN ARMY OF ROBOTS THAT HE CALLED KOBOTS, WHICH HE WOULD LEAD INTO BATTLE.
THROUGH HIS WORLD WIDE WEB ACCESS COMPANY, KOSHIDO TECHNOLOGIES, HE TRANSMITTED THE HYPNOTIC SUGGESTIONS.
NOW AT THE STROKE OF MIDNIGHT, HAVING DONED HIS BATTLE ARMOR, KOSHIDO CALLS OUT THE BATTLE CRY...
ATTACK!

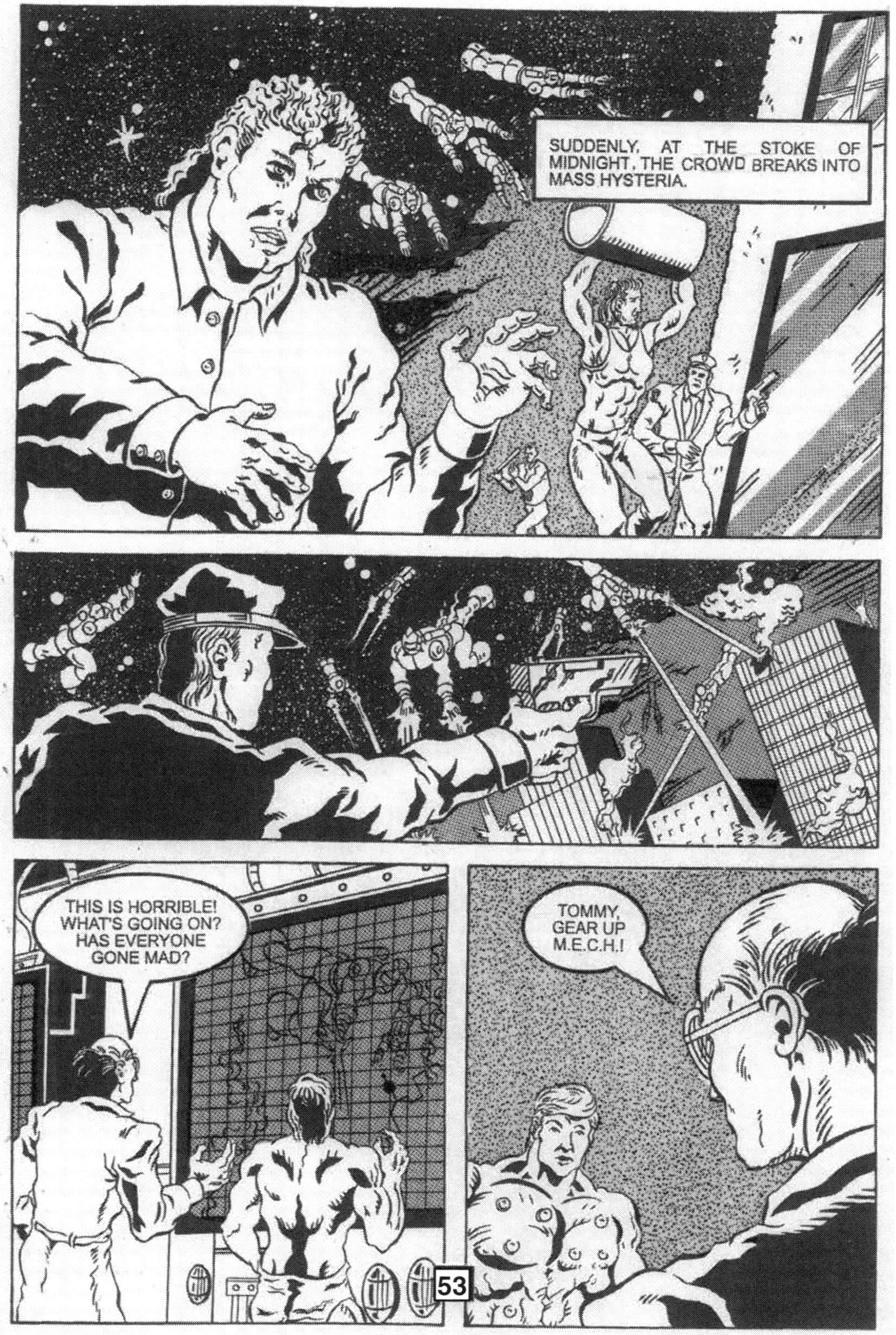
SUDDENLY, AT THE STOKE OF MIDNIGHT, THE CROWD BREAKS INTO MASS HYSTERIA.
THIS IS HORRIBLE! WHAT'S GOING ON? HAS EVERYONE GONE MAD?
TOMMY, GEAR UP M.E.C.H.I

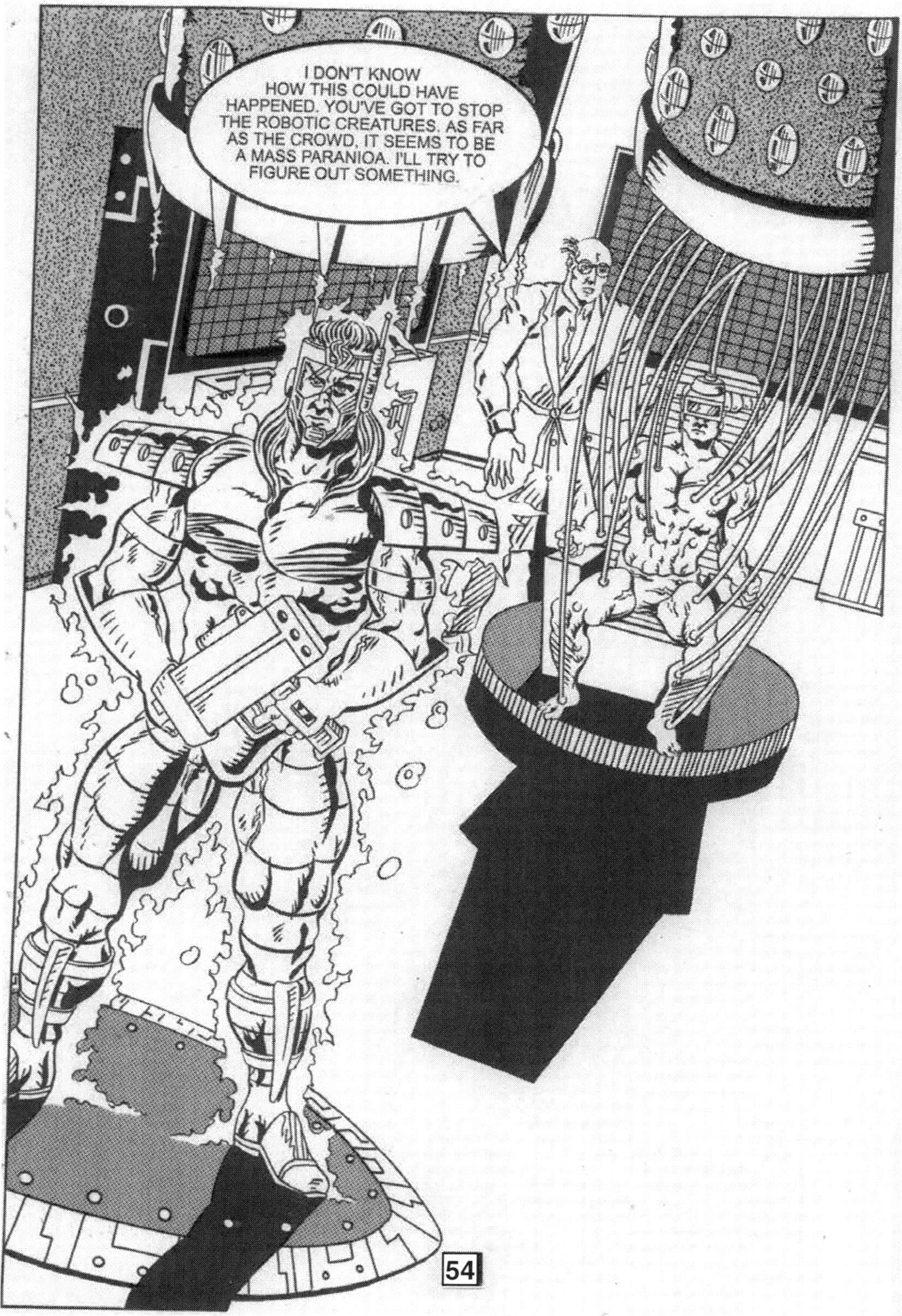
I DON'T KNOW HOW THIS COULD HAVE HAPPENED. YOU'VE GOT TO STOP THE ROBOTIC CREATURES. AS FAR AS THE CROWD, IT SEEMS TO BE A MASS PARANIOA. I'LL TRY TO FIGURE OUT SOMETHING.

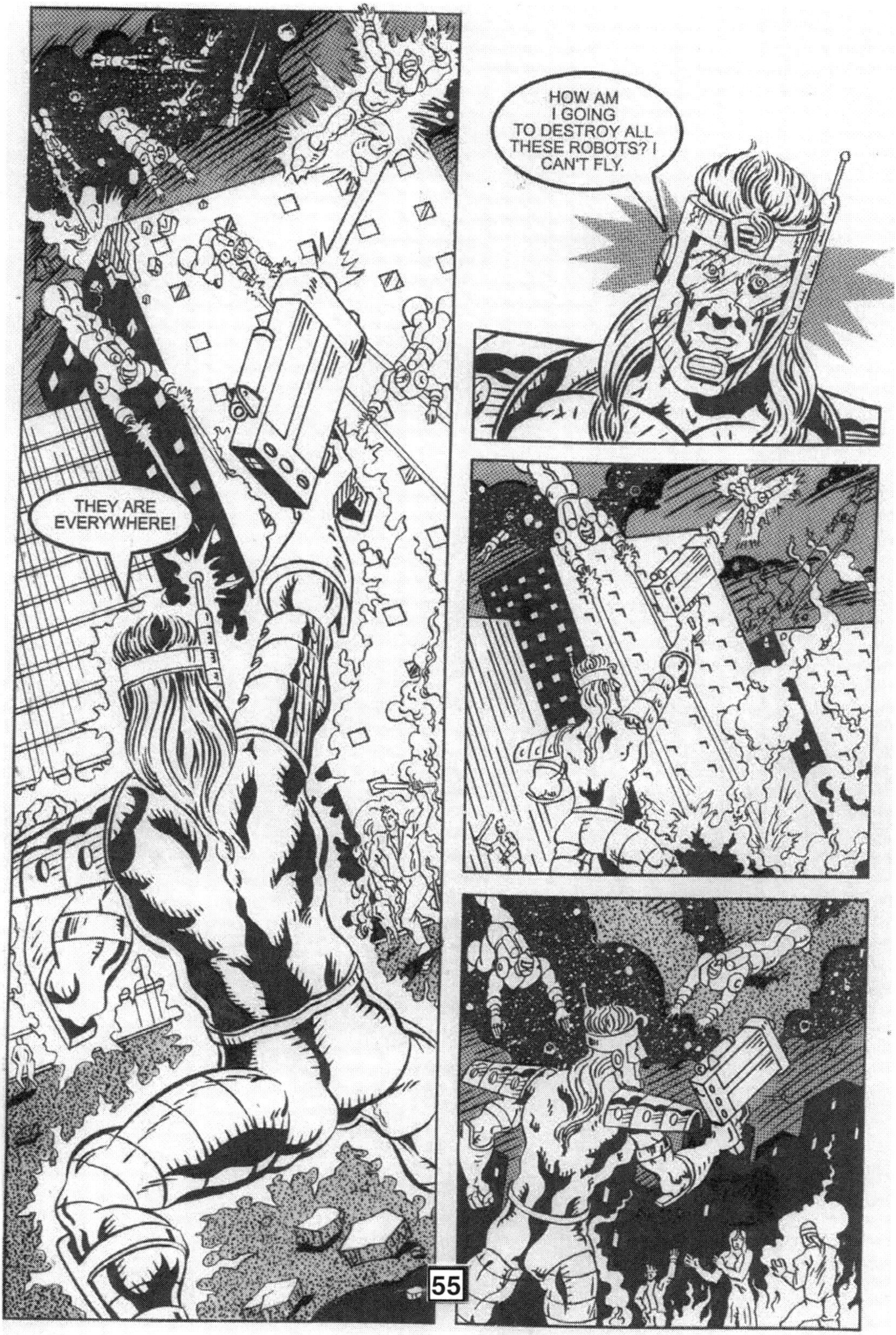
THEY ARE EVERYWHERE!
HOW AM I GOING TO DESTROY ALL THESE ROBOTS? I CAN'T FLY.

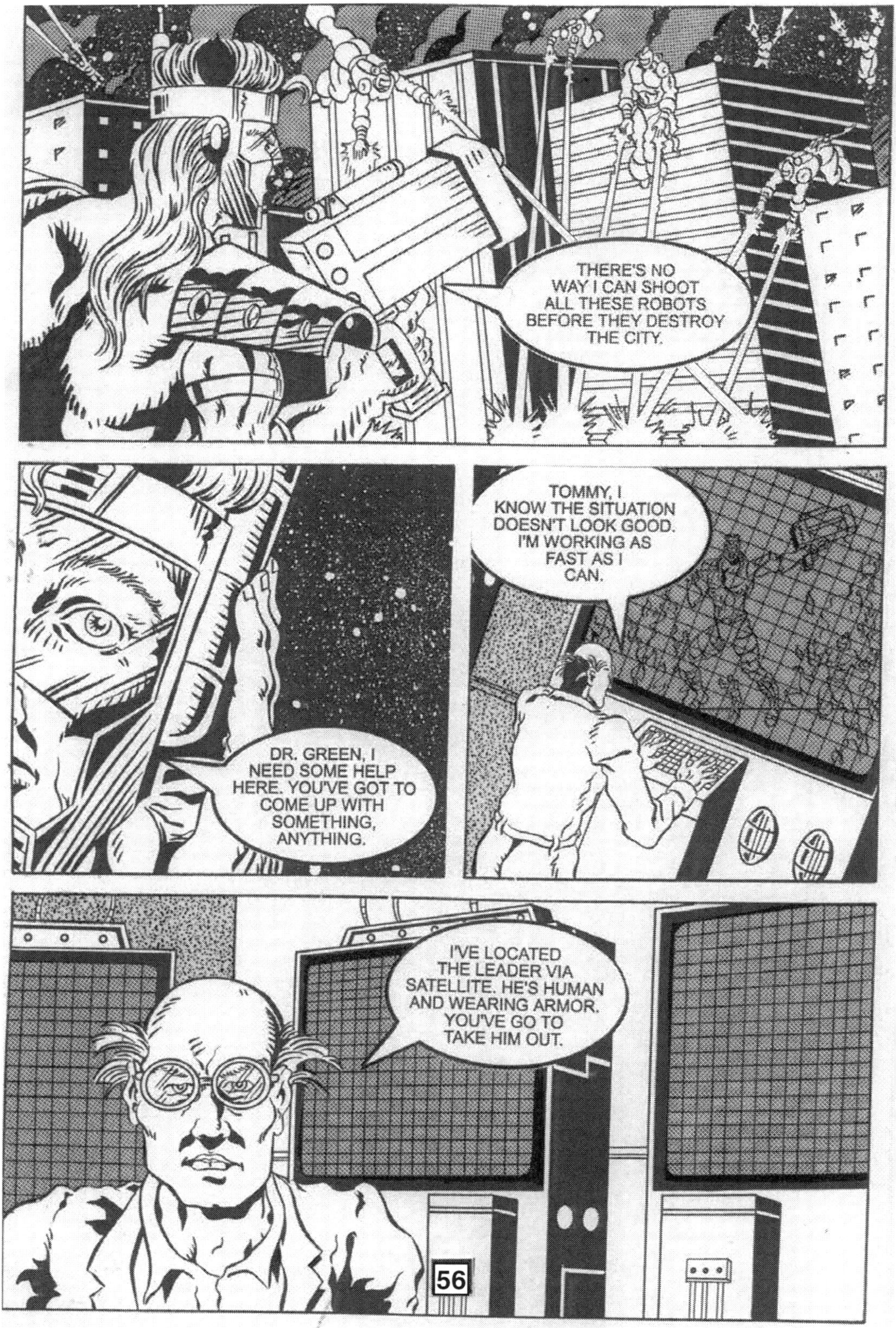
THERE'S NO WAY I CAN SHOOT ALL THESE ROBOTS BEFORE THEY DESTROY THE CITY.
DR. GREEN, I NEED SOME HELP HERE. YOU'VE GOT TO COME UP WITH SOMETHING, ANYTHING.
TOMMY, I KNOW THE SITUATION DOESN'T LOOK GOOD. I'M WORKING AS FAST AS I CAN.
I'VE LOCATED THE LEADER VIA SATELLITE. HE'S HUMAN AND WEARING ARMOR. YOU'VE GO TO TAKE HIM OUT.

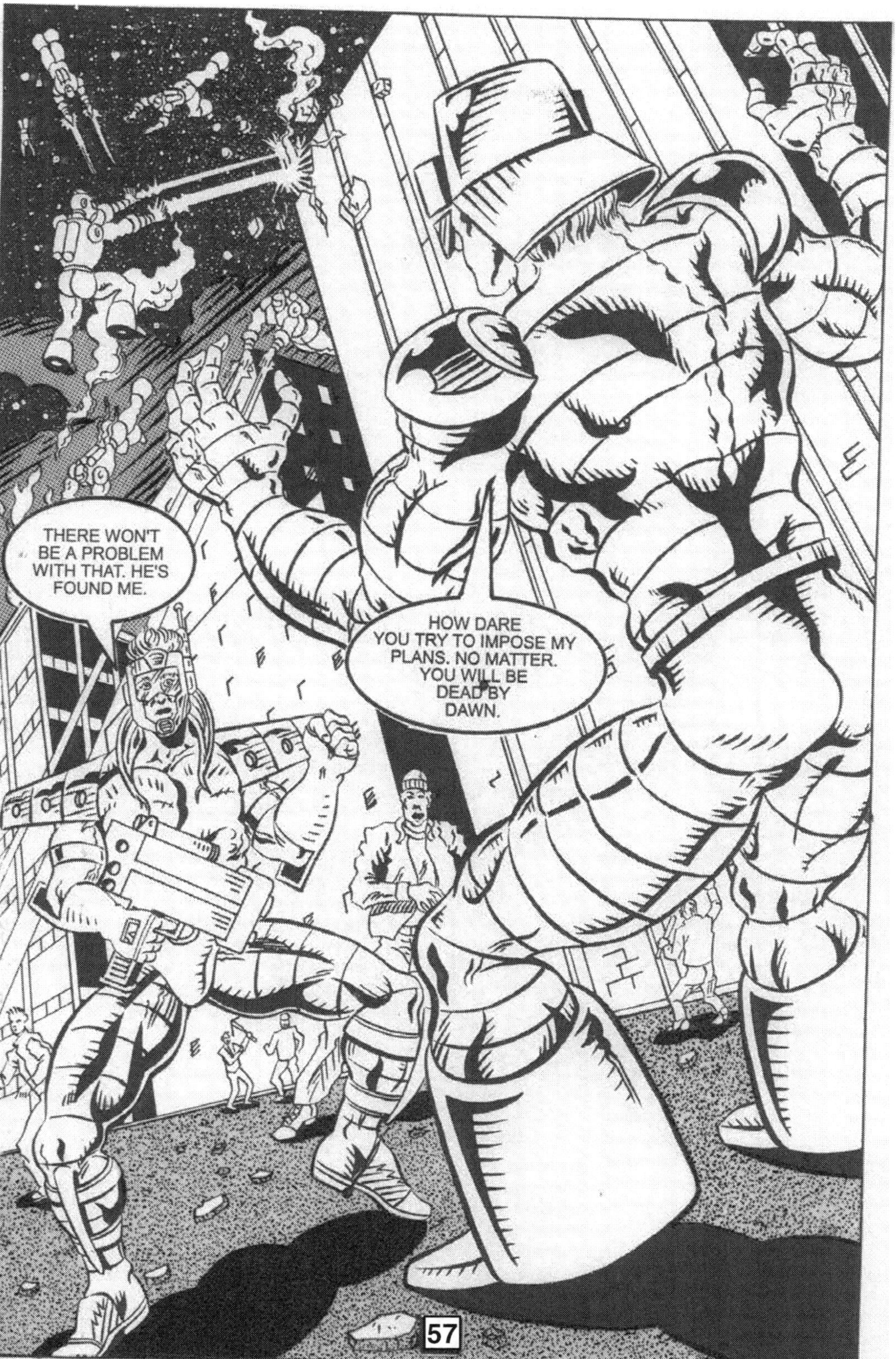
THERE WON'T BE A PROBLEM WITH THAT. HE'S FOUND ME.
HOW DARE YOU TRY TO IMPOSE MY PLANS. NO MATTER. YOU WILL BE DEAD BY DAWN.

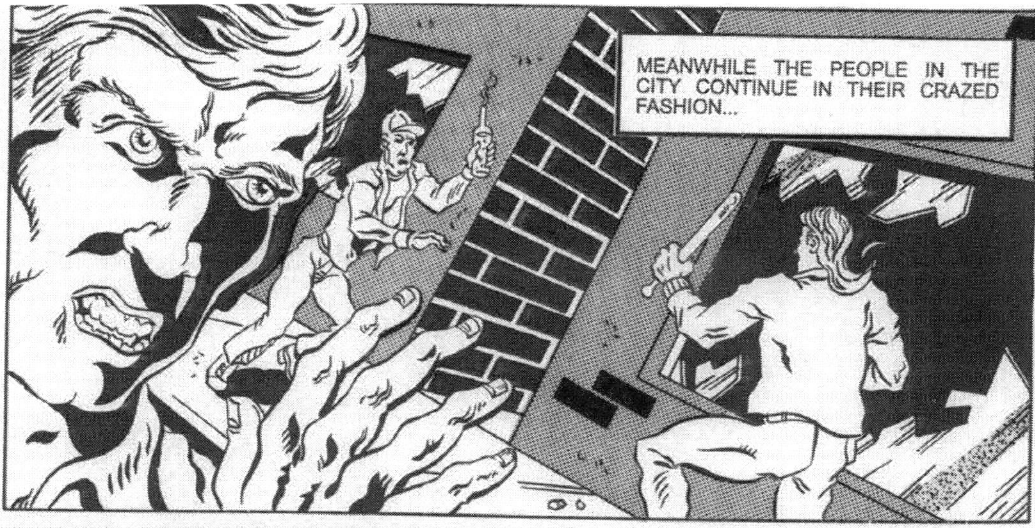
MEANWHILE THE PEOPLE IN THE CITY CONTINUE IN THEIR CRAZED FASHION...

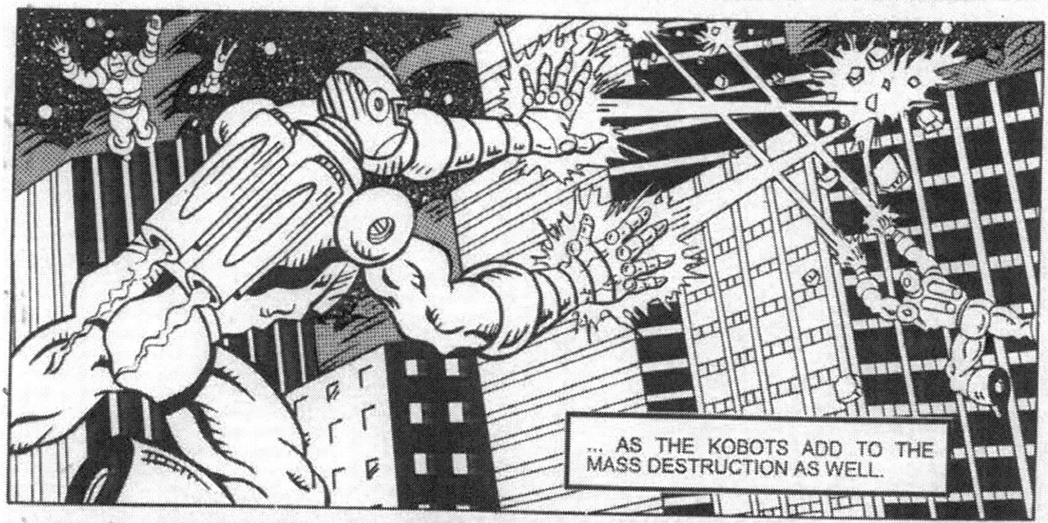
... AS THE KOBOTS ADD TO THE MASS DESTRUCTION AS WELL.

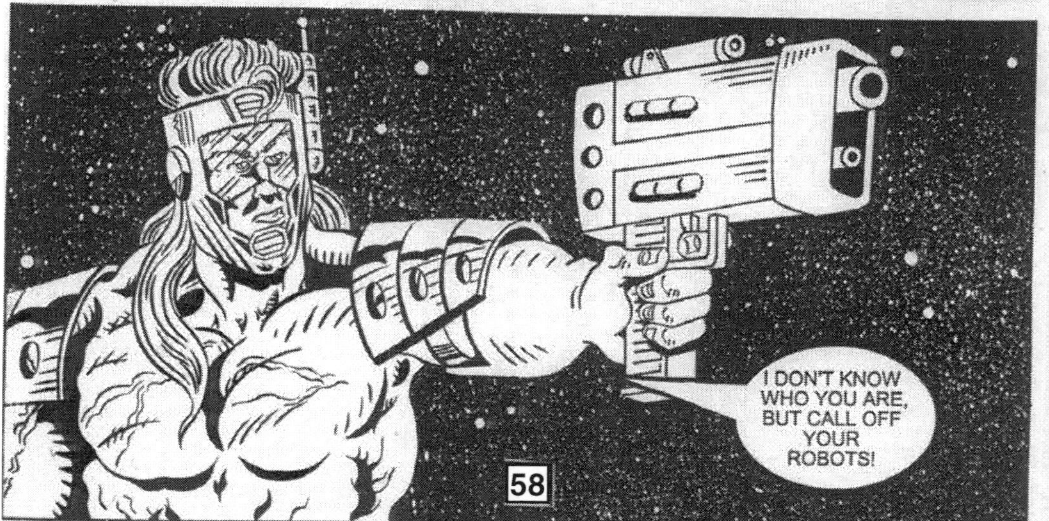
I DON'T KNOW WHO YOU ARE, BUT CALL OFF YOUR ROBOTS!

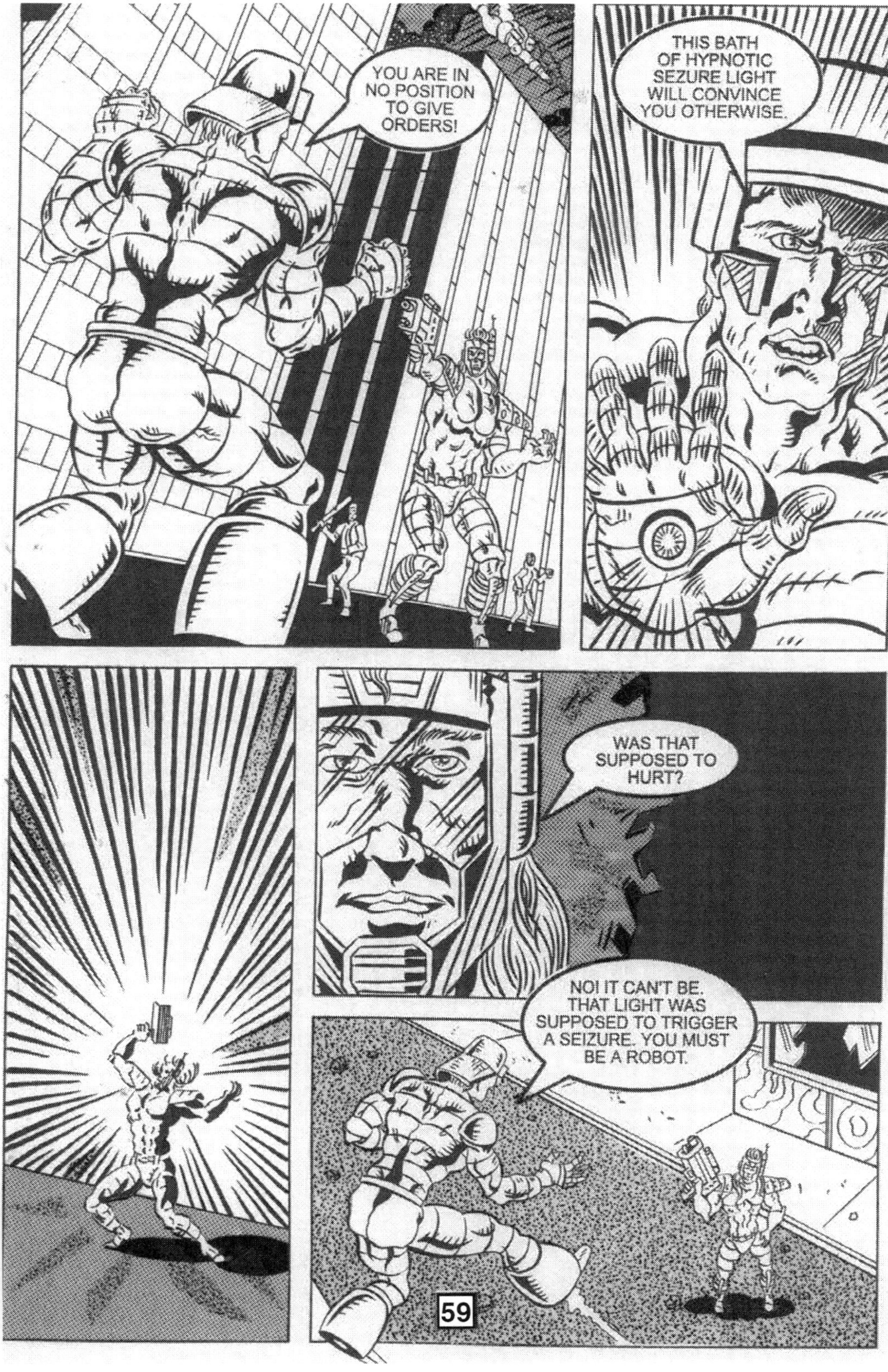
YOU ARE IN NO POSITION TO GIVE ORDERS!
THIS BATH OF HYPNOTIC SEZURE LIGHT WILL CONVINCE YOU OTHERWISE.
WAS THAT SUPPOSED TO HURT?
NO! IT CAN'T BE. THAT LIGHT WAS SUPPOSED TO TRIGGER A SEIZURE. YOU MUST BE A ROBOT.

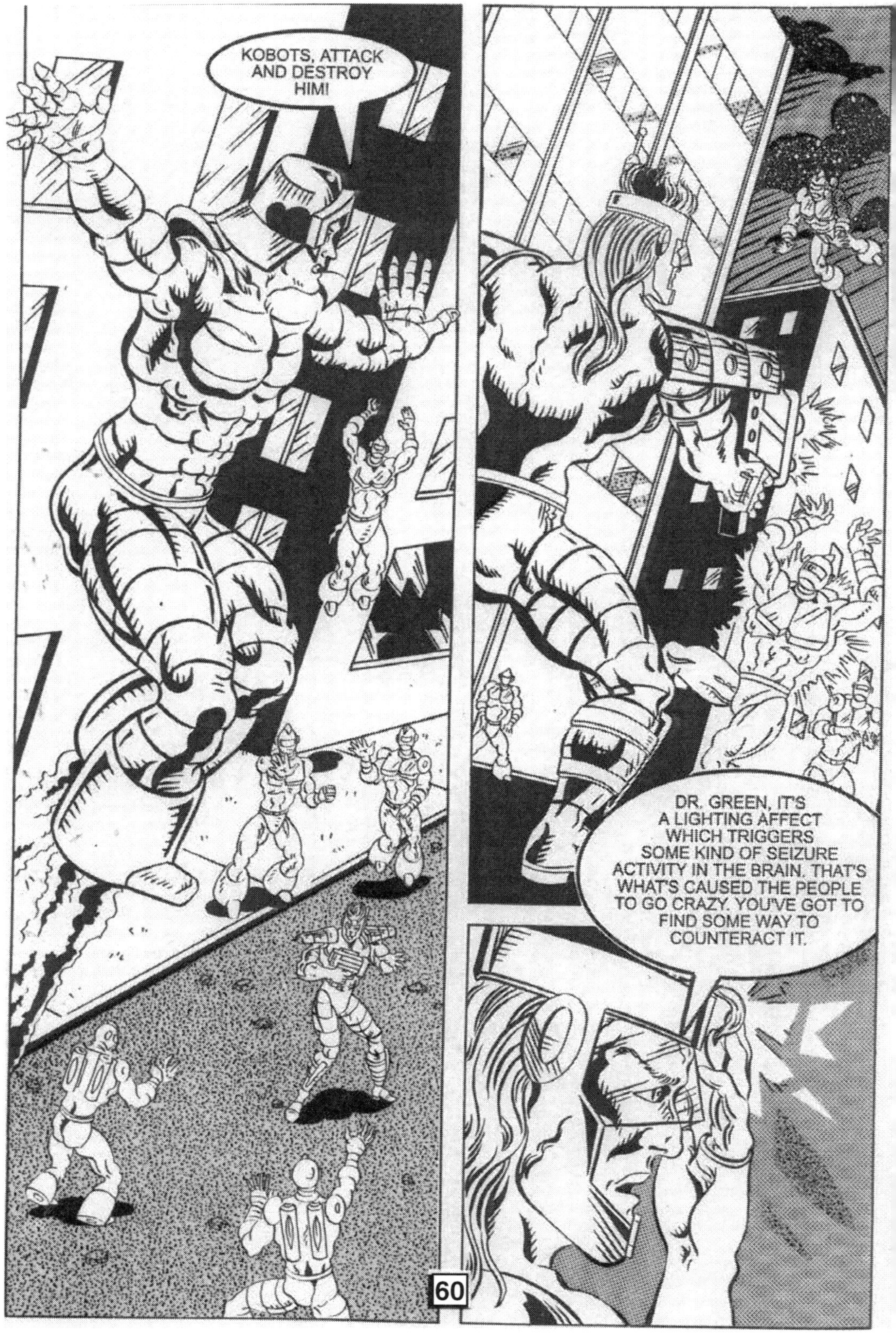
KOBOTS, ATTACK AND DESTROY HIM!
DR. GREEN, IT'S A LIGHTING AFFECT WHICH TRIGGERS SOME KIND OF SEIZURE ACTIVITY IN THE BRAIN. THAT'S WHAT'S CAUSED THE PEOPLE TO GO CRAZY. YOU'VE GOT TO FIND SOME WAY TO COUNTERACT IT.

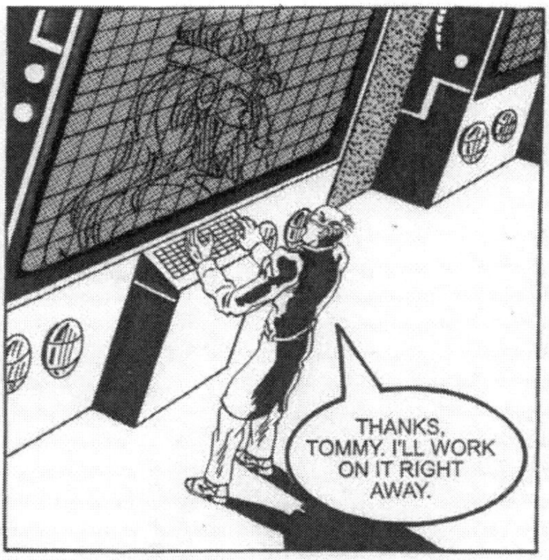
THANKS, TOMMY. I'LL WORK ON IT RIGHT AWAY.

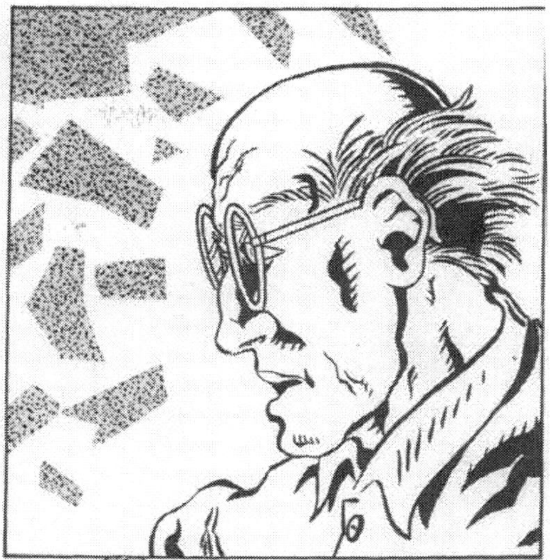

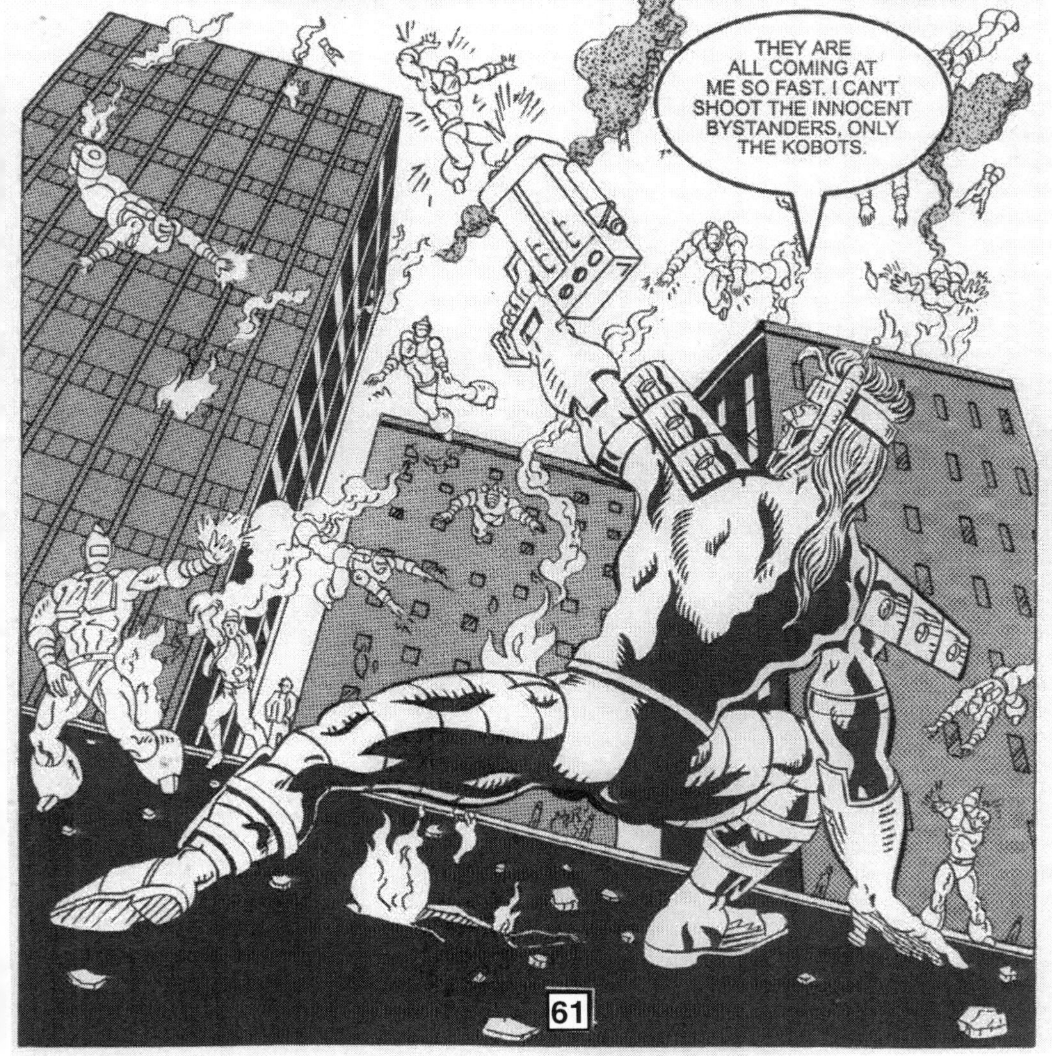
THEY ARE ALL COMING AT ME SO FAST. I CAN'T SHOOT THE INNOCENT BYSTANDERS, ONLY THE KOBOTS.

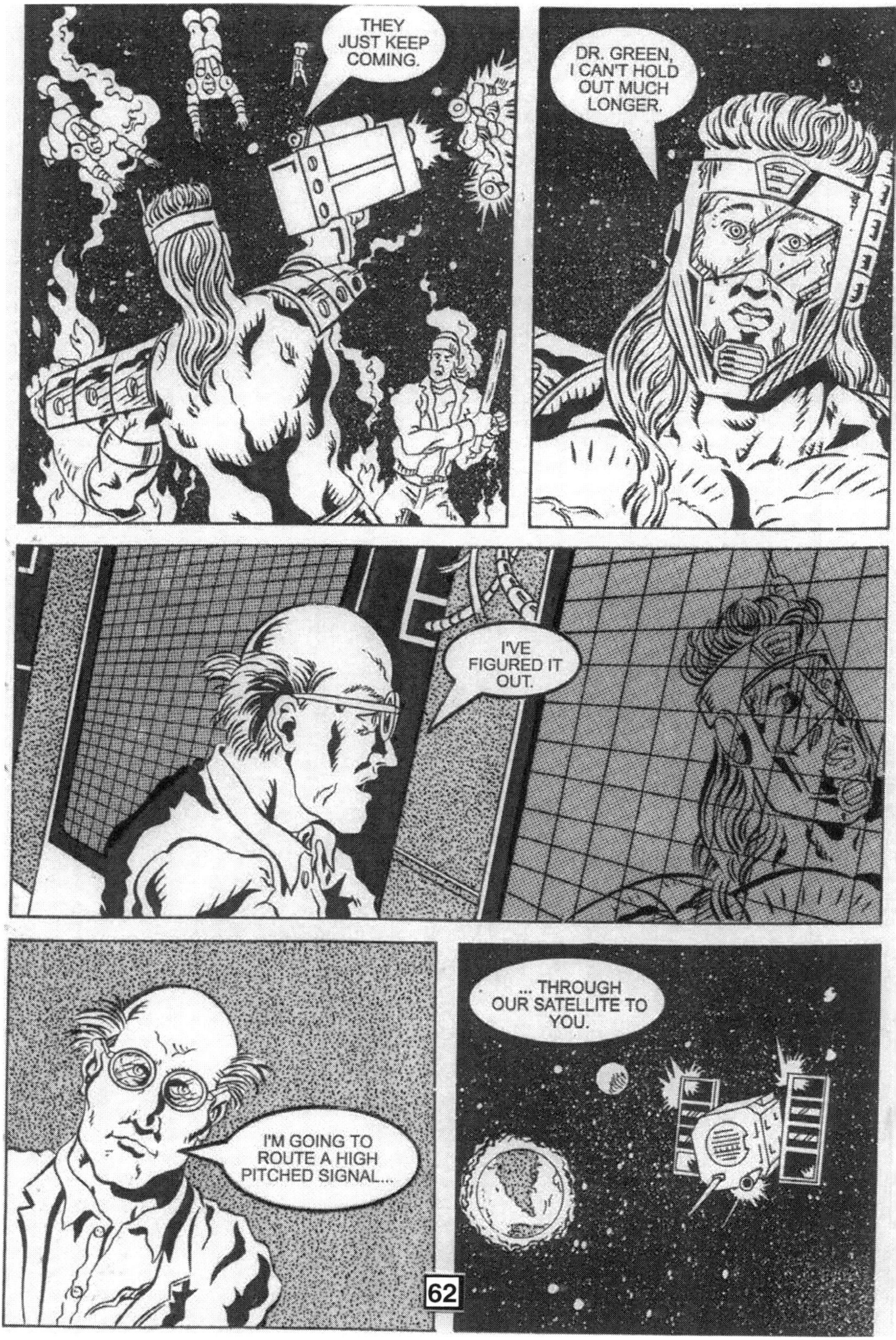
THEY JUST KEEP COMING.
DR. GREEN, I CAN'T HOLD OUT MUCH LONGER.
I'VE FIGURED IT OUT.
I'M GOING TO ROUTE A HIGH PITCHED SIGNAL...
... THROUGH OUR SATELLITE TO YOU.

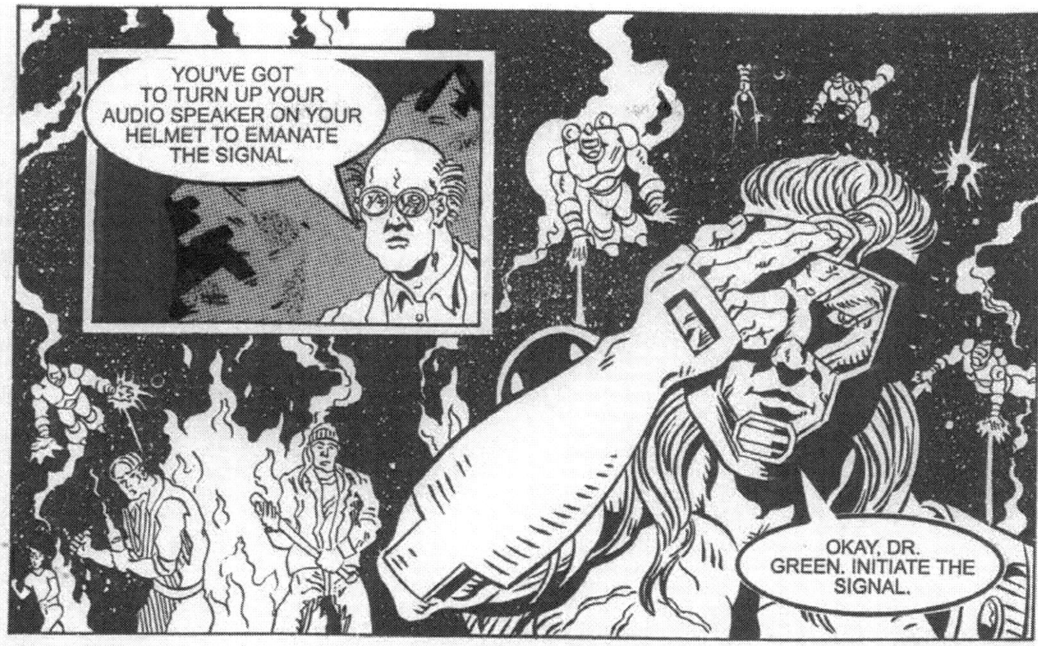
YOU'VE GOT TO TURN UP YOUR AUDIO SPEAKER ON YOUR HELMET TO EMANATE THE SIGNAL.
OKAY, DR. GREEN. INITIATE THE SIGNAL.

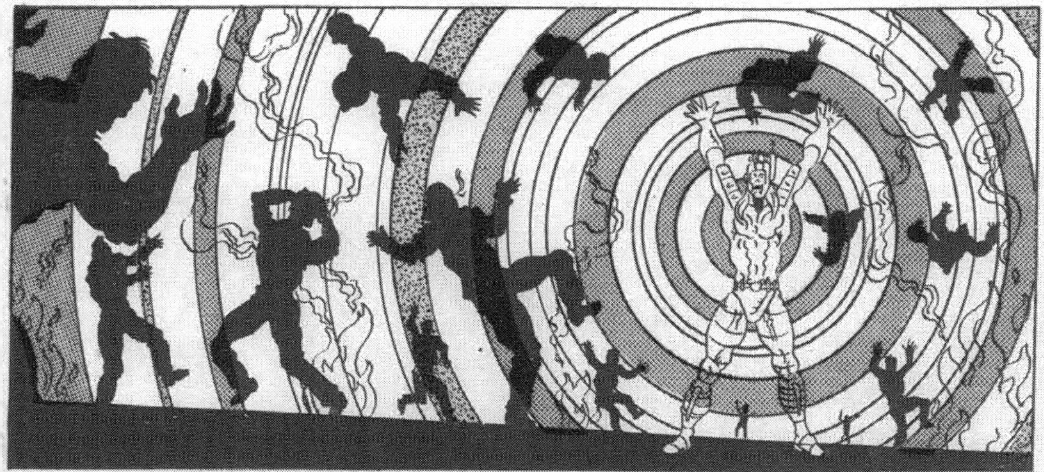

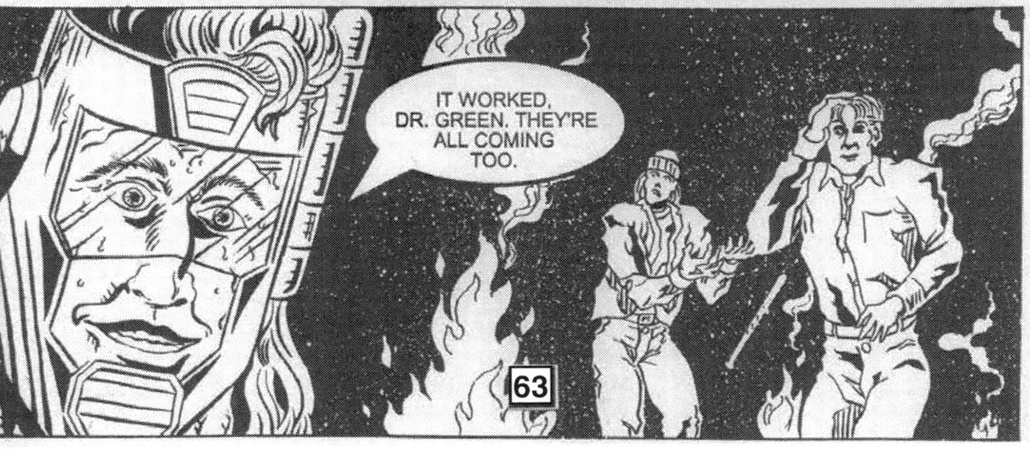
IT WORKED, DR. GREEN. THEY'RE ALL COMING TOO.

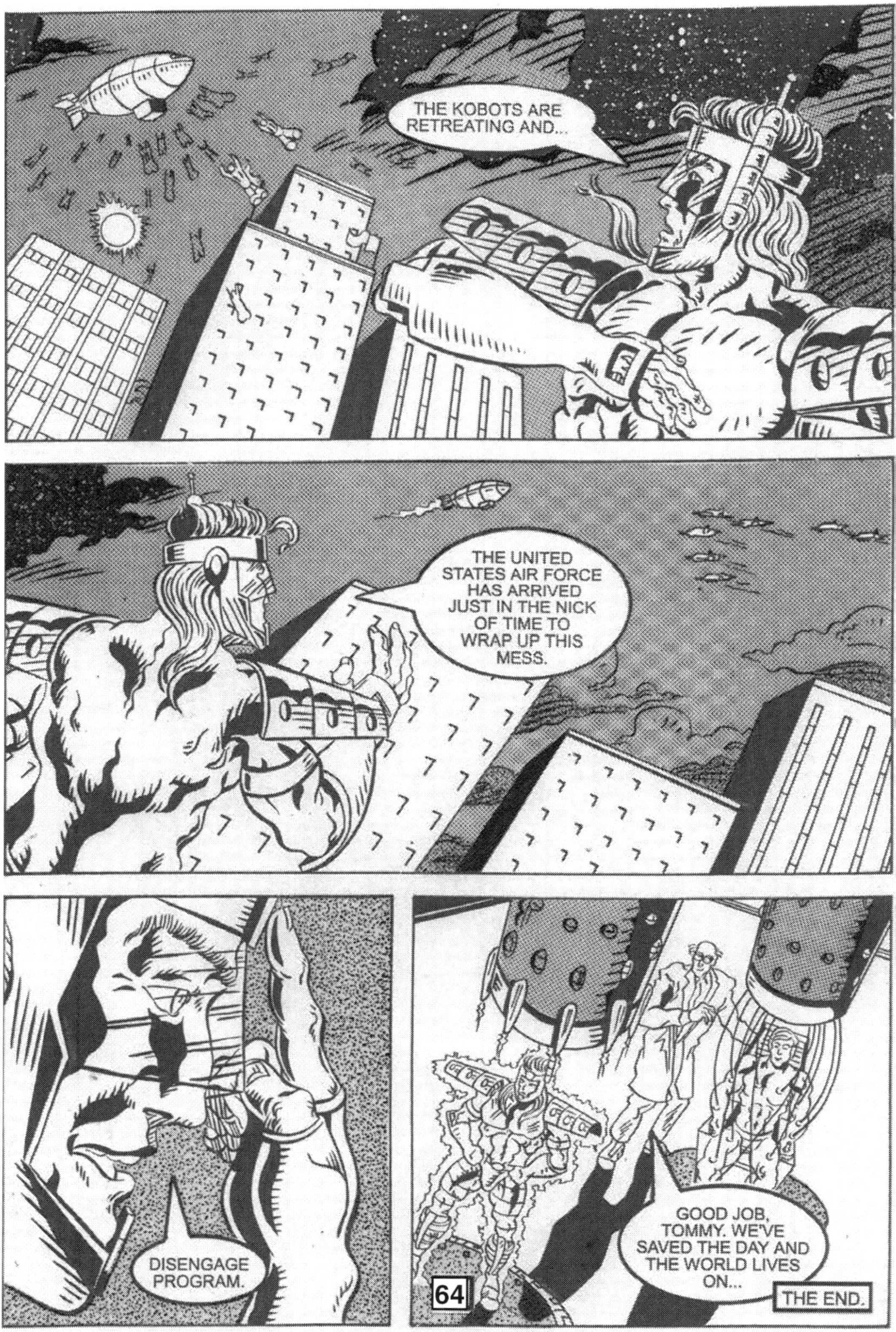
THE KOBOTS ARE RETREATING AND...
THE UNITED STATES AIR FORCE HAS ARRIVED JUST IN THE NICK OF TIME TO WRAP UP THIS MESS.
DISENGAGE PROGRAM.
GOOD JOB, TOMMY. WE'VE SAVED THE DAY AND THE WORLD LIVES ON...
THE END.

THEODORE RAYMOND RIDDLE'S

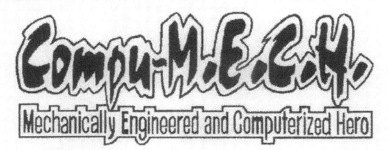

Mechanically Engineered and Computerized Hero

®

MONOLITH COMICS PRESENTS:

Welcome to the exciting adventures of Dr. Green, the inventor of the Compu-M.E.C.H. Program and Tommy Chase, the controller of the M.E.C.H. unit.

They unite there skills to combat the evils in the world with truth and justice. They are our protecters.

They are:
Compu-M.E.C.H.!

SPECIAL THANKS TO:
My loving wife, Melissa Jane Riddle. Plus all the people who believed in me and gave me a chance.

CHAPTER #2.

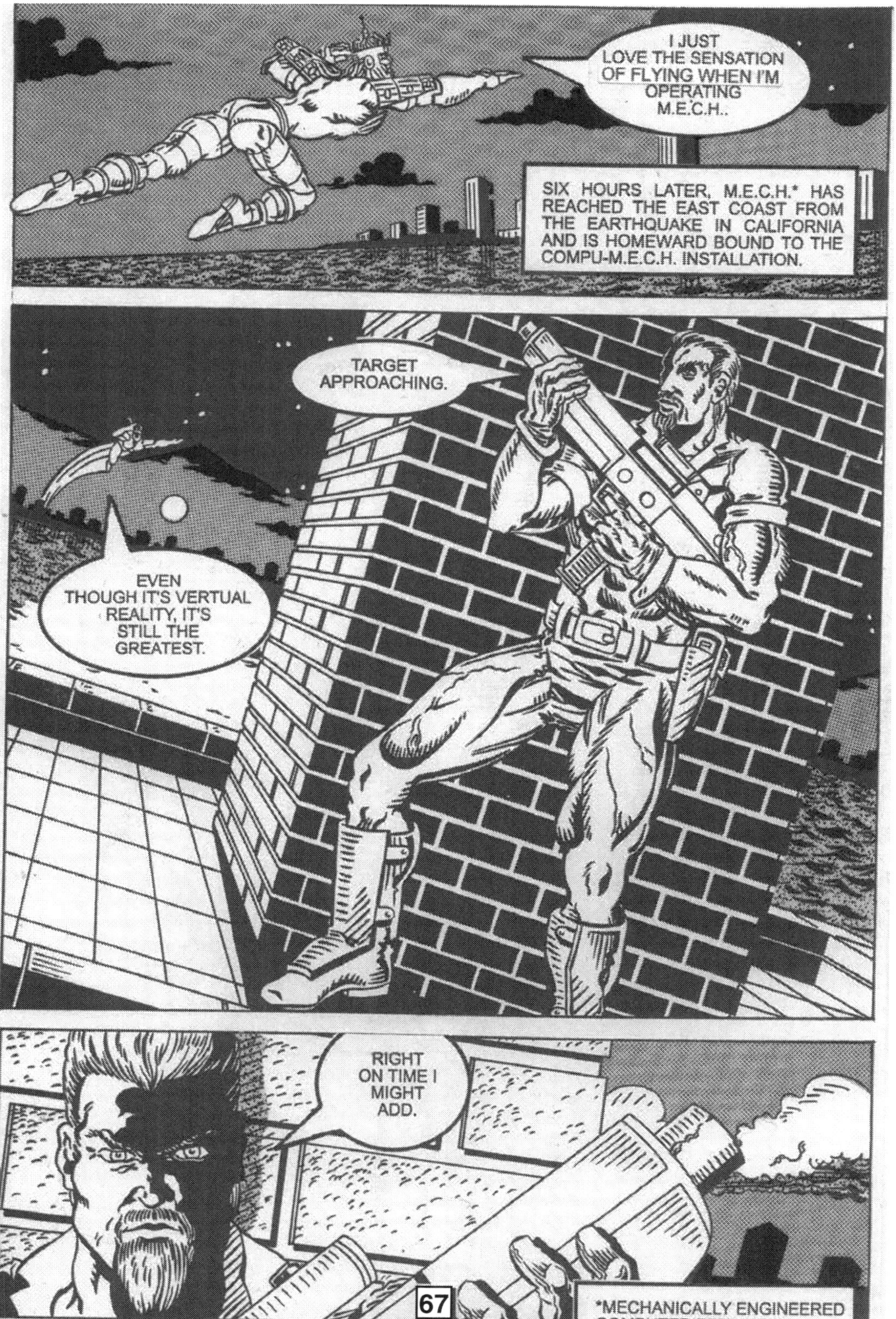
I JUST LOVE THE SENSATION OF FLYING WHEN I'M OPERATING M.E.C.H..
SIX HOURS LATER, M.E.C.H.* HAS REACHED THE EAST COAST FROM THE EARTHQUAKE IN CALIFORNIA AND IS HOMEWARD BOUND TO THE COMPU-M.E.C.H. INSTALLATION.
TARGET APPROACHING.
EVEN THOUGH IT'S VERTUAL REALITY, IT'S STILL THE GREATEST.
RIGHT ON TIME I MIGHT ADD.
*MECHANICALLY ENGINEERED COMPUTERIZED HERO.

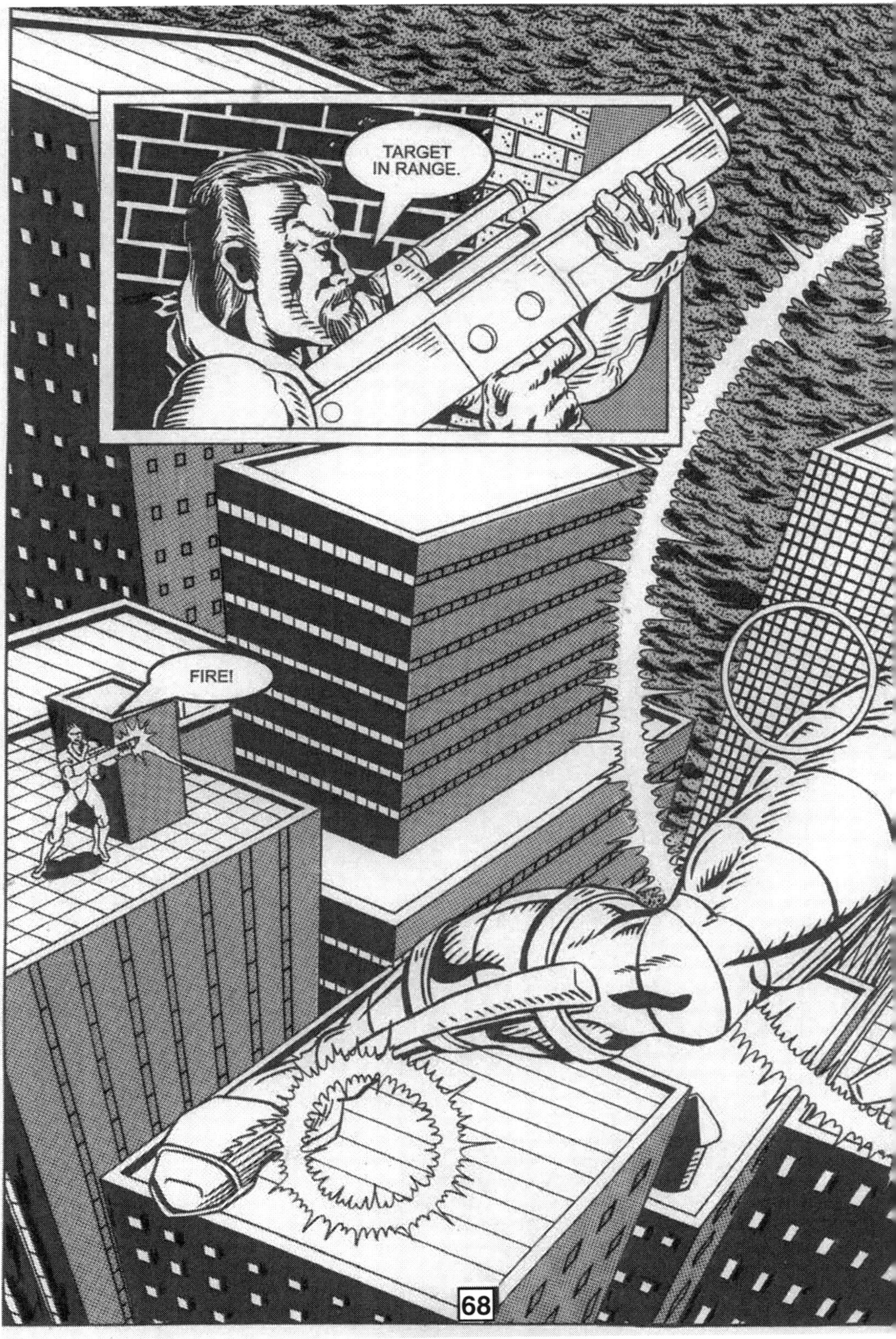
TARGET IN RANGE.
FIRE!

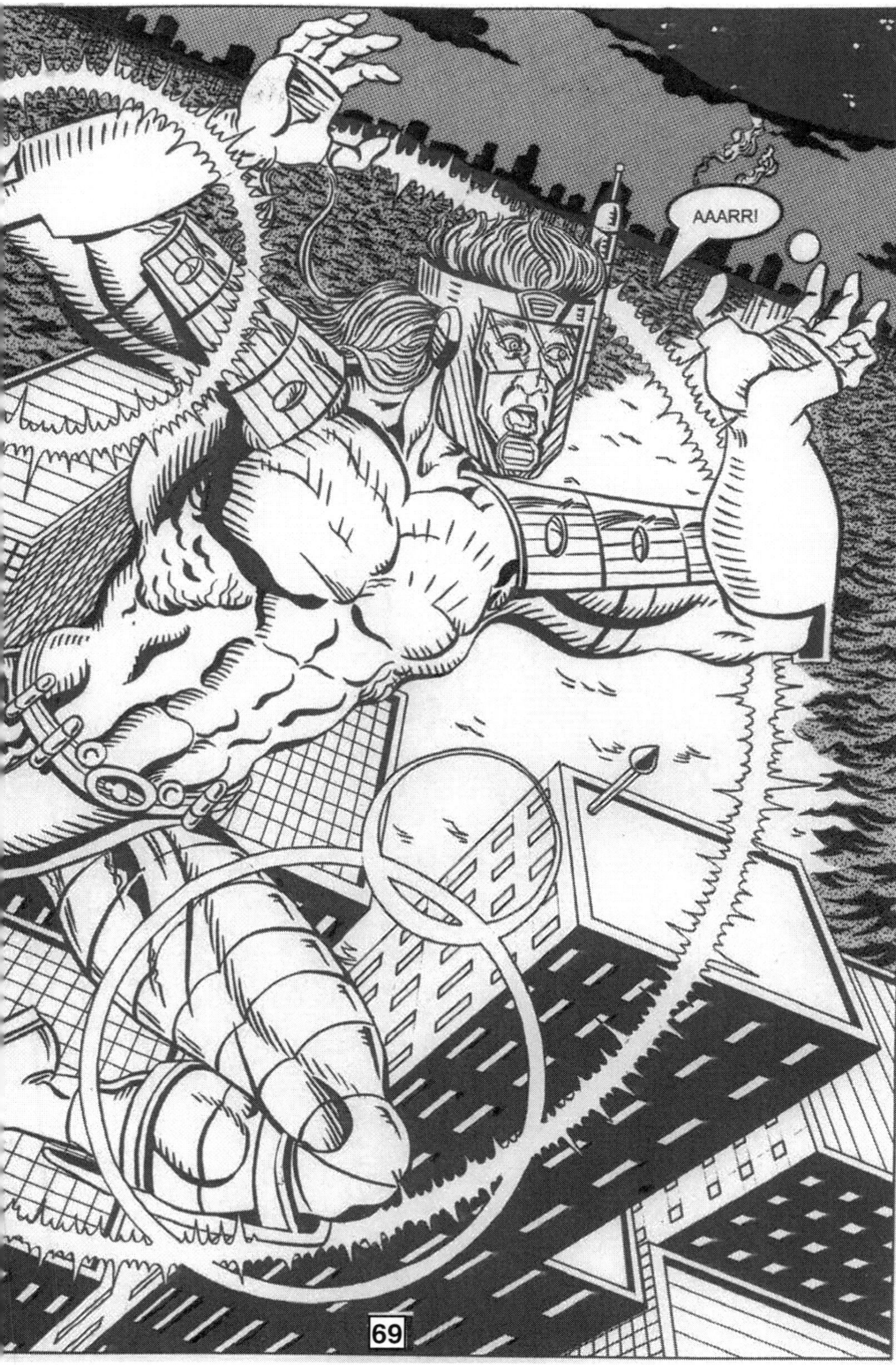
AAARR!

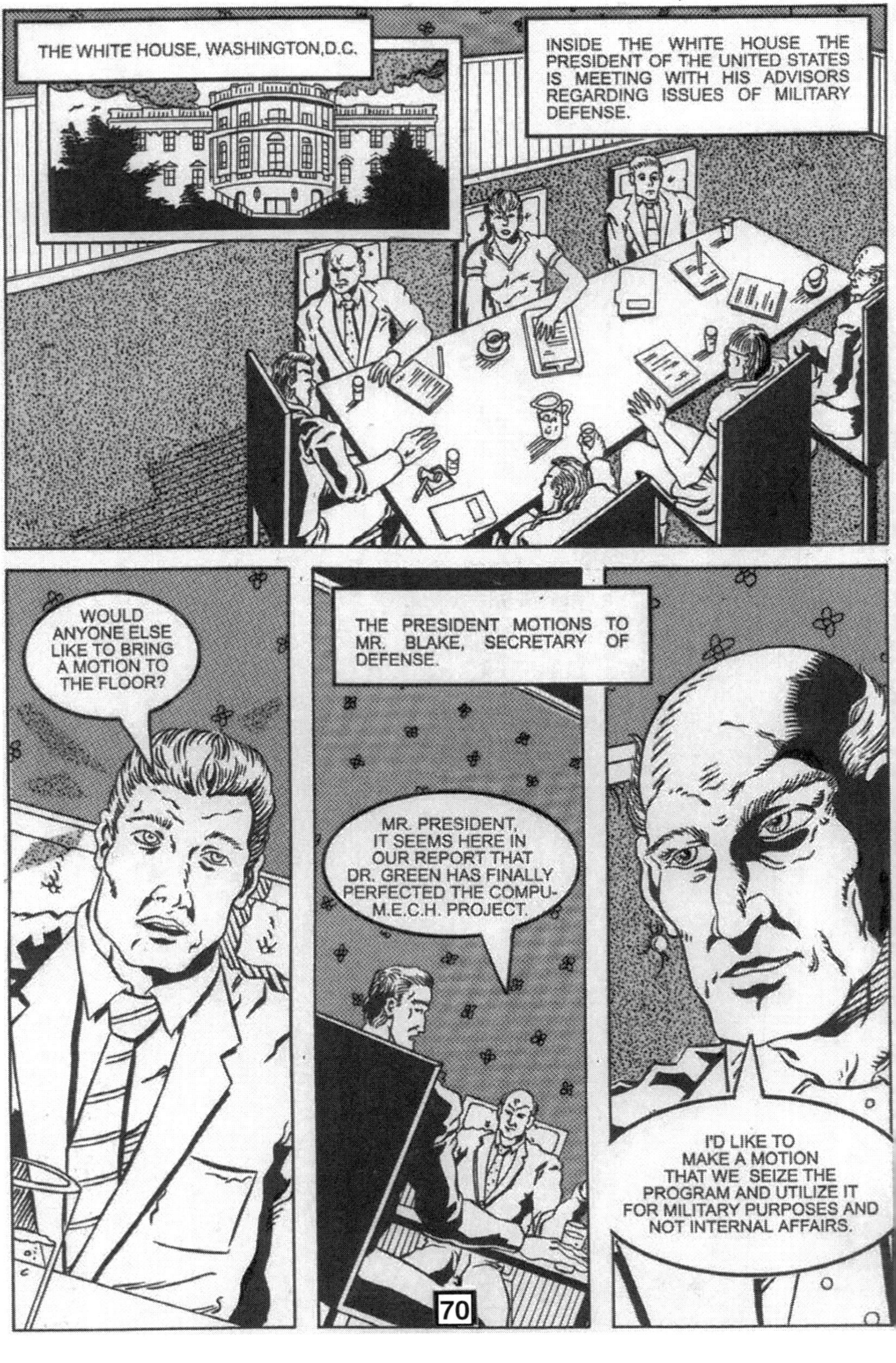
THE WHITE HOUSE, WASHINGTON,D.C.
INSIDE THE WHITE HOUSE THE PRESIDENT OF THE UNITED STATES IS MEETING WITH HIS ADVISORS REGARDING ISSUES OF MILITARY DEFENSE.
WOULD ANYONE ELSE LIKE TO BRING A MOTION TO THE FLOOR?
THE PRESIDENT MOTIONS TO MR. BLAKE, SECRETARY OF DEFENSE.
MR. PRESIDENT, IT SEEMS HERE IN OUR REPORT THAT DR. GREEN HAS FINALLY PERFECTED THE COMPU-M.E.C.H. PROJECT.
I'D LIKE TO MAKE A MOTION THAT WE SEIZE THE PROGRAM AND UTILIZE IT FOR MILITARY PURPOSES AND NOT INTERNAL AFFAIRS.

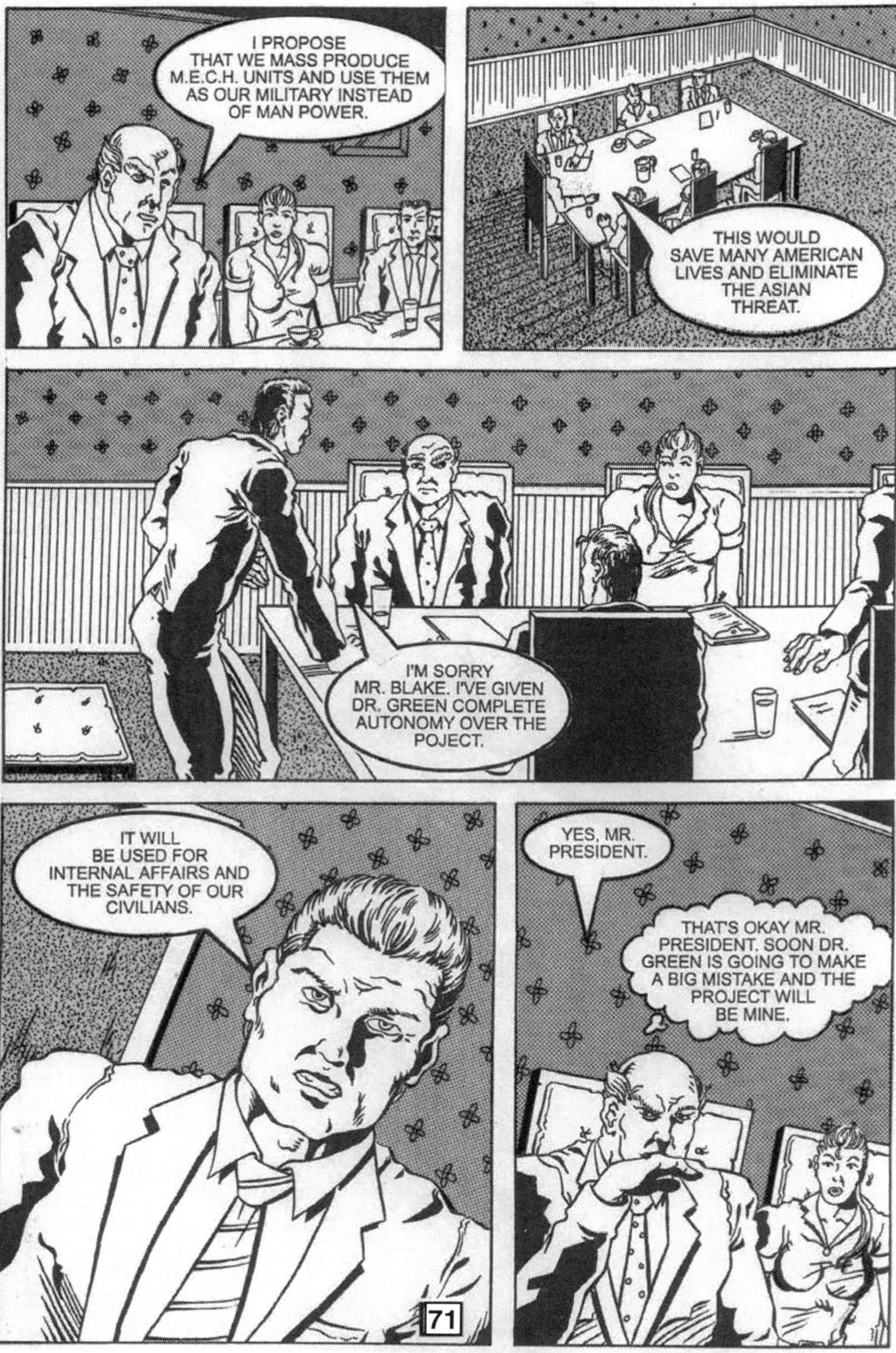
I PROPOSE THAT WE MASS PRODUCE M.E.C.H. UNITS AND USE THEM AS OUR MILITARY INSTEAD OF MAN POWER.
THIS WOULD SAVE MANY AMERICAN LIVES AND ELIMINATE THE ASIAN THREAT.
I'M SORRY MR. BLAKE. I'VE GIVEN DR. GREEN COMPLETE AUTONOMY OVER THE POJECT.
IT WILL BE USED FOR INTERNAL AFFAIRS AND THE SAFETY OF OUR CIVILIANS.
YES, MR. PRESIDENT.
THAT'S OKAY MR. PRESIDENT. SOON DR. GREEN IS GOING TO MAKE A BIG MISTAKE AND THE PROJECT WILL BE MINE.

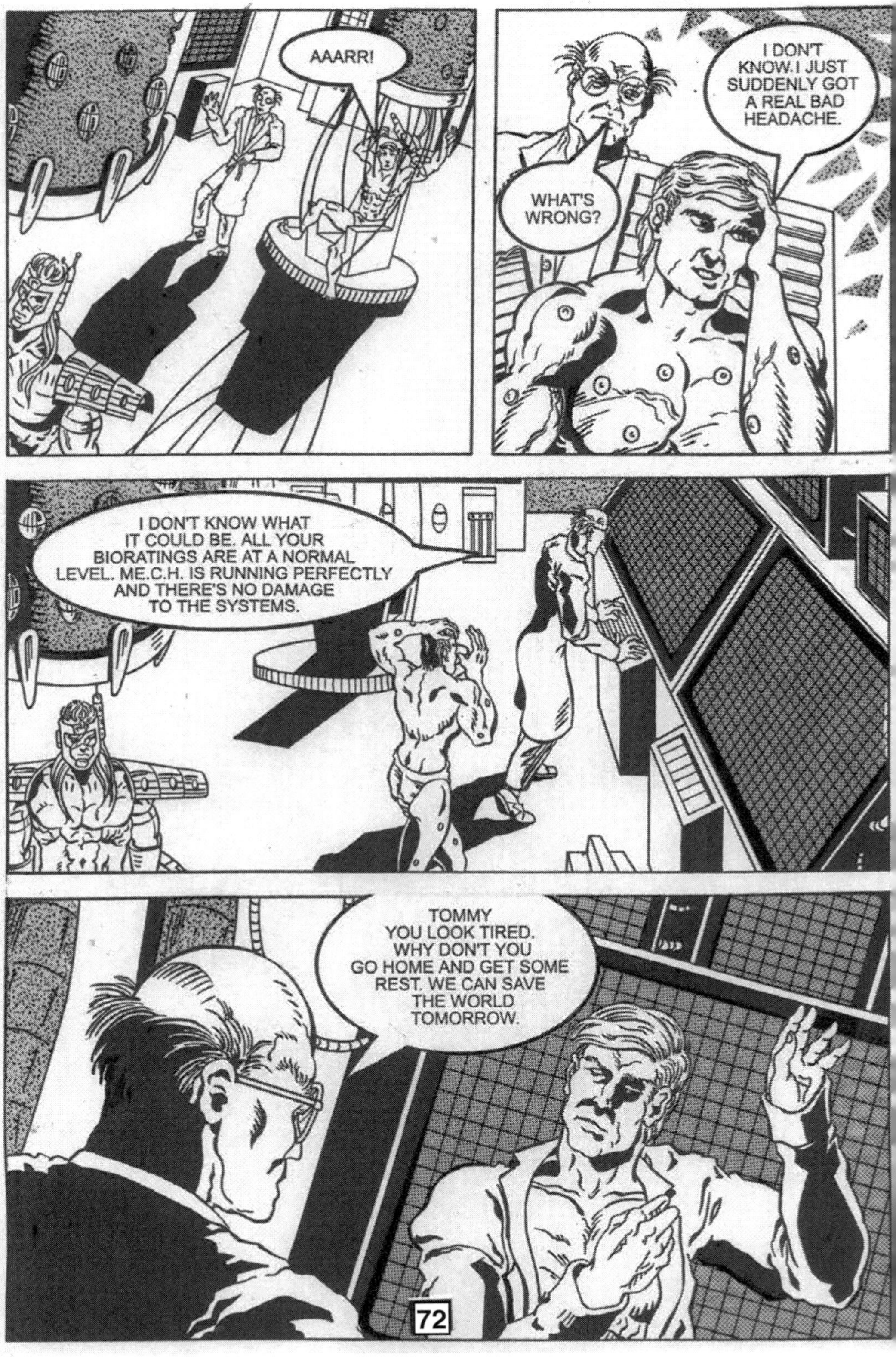
AAARR!
WHAT'S WRONG?
I DON'T KNOW. I JUST SUDDENLY GOT A REAL BAD HEADACHE.
I DON'T KNOW WHAT IT COULD BE. ALL YOUR BIORATINGS ARE AT A NORMAL LEVEL. ME.C.H. IS RUNNING PERFECTLY AND THERE'S NO DAMAGE TO THE SYSTEMS.
TOMMY YOU LOOK TIRED. WHY DON'T YOU GO HOME AND GET SOME REST. WE CAN SAVE THE WORLD TOMORROW.

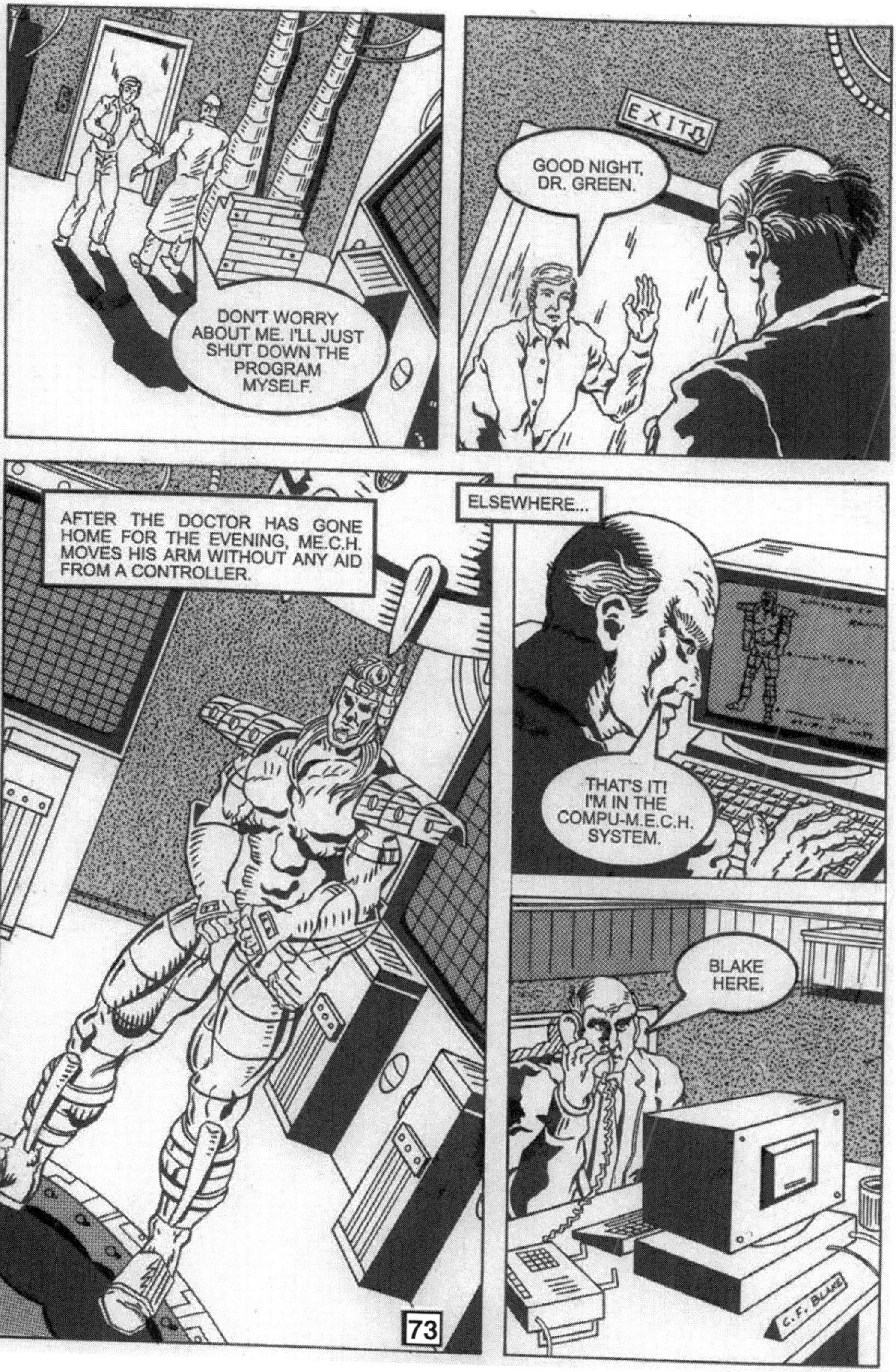
DON'T WORRY ABOUT ME. I'LL JUST SHUT DOWN THE PROGRAM MYSELF.
EXIT
GOOD NIGHT, DR. GREEN.
AFTER THE DOCTOR HAS GONE HOME FOR THE EVENING, ME.C.H. MOVES HIS ARM WITHOUT ANY AID FROM A CONTROLLER.
ELSEWHERE...
THAT'S IT! I'M IN THE COMPU-M.E.C.H. SYSTEM.
BLAKE HERE.
C.F. BLAKE

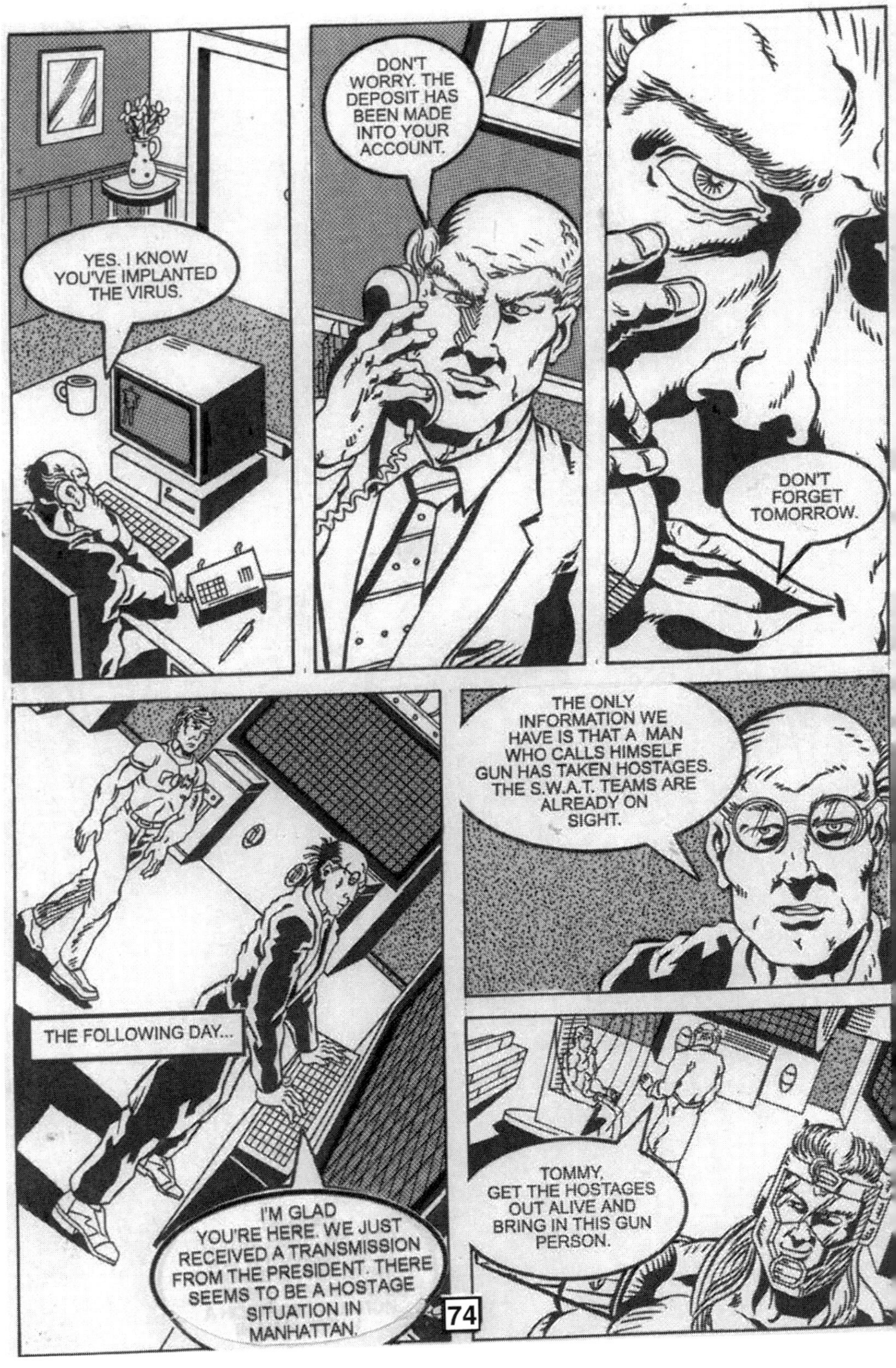

YES. I KNOW YOU'VE IMPLANTED THE VIRUS.
DON'T WORRY. THE DEPOSIT HAS BEEN MADE INTO YOUR ACCOUNT.
DON'T FORGET TOMORROW.
THE FOLLOWING DAY...
I'M GLAD YOU'RE HERE. WE JUST RECEIVED A TRANSMISSION FROM THE PRESIDENT. THERE SEEMS TO BE A HOSTAGE SITUATION IN MANHATTAN.
THE ONLY INFORMATION WE HAVE IS THAT A MAN WHO CALLS HIMSELF GUN HAS TAKEN HOSTAGES. THE S.W.A.T. TEAMS ARE ALREADY ON SIGHT.
TOMMY, GET THE HOSTAGES OUT ALIVE AND BRING IN THIS GUN PERSON.

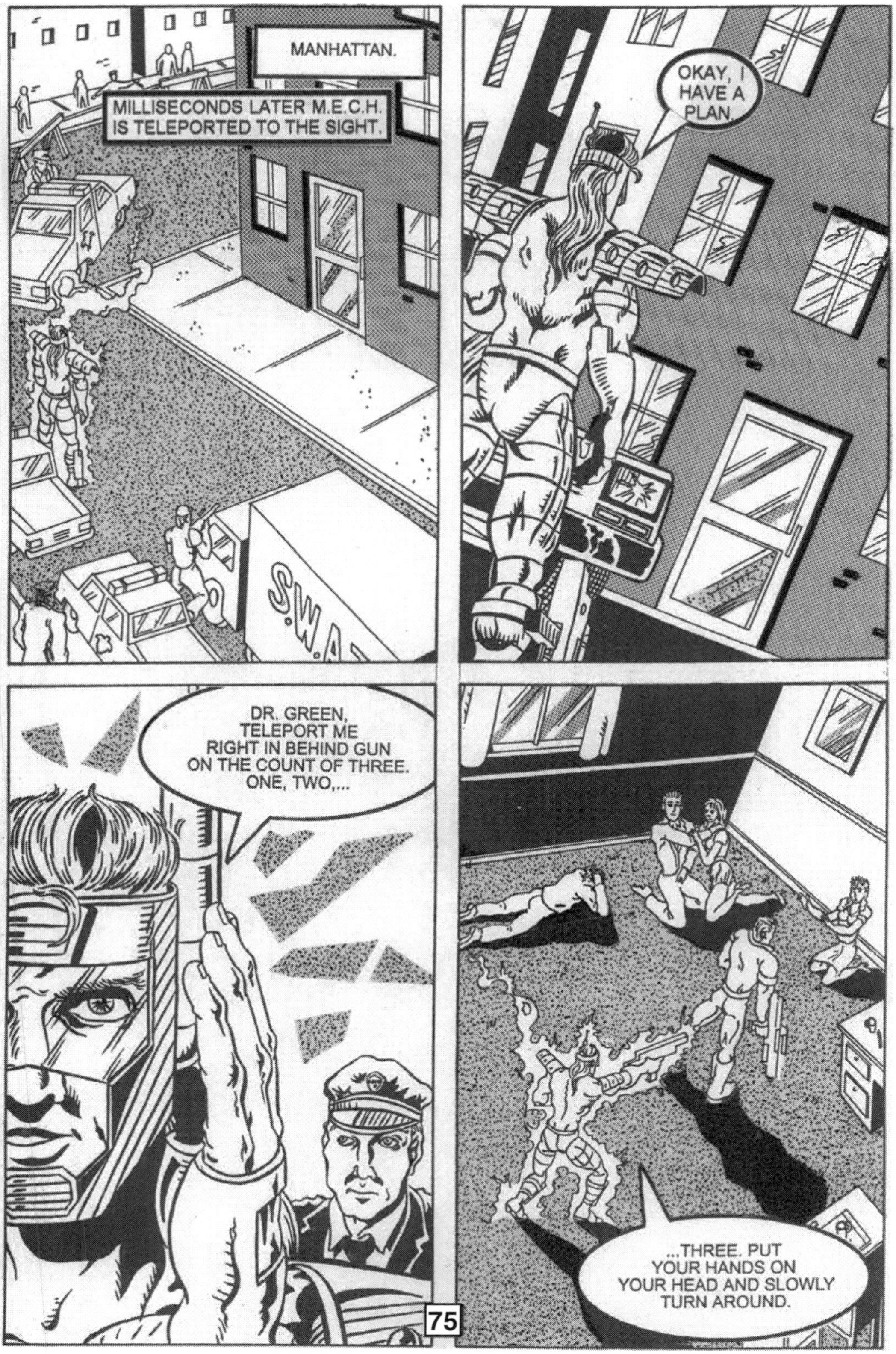
MANHATTAN.
MILLISECONDS LATER M.E.C.H. IS TELEPORTED TO THE SIGHT.
OKAY, I HAVE A PLAN.
DR. GREEN, TELEPORT ME RIGHT IN BEHIND GUN ON THE COUNT OF THREE. ONE, TWO,...
...THREE. PUT YOUR HANDS ON YOUR HEAD AND SLOWLY TURN AROUND.

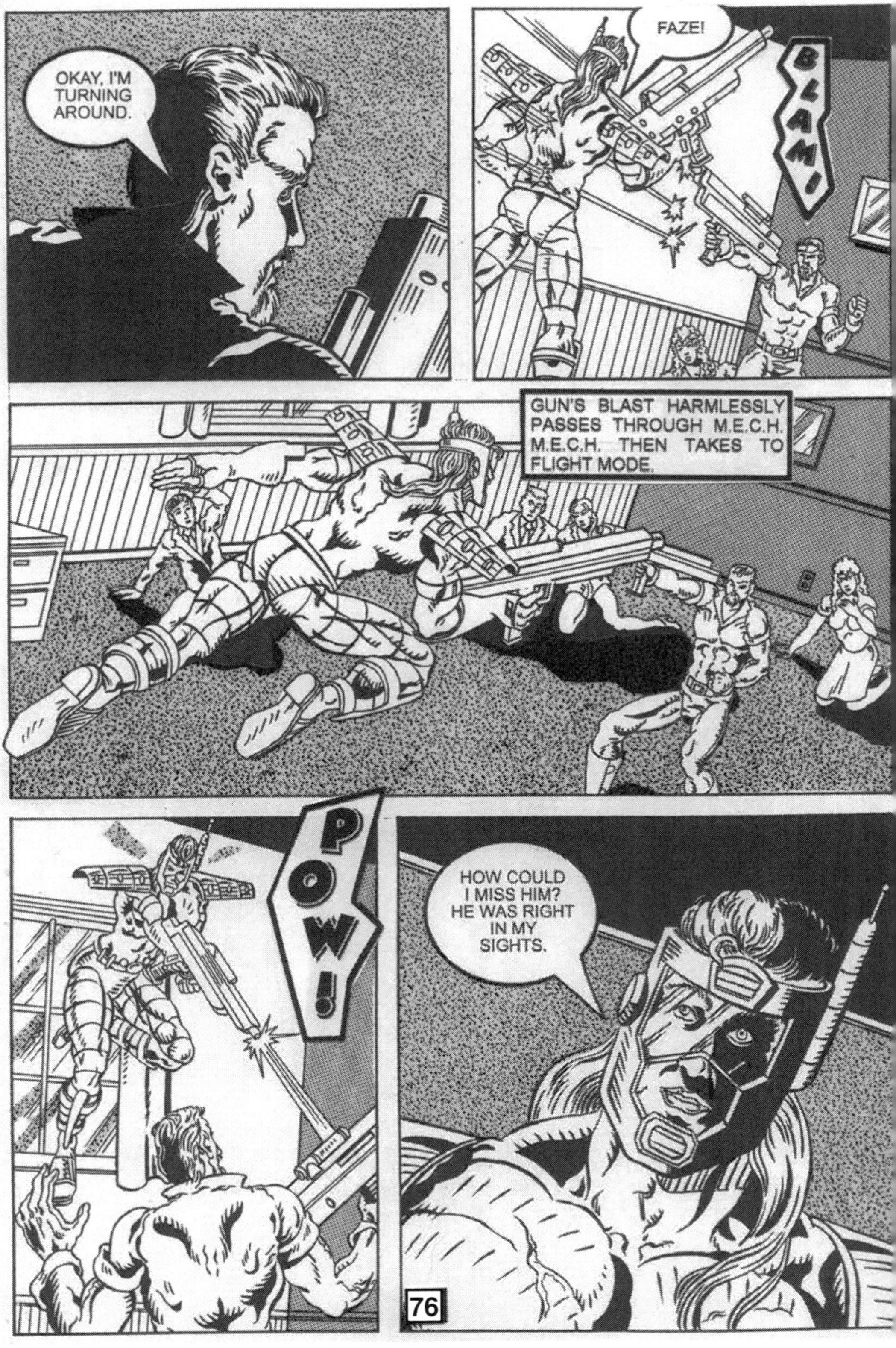
OKAY, I'M TURNING AROUND.
FAZE!
BLAM!
GUN'S BLAST HARMLESSLY PASSES THROUGH M.E.C.H. M.E.C.H. THEN TAKES TO FLIGHT MODE.
POW!
HOW COULD I MISS HIM? HE WAS RIGHT IN MY SIGHTS.

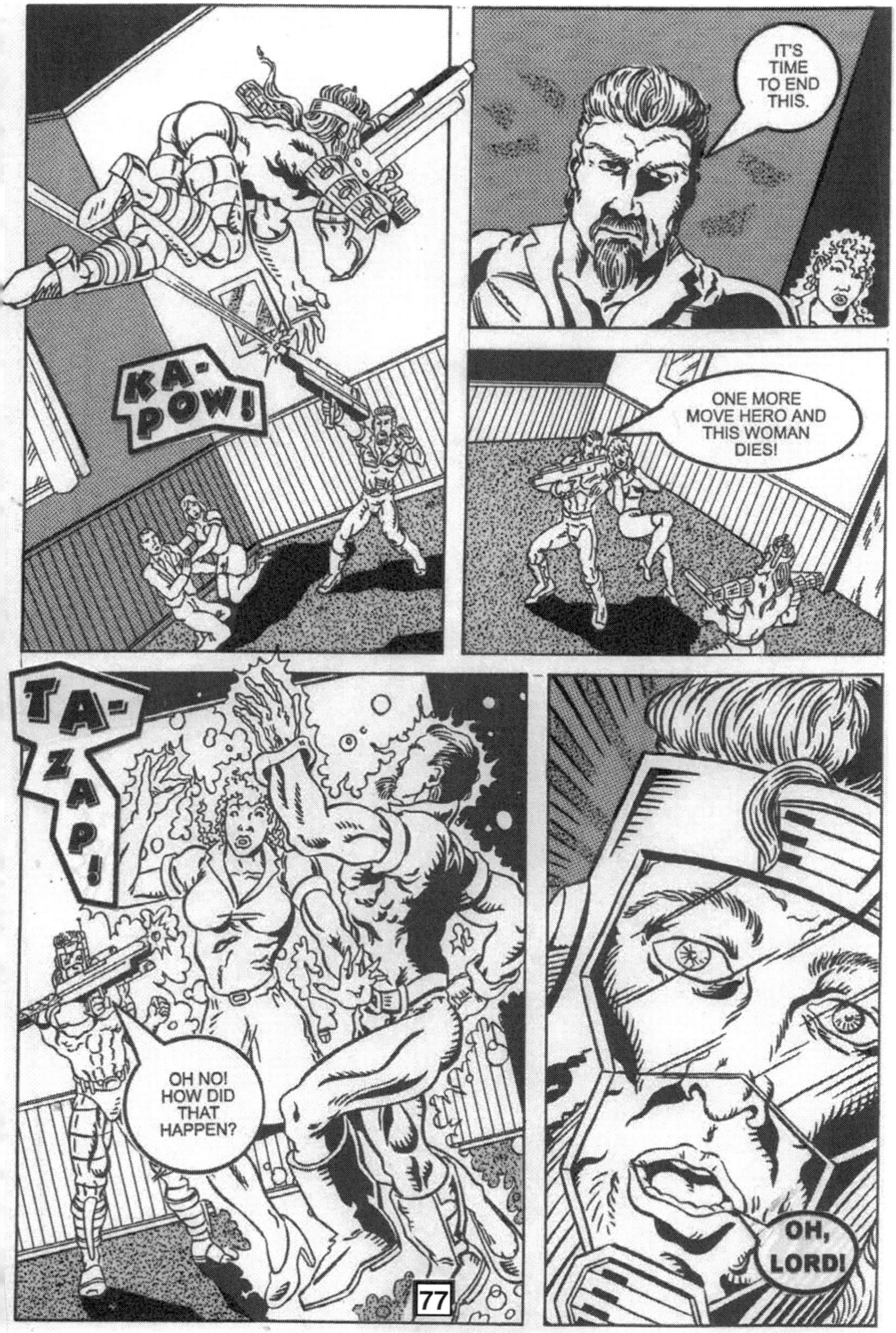
KA-POW!
IT'S TIME TO END THIS.
ONE MORE MOVE HERO AND THIS WOMAN DIES!
TA-ZAP!
OH NO! HOW DID THAT HAPPEN?
OH, LORD!

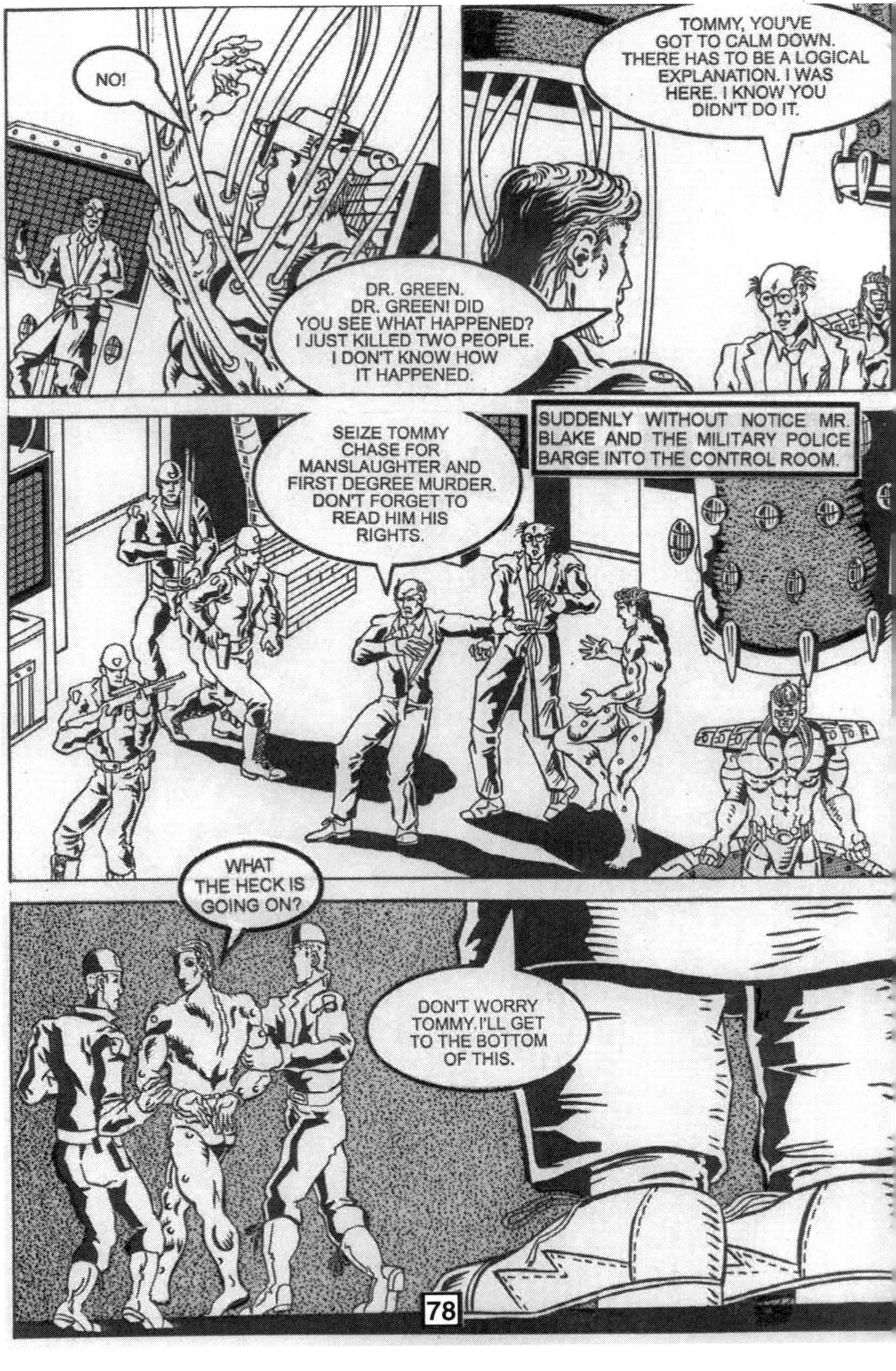
NO!
TOMMY, YOU'VE GOT TO CALM DOWN. THERE HAS TO BE A LOGICAL EXPLANATION. I WAS HERE. I KNOW YOU DIDN'T DO IT.
DR. GREEN. DR. GREEN! DID YOU SEE WHAT HAPPENED? I JUST KILLED TWO PEOPLE. I DON'T KNOW HOW IT HAPPENED.
SUDDENLY WITHOUT NOTICE MR. BLAKE AND THE MILITARY POLICE BARGE INTO THE CONTROL ROOM.
SEIZE TOMMY CHASE FOR MANSLAUGHTER AND FIRST DEGREE MURDER. DON'T FORGET TO READ HIM HIS RIGHTS.
WHAT THE HECK IS GOING ON?
DON'T WORRY TOMMY.I'LL GET TO THE BOTTOM OF THIS.

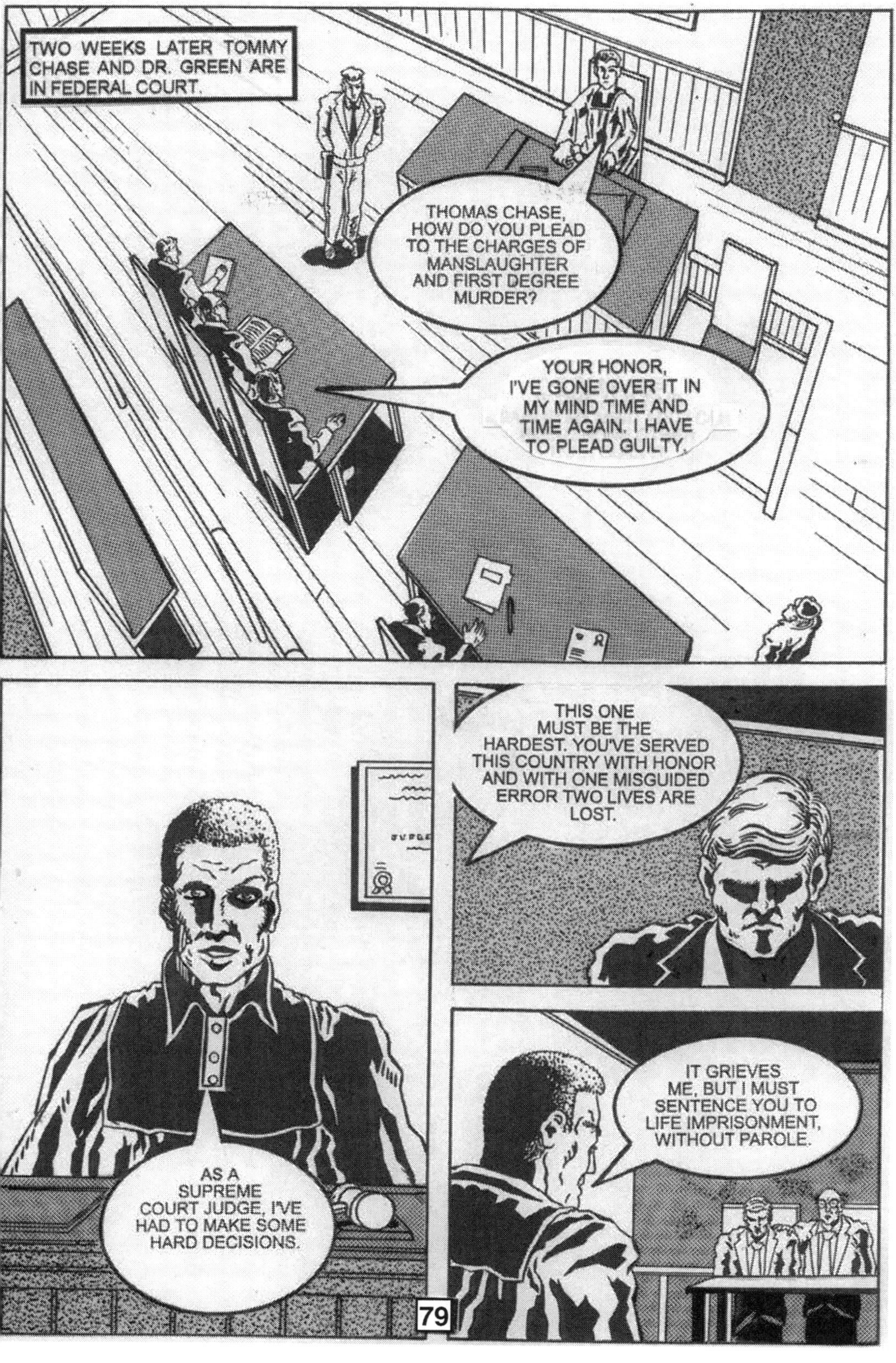
TWO WEEKS LATER TOMMY CHASE AND DR. GREEN ARE IN FEDERAL COURT.
THOMAS CHASE, HOW DO YOU PLEAD TO THE CHARGES OF MANSLAUGHTER AND FIRST DEGREE MURDER?
YOUR HONOR, I'VE GONE OVER IT IN MY MIND TIME AND TIME AGAIN. I HAVE TO PLEAD GUILTY.
AS A SUPREME COURT JUDGE, I'VE HAD TO MAKE SOME HARD DECISIONS.
THIS ONE MUST BE THE HARDEST. YOU'VE SERVED THIS COUNTRY WITH HONOR AND WITH ONE MISGUIDED ERROR TWO LIVES ARE LOST.
IT GRIEVES ME, BUT I MUST SENTENCE YOU TO LIFE IMPRISONMENT, WITHOUT PAROLE.

AFTER THE COURT CASE DR. GREEN IS VERY UPSET. HE GOES BACK TO THE COMPU-M.E.C.H. CONTROL CENTER TO FIND OUT WHAT WENT WRONG WITH THE SYSTEM.

I'VE GONE OVER THIS A THOUSAND TIMES AND I STILL DON'T KNOW WHAT WENT WRONG.

THE VERY SECOND THAT M.E.C.H. DISCHARGED THE WEAPON ALL OF THIS INSTALLATION RECORDING DEVICES HAVE A MEMORY SPIKE.

IT WAS LIKE IT NEVER HAPPENED, OR IT WAS MADE TO APPEAR THAT IT NEVER HAPPENED.

LET ME GO A LITTLE DEEPER INTO THE SYSTEM. THAT'S IT! WHY DIDN'T I THINK OF IT EARLIER?

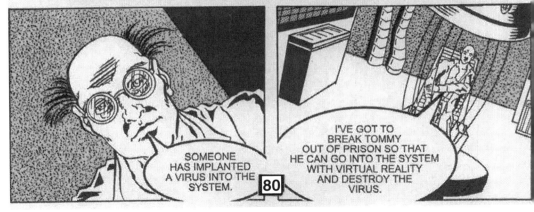

SOMEONE HAS IMPLANTED A VIRUS INTO THE SYSTEM.

80

I'VE GOT TO BREAK TOMMY OUT OF PRISON SO THAT HE CAN GO INTO THE SYSTEM WITH VIRTUAL REALITY AND DESTROY THE VIRUS.

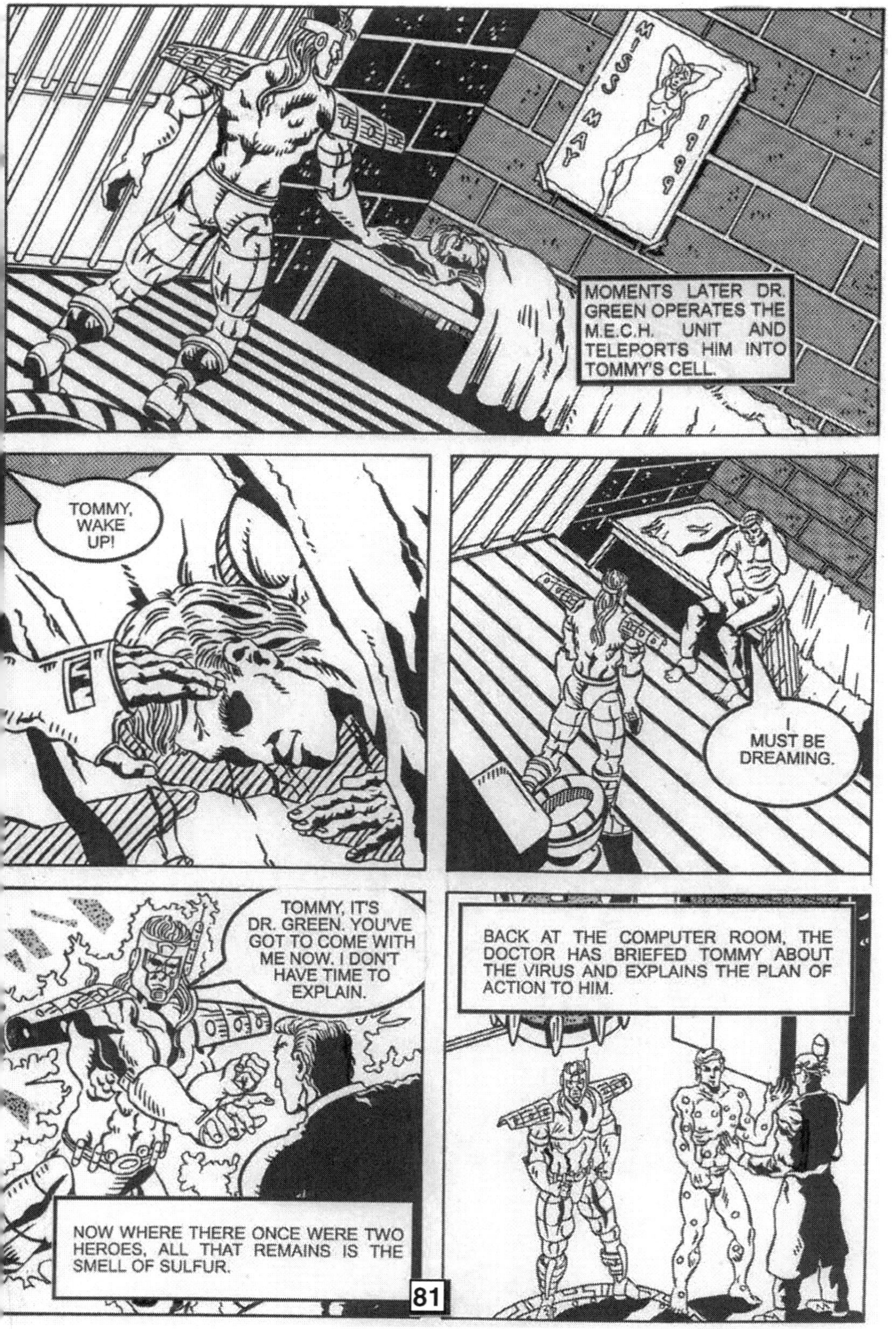

MISS MAY 1999
MOMENTS LATER DR. GREEN OPERATES THE M.E.C.H. UNIT AND TELEPORTS HIM INTO TOMMY'S CELL.
TOMMY, WAKE UP!
I MUST BE DREAMING.
TOMMY, IT'S DR. GREEN. YOU'VE GOT TO COME WITH ME NOW. I DON'T HAVE TIME TO EXPLAIN.
NOW WHERE THERE ONCE WERE TWO HEROES, ALL THAT REMAINS IS THE SMELL OF SULFUR.
BACK AT THE COMPUTER ROOM, THE DOCTOR HAS BRIEFED TOMMY ABOUT THE VIRUS AND EXPLAINS THE PLAN OF ACTION TO HIM.

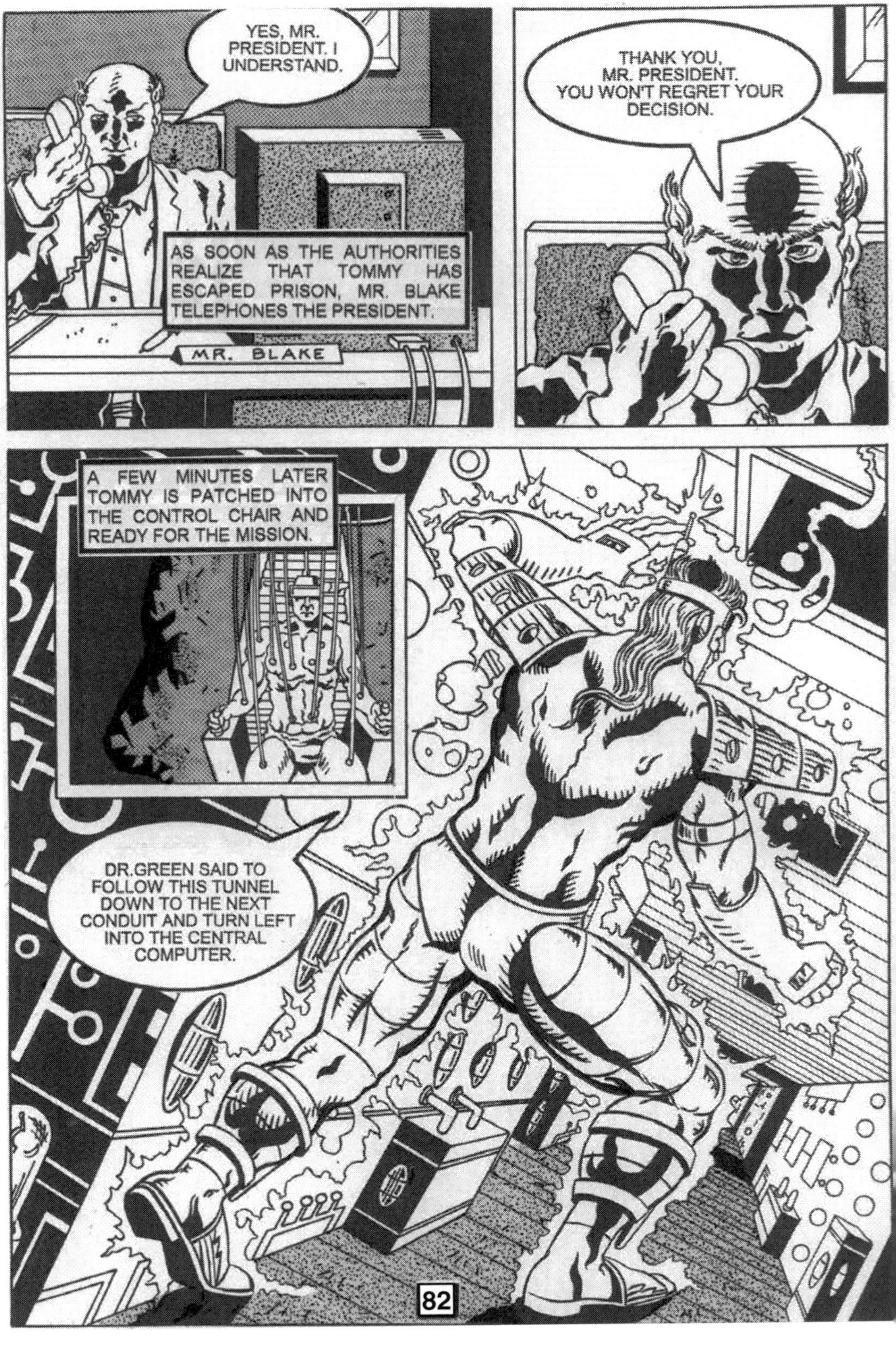
YES, MR. PRESIDENT. I UNDERSTAND.
AS SOON AS THE AUTHORITIES REALIZE THAT TOMMY HAS ESCAPED PRISON, MR. BLAKE TELEPHONES THE PRESIDENT.
MR. BLAKE
THANK YOU, MR. PRESIDENT. YOU WON'T REGRET YOUR DECISION.
A FEW MINUTES LATER TOMMY IS PATCHED INTO THE CONTROL CHAIR AND READY FOR THE MISSION.
DR.GREEN SAID TO FOLLOW THIS TUNNEL DOWN TO THE NEXT CONDUIT AND TURN LEFT INTO THE CENTRAL COMPUTER.

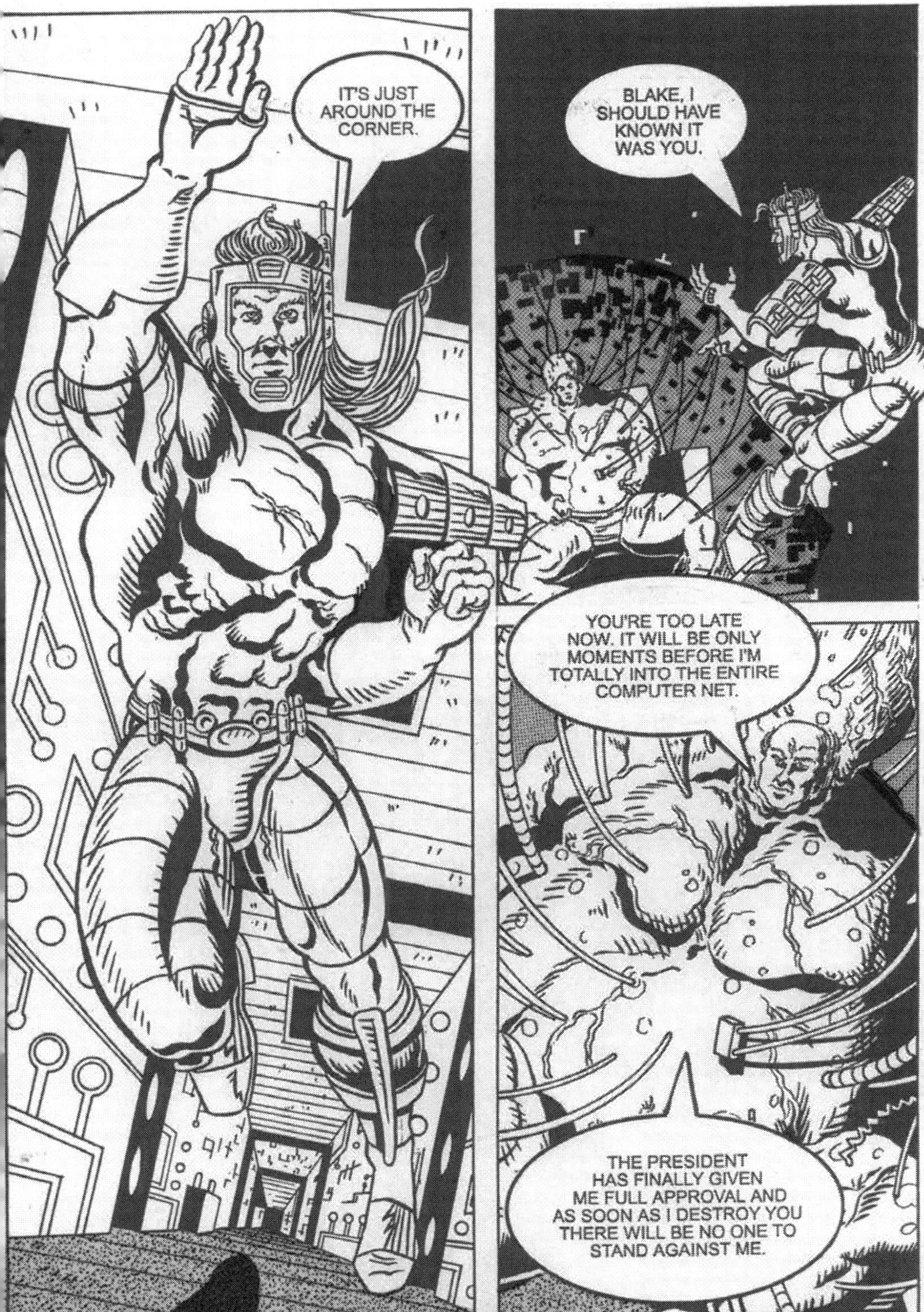
IT'S JUST AROUND THE CORNER.
BLAKE, I SHOULD HAVE KNOWN IT WAS YOU.
YOU'RE TOO LATE NOW. IT WILL BE ONLY MOMENTS BEFORE I'M TOTALLY INTO THE ENTIRE COMPUTER NET.
THE PRESIDENT HAS FINALLY GIVEN ME FULL APPROVAL AND AS SOON AS I DESTROY YOU THERE WILL BE NO ONE TO STAND AGAINST ME.

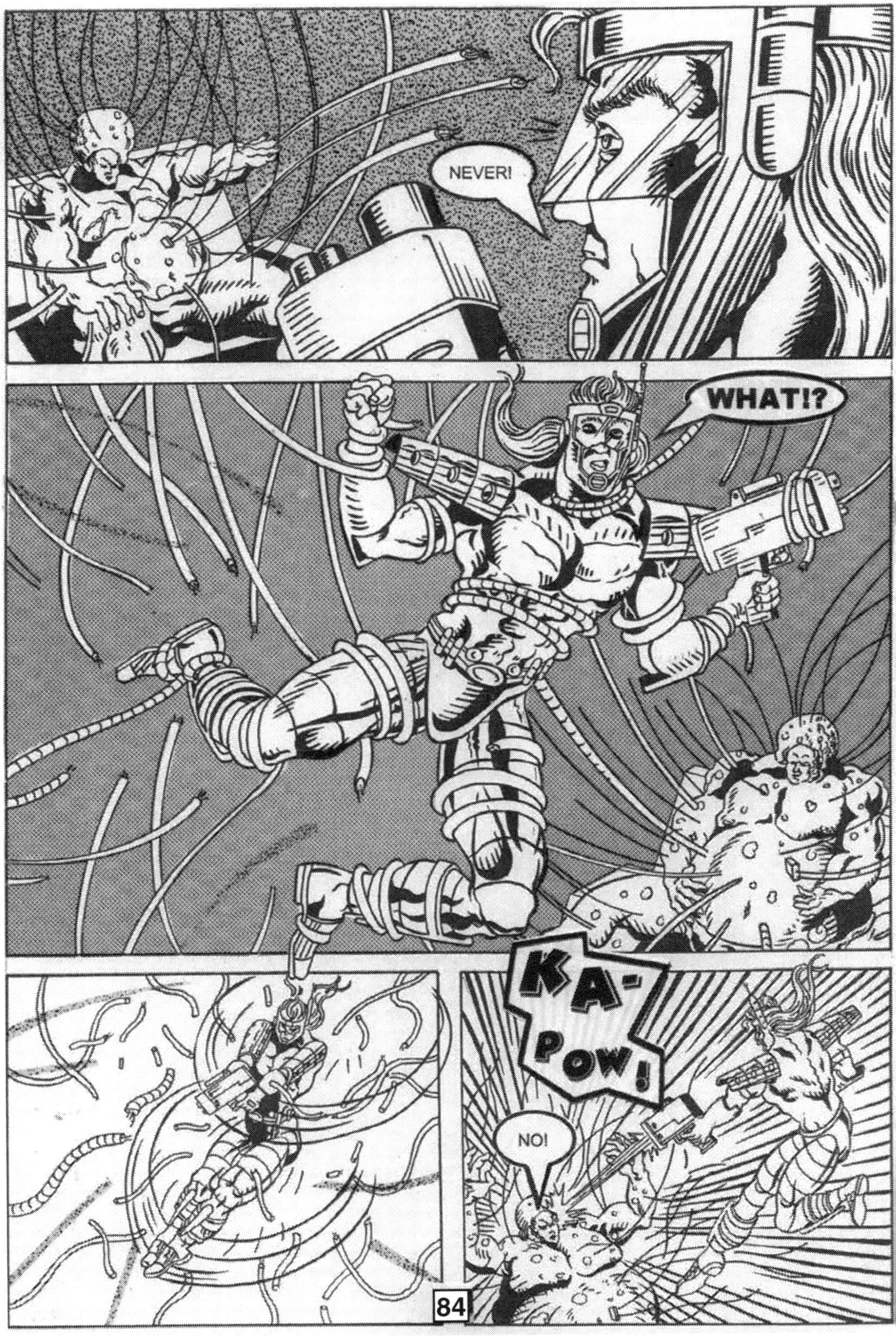
NEVER!
WHAT!?
KA-POW!
NO!

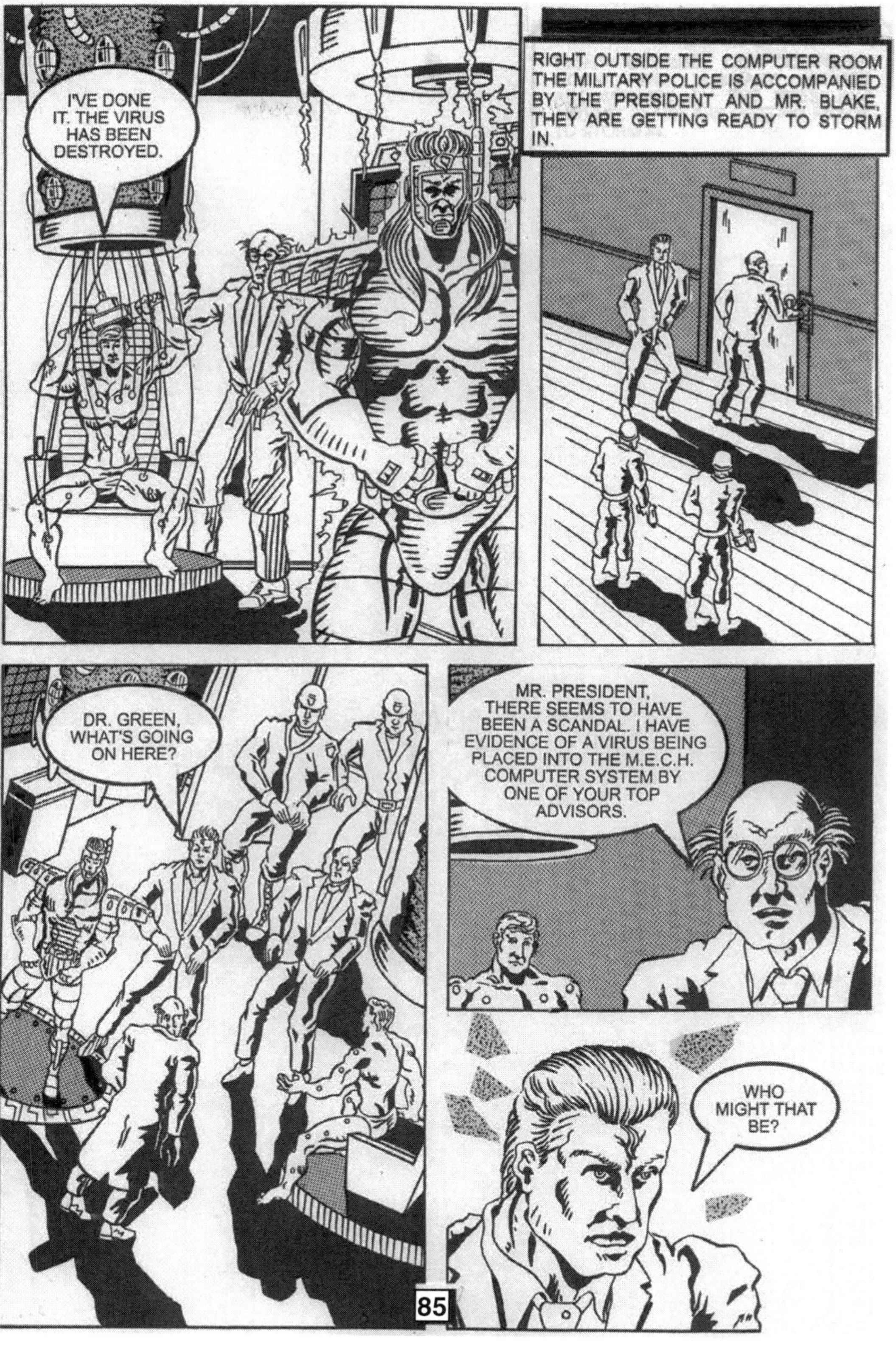

I'VE DONE IT. THE VIRUS HAS BEEN DESTROYED.
RIGHT OUTSIDE THE COMPUTER ROOM THE MILITARY POLICE IS ACCOMPANIED BY THE PRESIDENT AND MR. BLAKE, THEY ARE GETTING READY TO STORM IN.
DR. GREEN, WHAT'S GOING ON HERE?
MR. PRESIDENT, THERE SEEMS TO HAVE BEEN A SCANDAL. I HAVE EVIDENCE OF A VIRUS BEING PLACED INTO THE M.E.C.H. COMPUTER SYSTEM BY ONE OF YOUR TOP ADVISORS.
WHO MIGHT THAT BE?

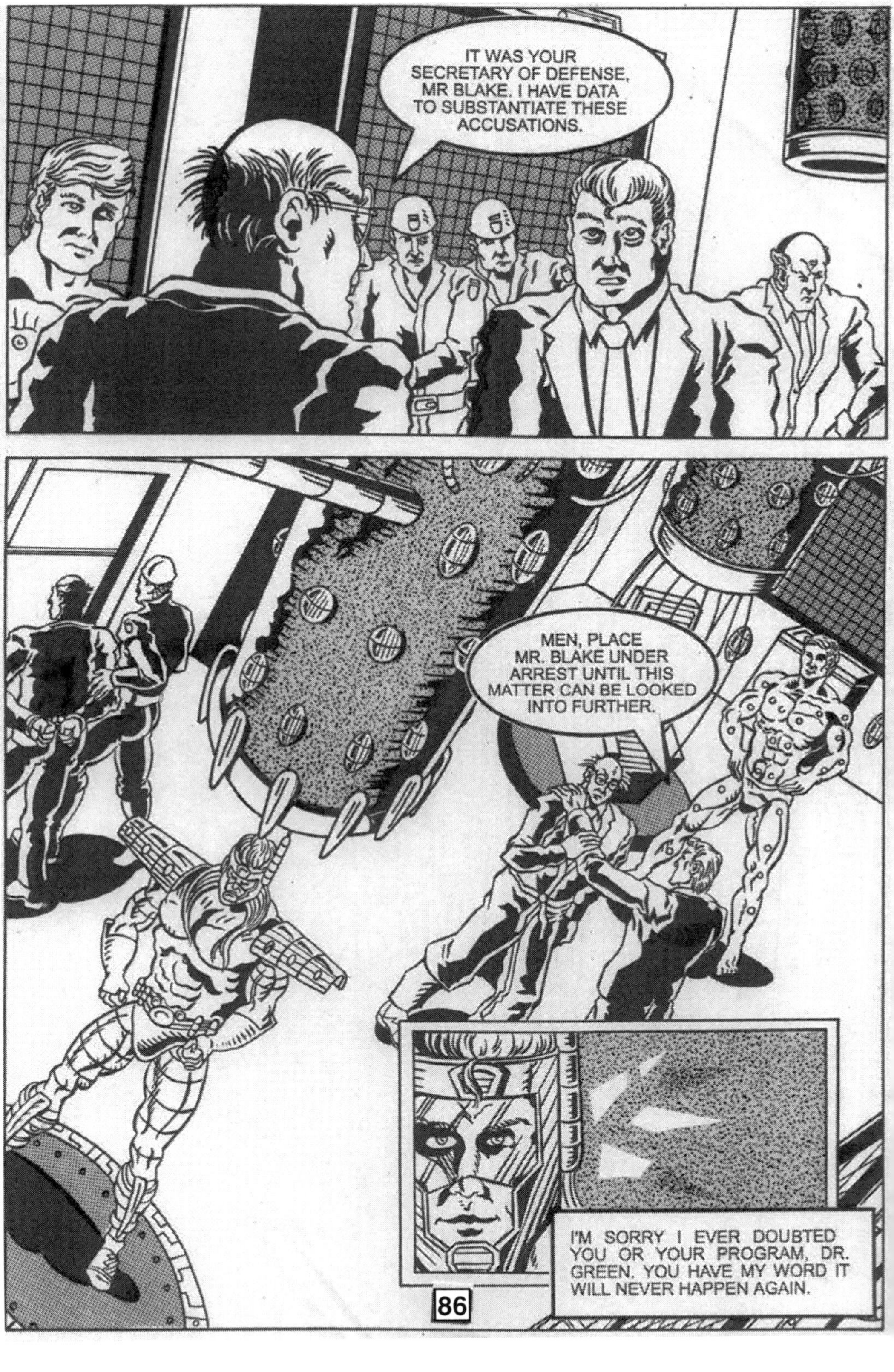
IT WAS YOUR SECRETARY OF DEFENSE, MR BLAKE. I HAVE DATA TO SUBSTANTIATE THESE ACCUSATIONS.
MEN, PLACE MR. BLAKE UNDER ARREST UNTIL THIS MATTER CAN BE LOOKED INTO FURTHER.
I'M SORRY I EVER DOUBTED YOU OR YOUR PROGRAM, DR. GREEN. YOU HAVE MY WORD IT WILL NEVER HAPPEN AGAIN.

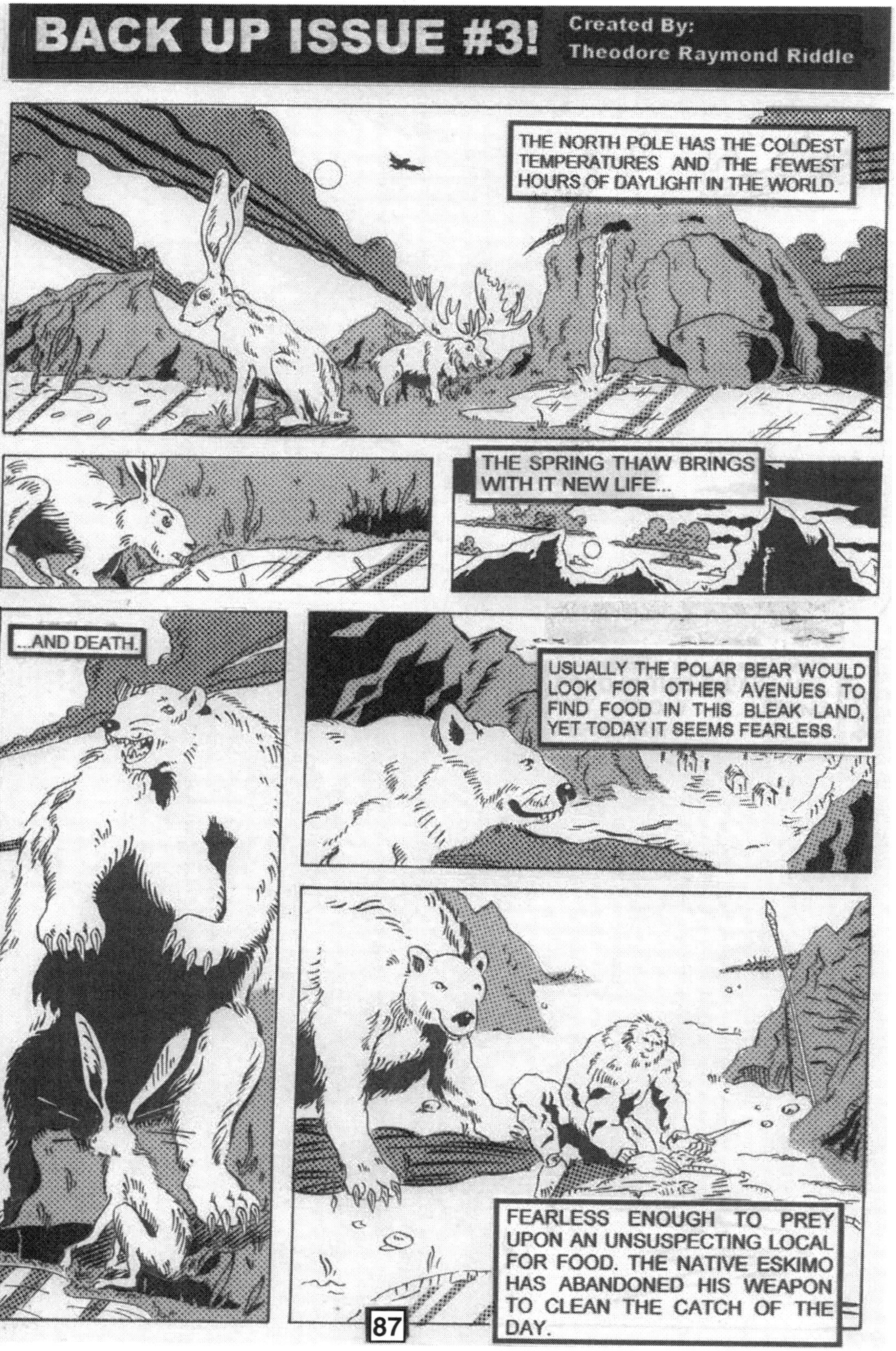
BACK UP ISSUE #3!
Created By:
Theodore Raymond Riddle
THE NORTH POLE HAS THE COLDEST TEMPERATURES AND THE FEWEST HOURS OF DAYLIGHT IN THE WORLD.
THE SPRING THAW BRINGS WITH IT NEW LIFE...
...AND DEATH.
USUALLY THE POLAR BEAR WOULD LOOK FOR OTHER AVENUES TO FIND FOOD IN THIS BLEAK LAND, YET TODAY IT SEEMS FEARLESS.
FEARLESS ENOUGH TO PREY UPON AN UNSUSPECTING LOCAL FOR FOOD. THE NATIVE ESKIMO HAS ABANDONED HIS WEAPON TO CLEAN THE CATCH OF THE DAY.

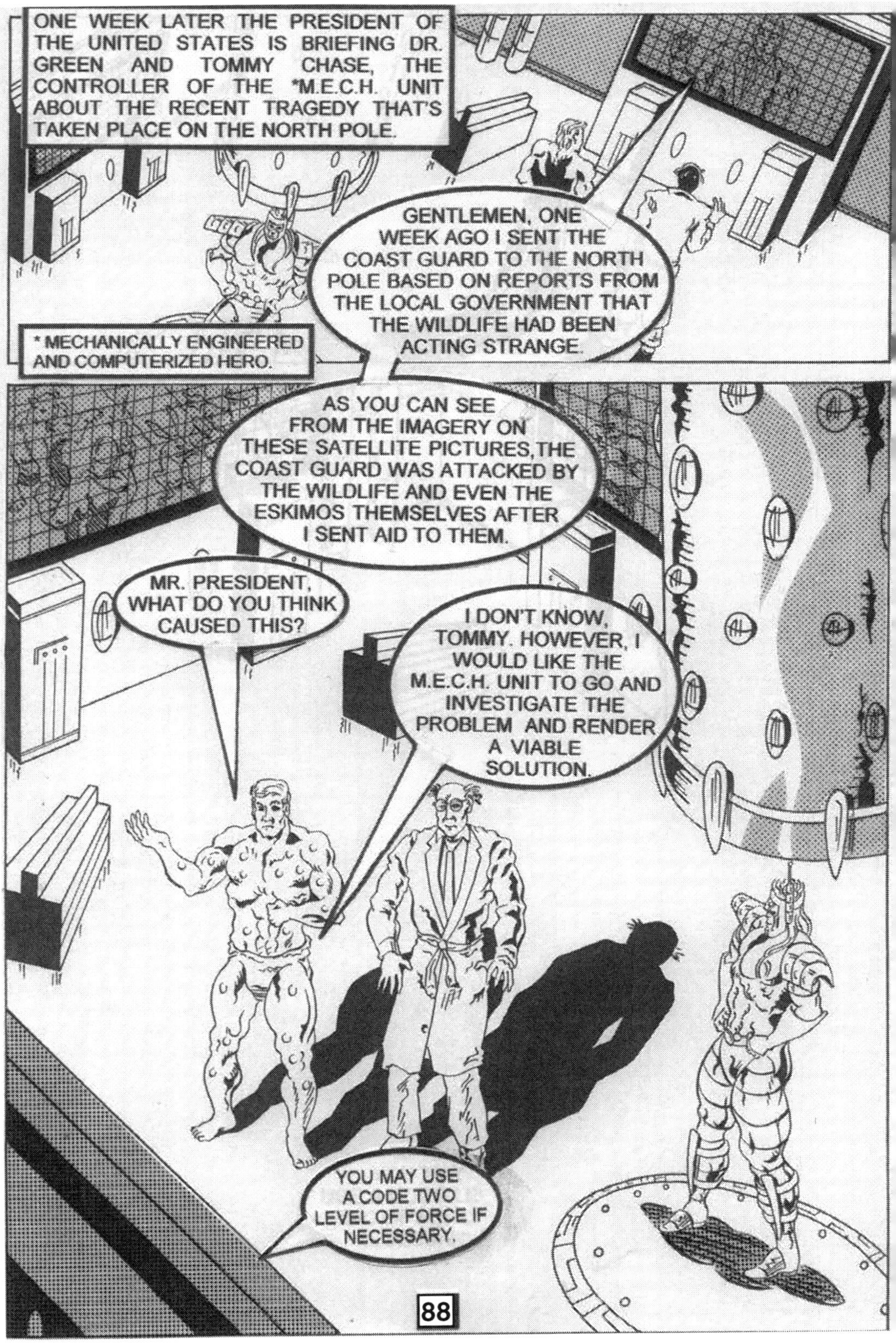
ONE WEEK LATER THE PRESIDENT OF THE UNITED STATES IS BRIEFING DR. GREEN AND TOMMY CHASE, THE CONTROLLER OF THE *M.E.C.H. UNIT ABOUT THE RECENT TRAGEDY THAT'S TAKEN PLACE ON THE NORTH POLE.
GENTLEMEN, ONE WEEK AGO I SENT THE COAST GUARD TO THE NORTH POLE BASED ON REPORTS FROM THE LOCAL GOVERNMENT THAT THE WILDLIFE HAD BEEN ACTING STRANGE.
* MECHANICALLY ENGINEERED AND COMPUTERIZED HERO.
AS YOU CAN SEE FROM THE IMAGERY ON THESE SATELLITE PICTURES,THE COAST GUARD WAS ATTACKED BY THE WILDLIFE AND EVEN THE ESKIMOS THEMSELVES AFTER I SENT AID TO THEM.
MR. PRESIDENT, WHAT DO YOU THINK CAUSED THIS?
I DON'T KNOW, TOMMY. HOWEVER, I WOULD LIKE THE M.E.C.H. UNIT TO GO AND INVESTIGATE THE PROBLEM AND RENDER A VIABLE SOLUTION.
YOU MAY USE A CODE TWO LEVEL OF FORCE IF NECESSARY.

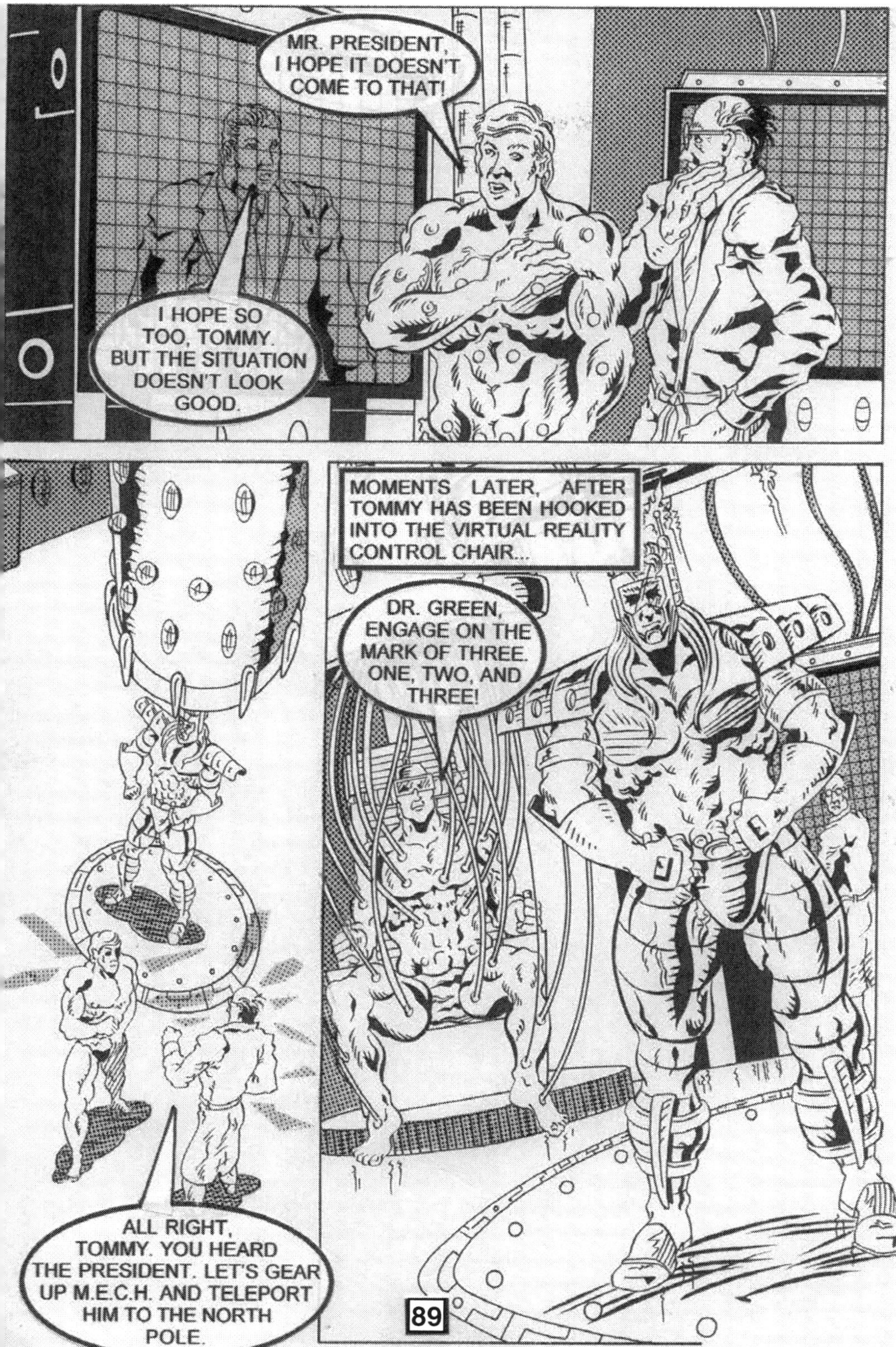
MR. PRESIDENT, I HOPE IT DOESN'T COME TO THAT!
I HOPE SO TOO, TOMMY. BUT THE SITUATION DOESN'T LOOK GOOD.
ALL RIGHT, TOMMY. YOU HEARD THE PRESIDENT. LET'S GEAR UP M.E.C.H. AND TELEPORT HIM TO THE NORTH POLE.
MOMENTS LATER, AFTER TOMMY HAS BEEN HOOKED INTO THE VIRTUAL REALITY CONTROL CHAIR...
DR. GREEN, ENGAGE ON THE MARK OF THREE. ONE, TWO, AND THREE!

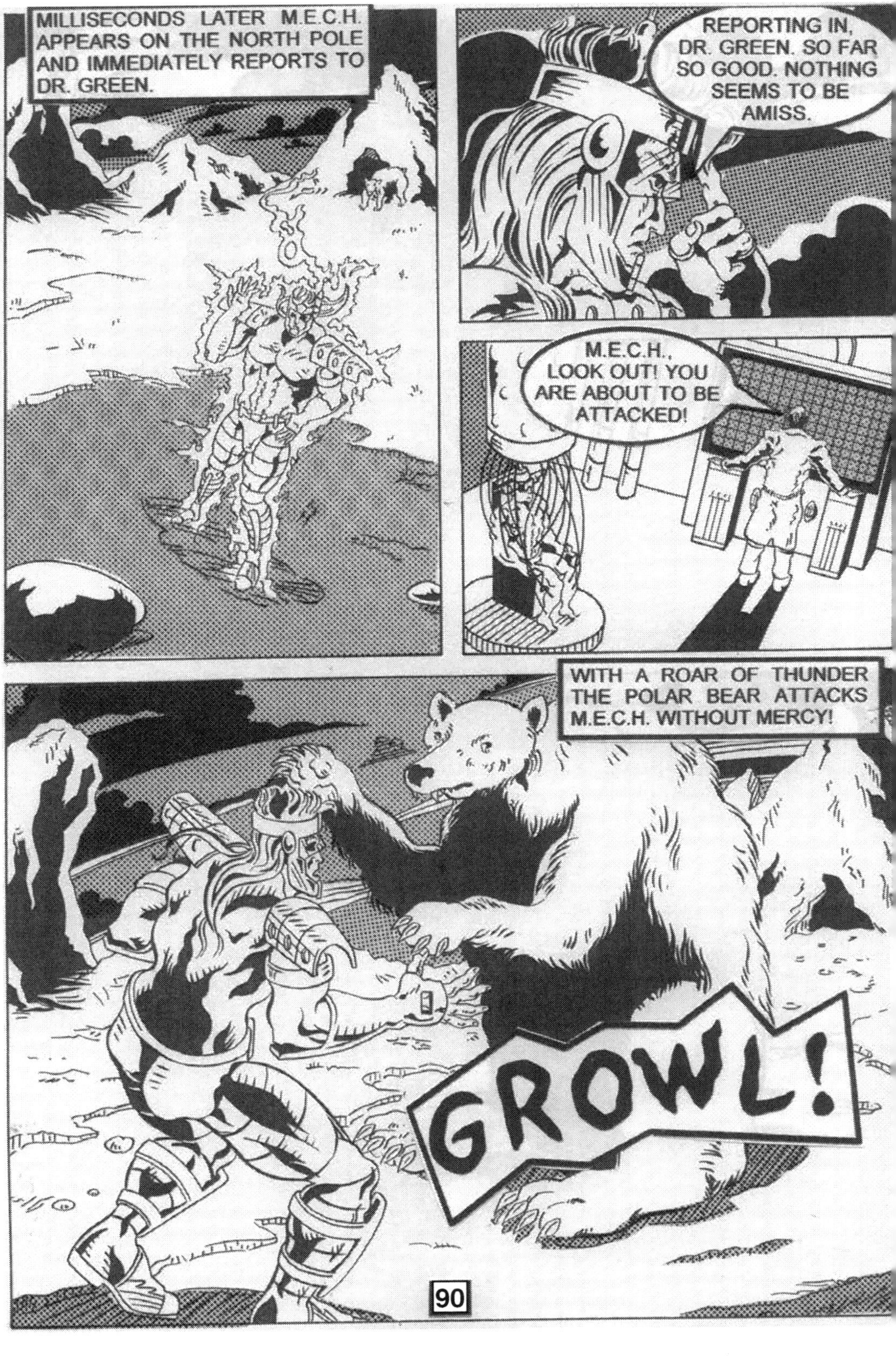
MILLISECONDS LATER M.E.C.H. APPEARS ON THE NORTH POLE AND IMMEDIATELY REPORTS TO DR. GREEN.
REPORTING IN, DR. GREEN. SO FAR SO GOOD. NOTHING SEEMS TO BE AMISS.
M.E.C.H., LOOK OUT! YOU ARE ABOUT TO BE ATTACKED!
WITH A ROAR OF THUNDER THE POLAR BEAR ATTACKS M.E.C.H. WITHOUT MERCY!
GROWL!

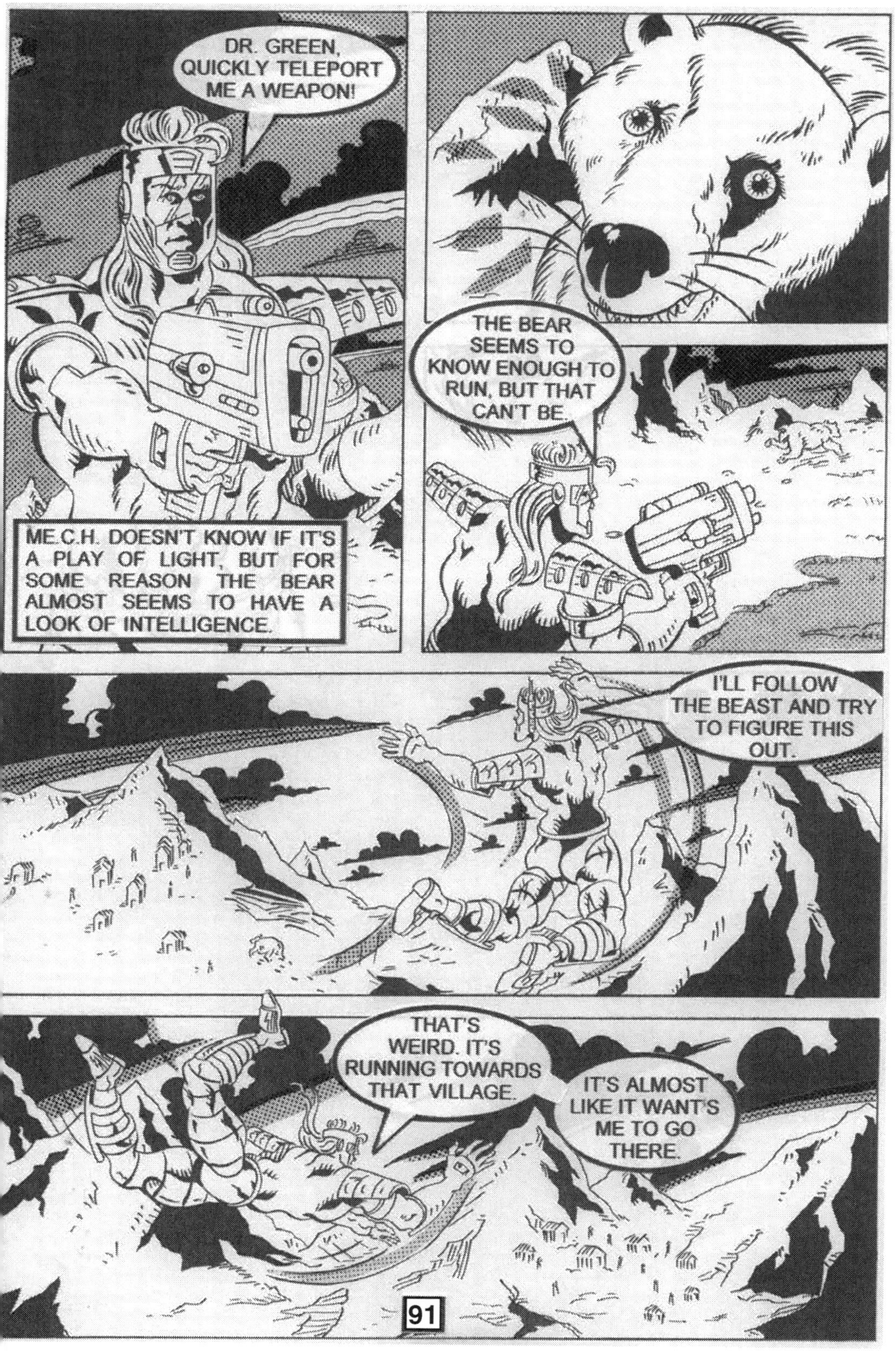
DR. GREEN, QUICKLY TELEPORT ME A WEAPON!
ME.C.H. DOESN'T KNOW IF IT'S A PLAY OF LIGHT, BUT FOR SOME REASON THE BEAR ALMOST SEEMS TO HAVE A LOOK OF INTELLIGENCE.
THE BEAR SEEMS TO KNOW ENOUGH TO RUN, BUT THAT CAN'T BE.
I'LL FOLLOW THE BEAST AND TRY TO FIGURE THIS OUT.
THAT'S WEIRD. IT'S RUNNING TOWARDS THAT VILLAGE.
IT'S ALMOST LIKE IT WANT'S ME TO GO THERE.

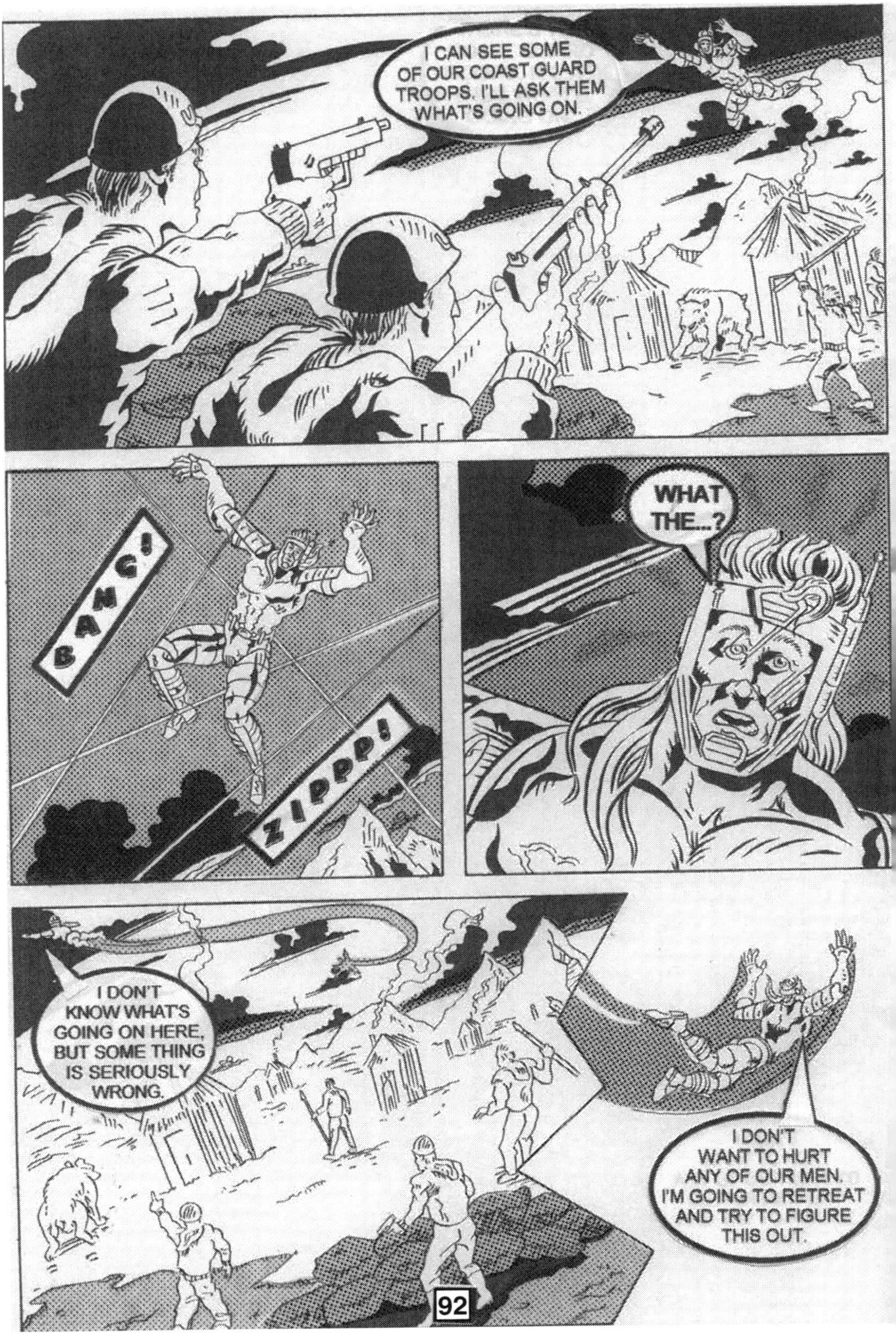
I CAN SEE SOME OF OUR COAST GUARD TROOPS. I'LL ASK THEM WHAT'S GOING ON.
BANG!
ZIPPP!
WHAT THE...?
I DON'T KNOW WHAT'S GOING ON HERE, BUT SOME THING IS SERIOUSLY WRONG.
I DON'T WANT TO HURT ANY OF OUR MEN. I'M GOING TO RETREAT AND TRY TO FIGURE THIS OUT.

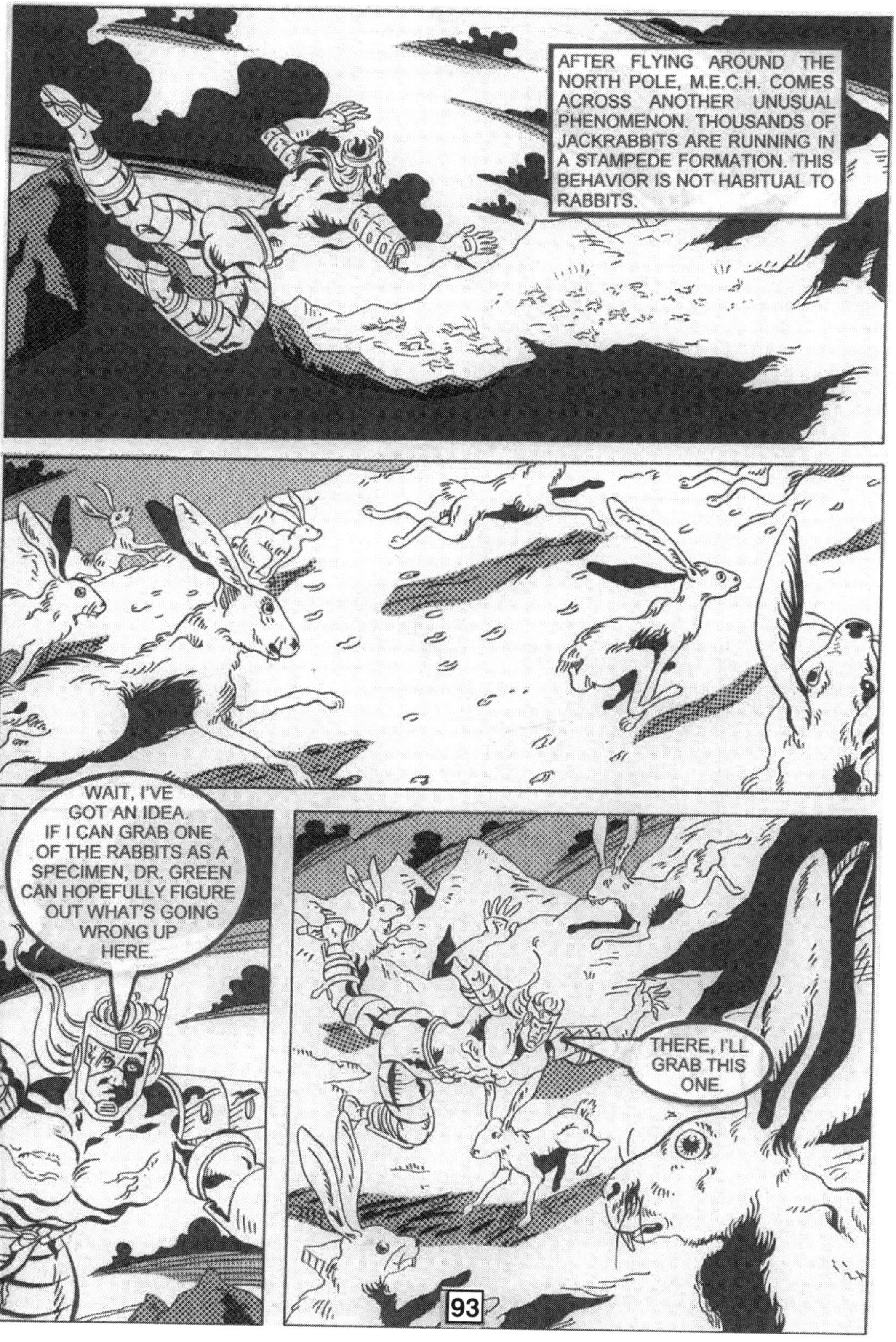
AFTER FLYING AROUND THE NORTH POLE, M.E.C.H. COMES ACROSS ANOTHER UNUSUAL PHENOMENON. THOUSANDS OF JACKRABBITS ARE RUNNING IN A STAMPEDE FORMATION. THIS BEHAVIOR IS NOT HABITUAL TO RABBITS.
WAIT, I'VE GOT AN IDEA. IF I CAN GRAB ONE OF THE RABBITS AS A SPECIMEN, DR. GREEN CAN HOPEFULLY FIGURE OUT WHAT'S GOING WRONG UP HERE.
THERE, I'LL GRAB THIS ONE.

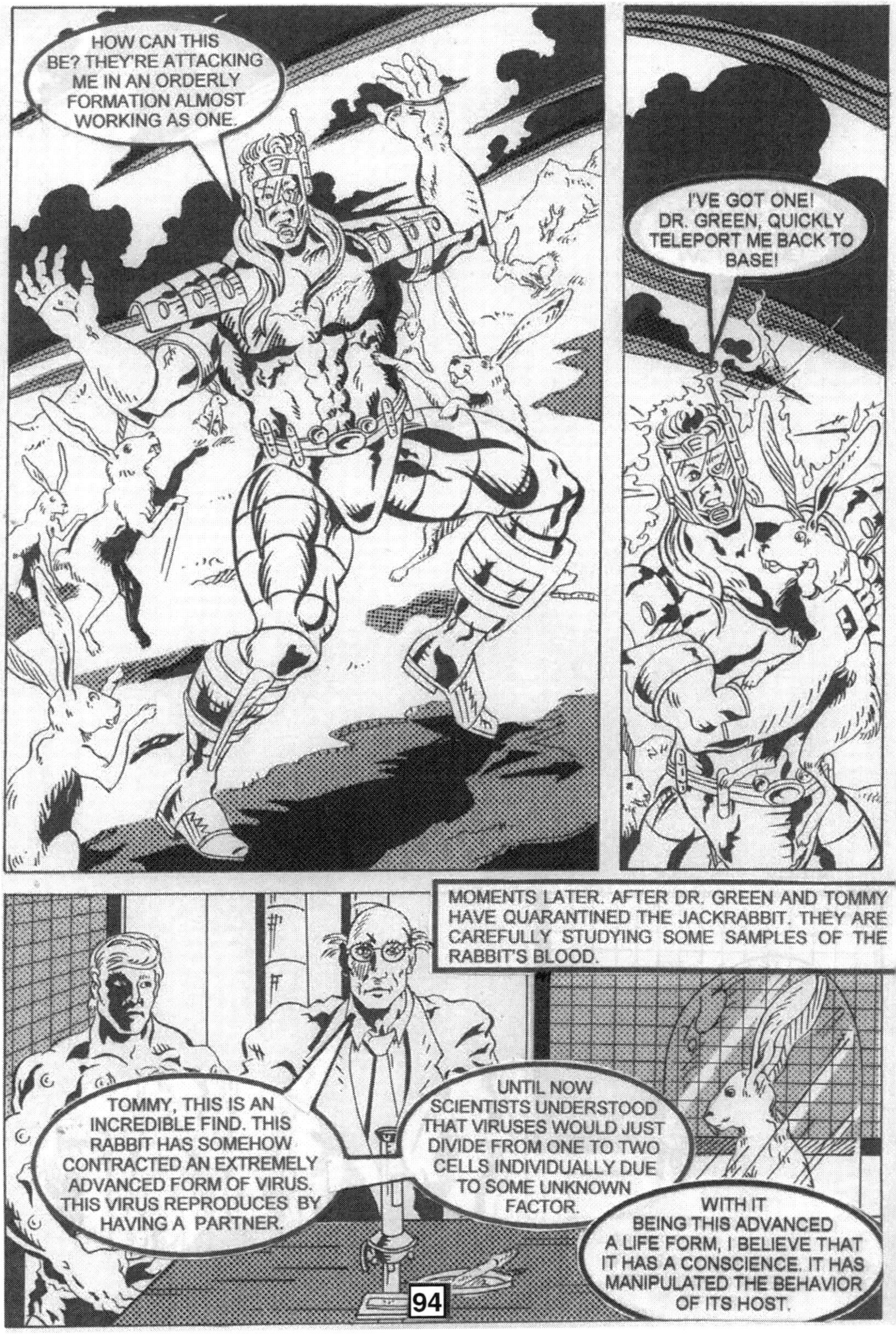

HOW CAN THIS BE? THEY'RE ATTACKING ME IN AN ORDERLY FORMATION ALMOST WORKING AS ONE.
I'VE GOT ONE! DR. GREEN, QUICKLY TELEPORT ME BACK TO BASE!
MOMENTS LATER. AFTER DR. GREEN AND TOMMY HAVE QUARANTINED THE JACKRABBIT. THEY ARE CAREFULLY STUDYING SOME SAMPLES OF THE RABBIT'S BLOOD.
TOMMY, THIS IS AN INCREDIBLE FIND. THIS RABBIT HAS SOMEHOW CONTRACTED AN EXTREMELY ADVANCED FORM OF VIRUS. THIS VIRUS REPRODUCES BY HAVING A PARTNER.
UNTIL NOW SCIENTISTS UNDERSTOOD THAT VIRUSES WOULD JUST DIVIDE FROM ONE TO TWO CELLS INDIVIDUALLY DUE TO SOME UNKNOWN FACTOR.
WITH IT BEING THIS ADVANCED A LIFE FORM, I BELIEVE THAT IT HAS A CONSCIENCE. IT HAS MANIPULATED THE BEHAVIOR OF ITS HOST.

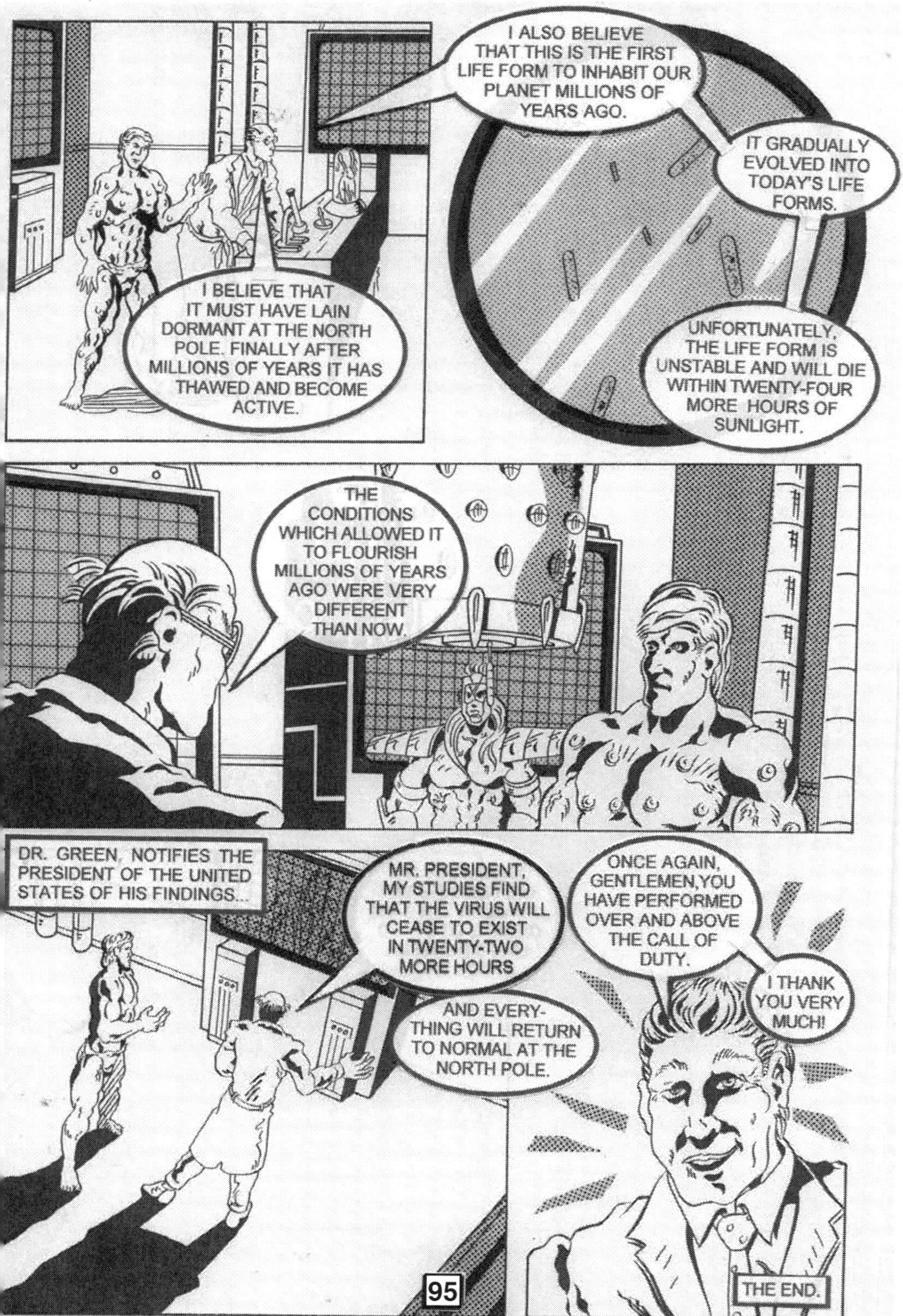
I BELIEVE THAT IT MUST HAVE LAIN DORMANT AT THE NORTH POLE. FINALLY AFTER MILLIONS OF YEARS IT HAS THAWED AND BECOME ACTIVE.
I ALSO BELIEVE THAT THIS IS THE FIRST LIFE FORM TO INHABIT OUR PLANET MILLIONS OF YEARS AGO.
IT GRADUALLY EVOLVED INTO TODAY'S LIFE FORMS.
UNFORTUNATELY, THE LIFE FORM IS UNSTABLE AND WILL DIE WITHIN TWENTY-FOUR MORE HOURS OF SUNLIGHT.
THE CONDITIONS WHICH ALLOWED IT TO FLOURISH MILLIONS OF YEARS AGO WERE VERY DIFFERENT THAN NOW.
DR. GREEN, NOTIFIES THE PRESIDENT OF THE UNITED STATES OF HIS FINDINGS...
MR. PRESIDENT, MY STUDIES FIND THAT THE VIRUS WILL CEASE TO EXIST IN TWENTY-TWO MORE HOURS
AND EVERY-THING WILL RETURN TO NORMAL AT THE NORTH POLE.
ONCE AGAIN, GENTLEMEN,YOU HAVE PERFORMED OVER AND ABOVE THE CALL OF DUTY.
I THANK YOU VERY MUCH!
THE END.

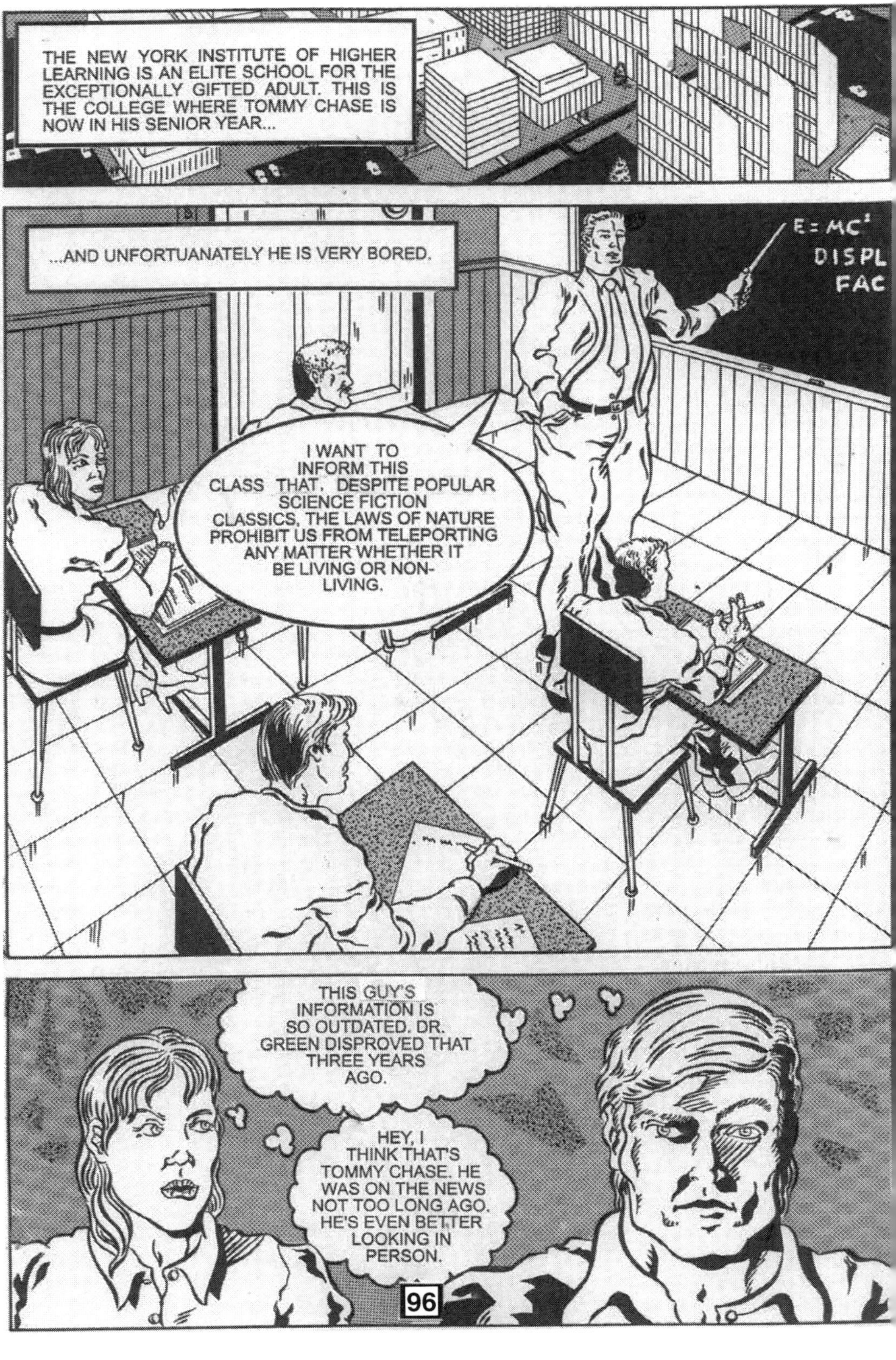
THE NEW YORK INSTITUTE OF HIGHER LEARNING IS AN ELITE SCHOOL FOR THE EXCEPTIONALLY GIFTED ADULT. THIS IS THE COLLEGE WHERE TOMMY CHASE IS NOW IN HIS SENIOR YEAR...
...AND UNFORTUANATELY HE IS VERY BORED.
$E = MC^2$
I WANT TO INFORM THIS CLASS THAT. DESPITE POPULAR SCIENCE FICTION CLASSICS, THE LAWS OF NATURE PROHIBIT US FROM TELEPORTING ANY MATTER WHETHER IT BE LIVING OR NON-LIVING.
THIS GUY'S INFORMATION IS SO OUTDATED. DR. GREEN DISPROVED THAT THREE YEARS AGO.
HEY, I THINK THAT'S TOMMY CHASE. HE WAS ON THE NEWS NOT TOO LONG AGO. HE'S EVEN BETTER LOOKING IN PERSON.

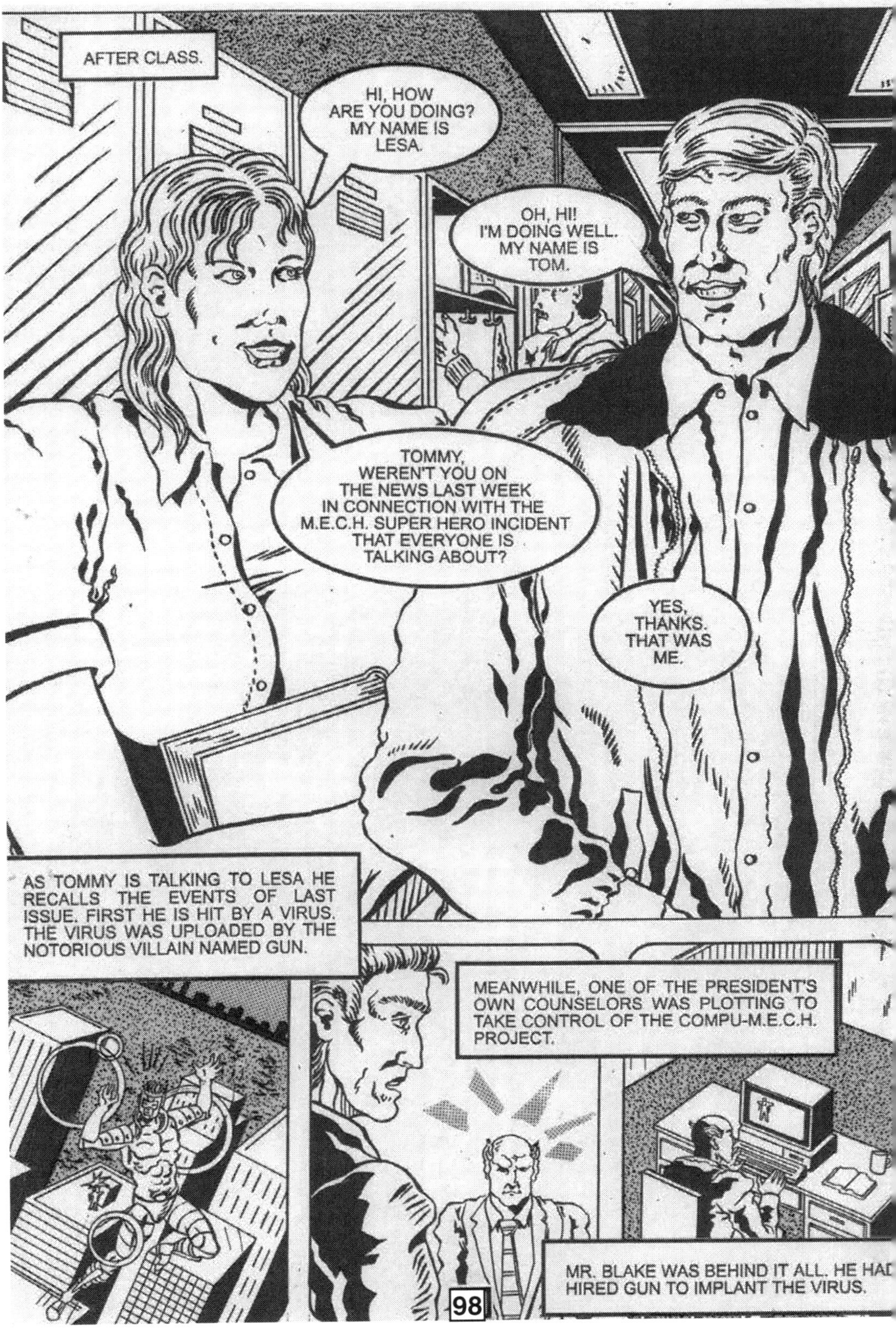
AFTER CLASS.
HI, HOW ARE YOU DOING? MY NAME IS LESA.
OH, HI! I'M DOING WELL. MY NAME IS TOM.
TOMMY, WEREN'T YOU ON THE NEWS LAST WEEK IN CONNECTION WITH THE M.E.C.H. SUPER HERO INCIDENT THAT EVERYONE IS TALKING ABOUT?
YES, THANKS. THAT WAS ME.
AS TOMMY IS TALKING TO LESA HE RECALLS THE EVENTS OF LAST ISSUE. FIRST HE IS HIT BY A VIRUS. THE VIRUS WAS UPLOADED BY THE NOTORIOUS VILLAIN NAMED GUN.
MEANWHILE, ONE OF THE PRESIDENT'S OWN COUNSELORS WAS PLOTTING TO TAKE CONTROL OF THE COMPU-M.E.C.H. PROJECT.
MR. BLAKE WAS BEHIND IT ALL. HE HAD HIRED GUN TO IMPLANT THE VIRUS.

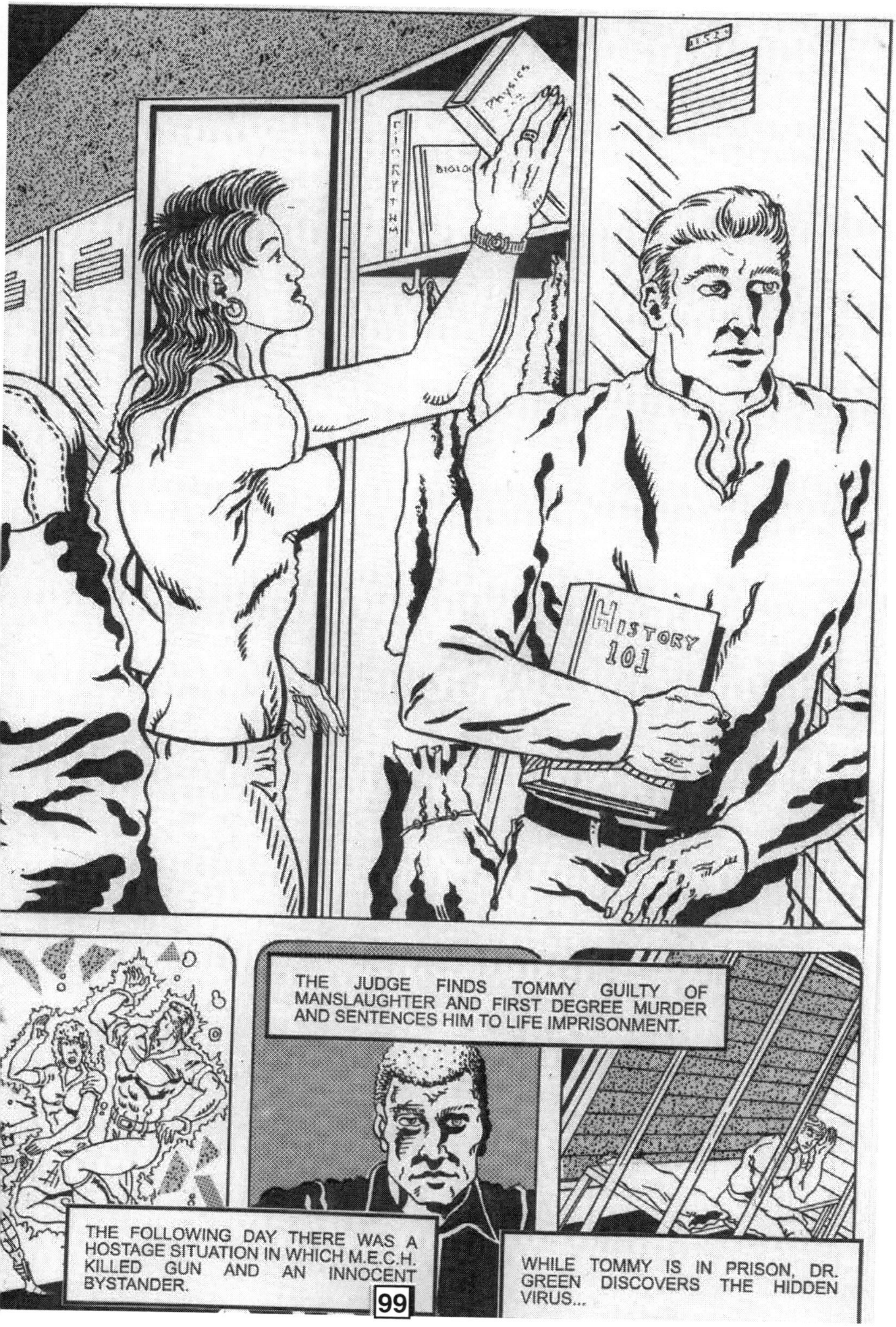
HISTORY 101
THE JUDGE FINDS TOMMY GUILTY OF MANSLAUGHTER AND FIRST DEGREE MURDER AND SENTENCES HIM TO LIFE IMPRISONMENT.
THE FOLLOWING DAY THERE WAS A HOSTAGE SITUATION IN WHICH M.E.C.H. KILLED GUN AND AN INNOCENT BYSTANDER.
WHILE TOMMY IS IN PRISON, DR. GREEN DISCOVERS THE HIDDEN VIRUS...

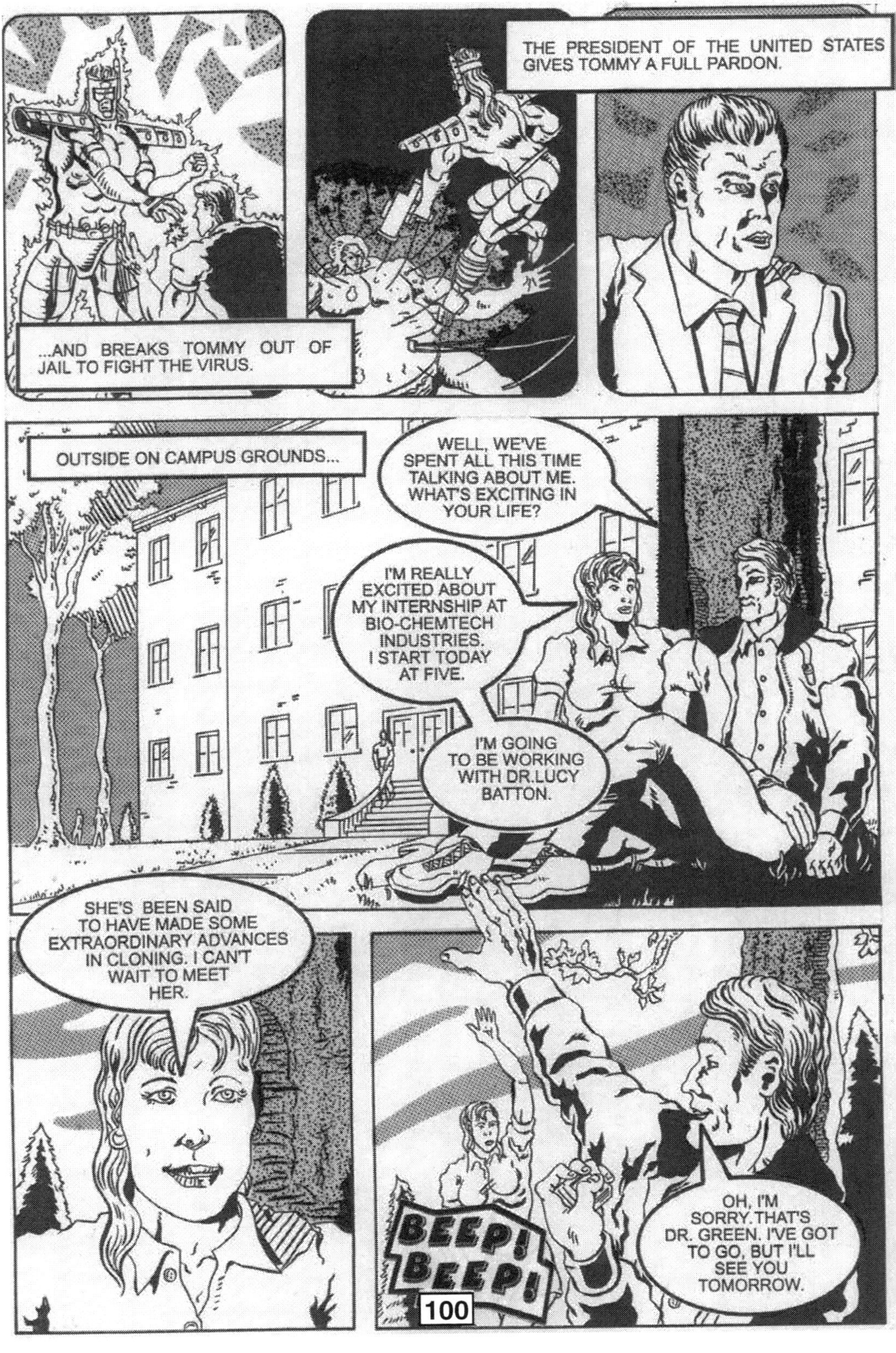

...AND BREAKS TOMMY OUT OF JAIL TO FIGHT THE VIRUS.
THE PRESIDENT OF THE UNITED STATES GIVES TOMMY A FULL PARDON.
OUTSIDE ON CAMPUS GROUNDS...
WELL, WE'VE SPENT ALL THIS TIME TALKING ABOUT ME. WHAT'S EXCITING IN YOUR LIFE?
I'M REALLY EXCITED ABOUT MY INTERNSHIP AT BIO-CHEMTECH INDUSTRIES. I START TODAY AT FIVE.
I'M GOING TO BE WORKING WITH DR.LUCY BATTON.
SHE'S BEEN SAID TO HAVE MADE SOME EXTRAORDINARY ADVANCES IN CLONING. I CAN'T WAIT TO MEET HER.
BEEP! BEEP!
OH, I'M SORRY. THAT'S DR. GREEN. I'VE GOT TO GO, BUT I'LL SEE YOU TOMORROW.

ONLY ONE MINUTE LATE.

I KNOW HOW THAT UPSETS DR. GREEN.

MOMENTS LATER AT THE COMPU-M.E.C.H. CONTROL CENTER TOMMY IS PUNCHING IN HIS ACCESS CODE.

WHAT HAPPENED?

I MET THIS REALLY NICE WOMAN NAMED LESA.

THAT'S GREAT TOMMY, BUT WE'VE GOT AN EMERGENCY SITUATION IN RUSSIA. WE'LL HAVE TO TALK LATER.

THE PRESIDENT IS HERE TO INFORM US ON A PLAN OF ACTION.

GENTLEMEN, WE HAVE A CODE. ONE PRIORITY IN RUSSIA. IT SEEMS THAT ANOTHER ONE OF THE NUCLEAR REACTORS IS GOING TO MELT DOWN.

THE REPORTS COMING IN VARY FROM TEN TO FIFTEEN MINUTES TO TOTAL MELT DOWN. THAT MUST NOT HAPPEN. GET THAT CORE SHUT DOWN.

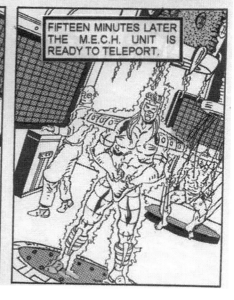

FIFTEEN MINUTES LATER THE M.E.C.H. UNIT IS READY TO TELEPORT.

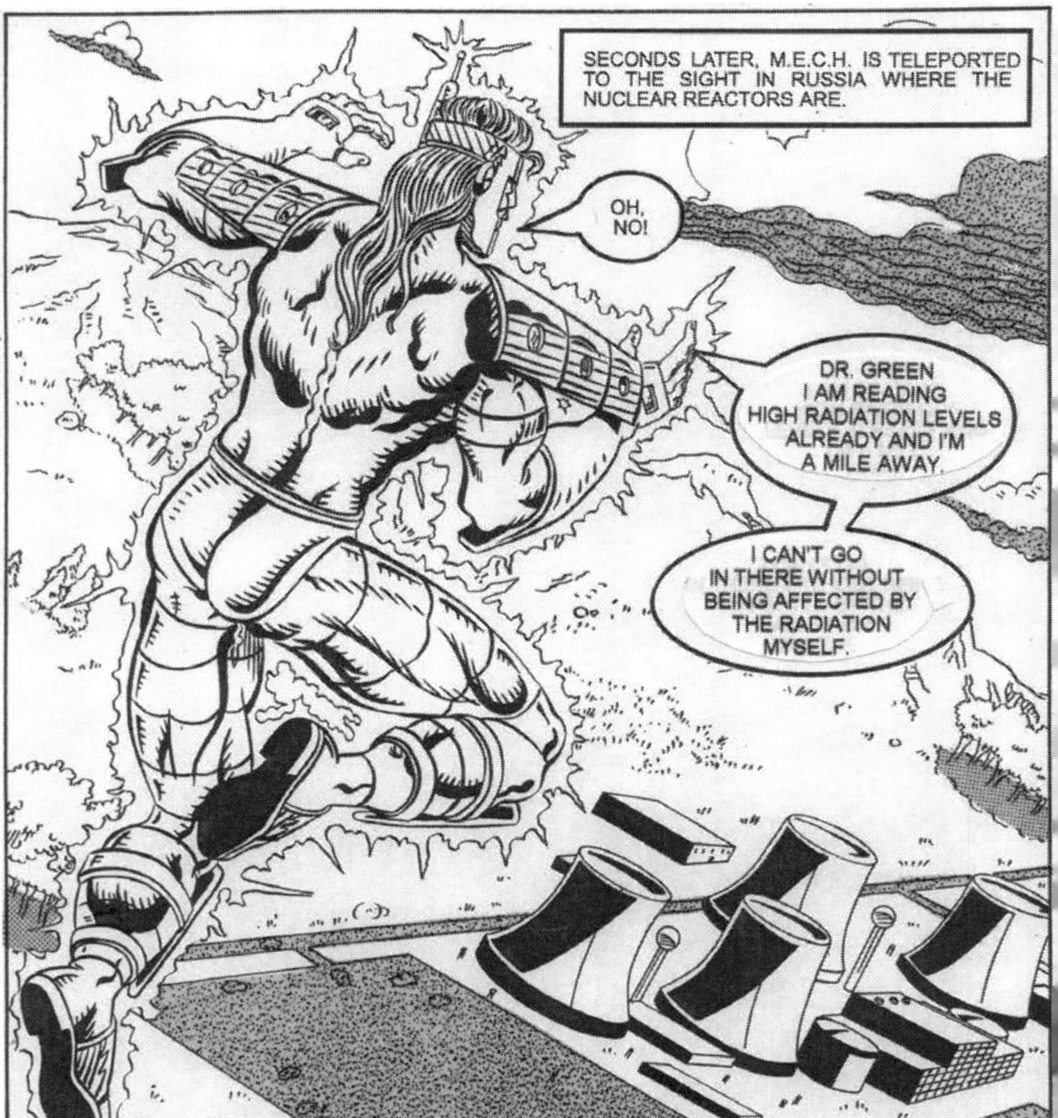
SECONDS LATER, M.E.C.H. IS TELEPORTED TO THE SIGHT IN RUSSIA WHERE THE NUCLEAR REACTORS ARE.
OH, NO!
DR. GREEN I AM READING HIGH RADIATION LEVELS ALREADY AND I'M A MILE AWAY.
I CAN'T GO IN THERE WITHOUT BEING AFFECTED BY THE RADIATION MYSELF.

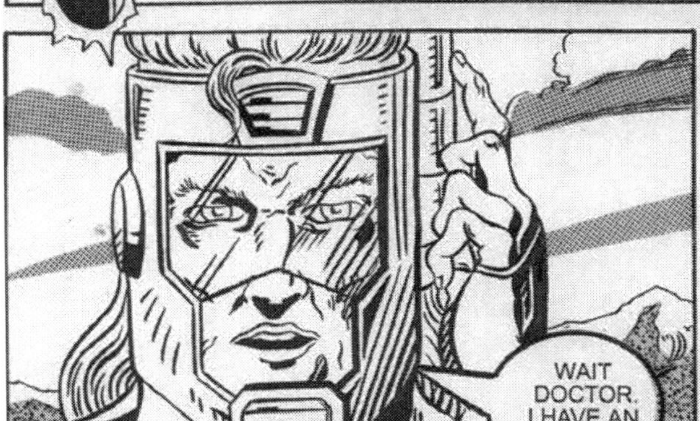
WAIT DOCTOR. I HAVE AN IDEA.

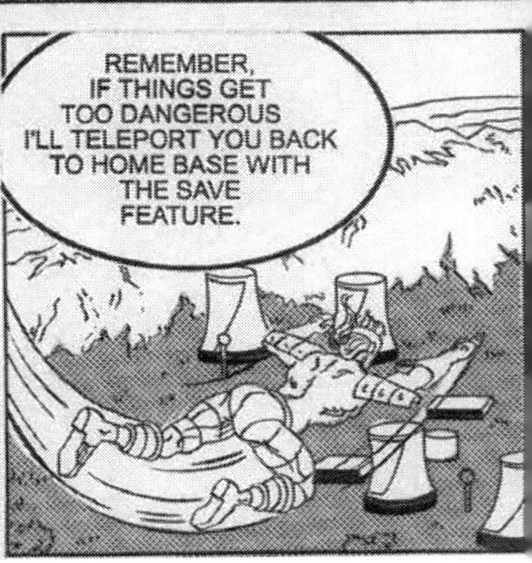
REMEMBER, IF THINGS GET TOO DANGEROUS I'LL TELEPORT YOU BACK TO HOME BASE WITH THE SAVE FEATURE.

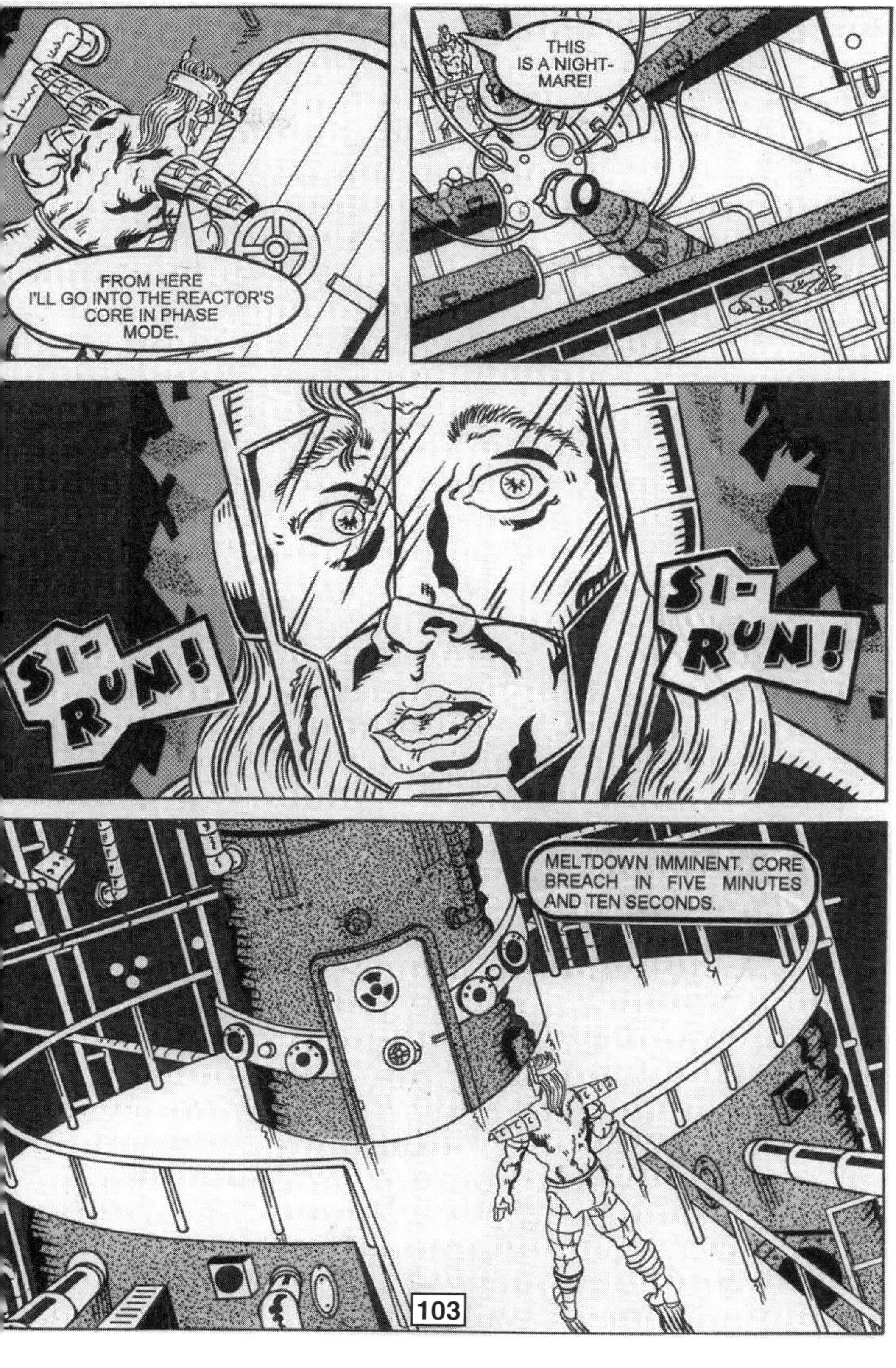
FROM HERE I'LL GO INTO THE REACTOR'S CORE IN PHASE MODE.
THIS IS A NIGHT-MARE!
SI-RUN!
SI-RUN!
MELTDOWN IMMINENT. CORE BREACH IN FIVE MINUTES AND TEN SECONDS.

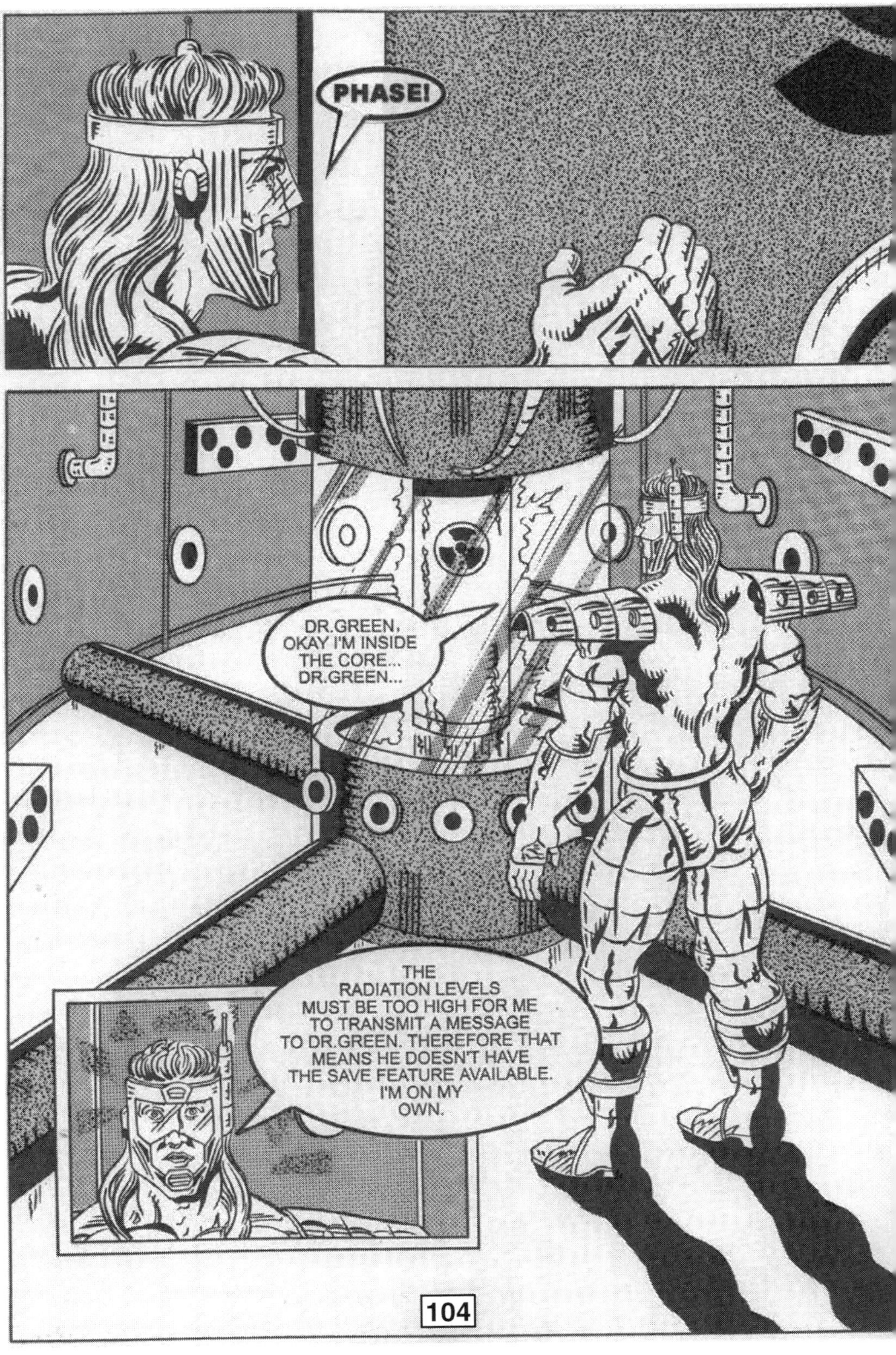
PHASE!
DR.GREEN, OKAY I'M INSIDE THE CORE... DR.GREEN...
THE RADIATION LEVELS MUST BE TOO HIGH FOR ME TO TRANSMIT A MESSAGE TO DR.GREEN. THEREFORE THAT MEANS HE DOESN'T HAVE THE SAVE FEATURE AVAILABLE. I'M ON MY OWN.

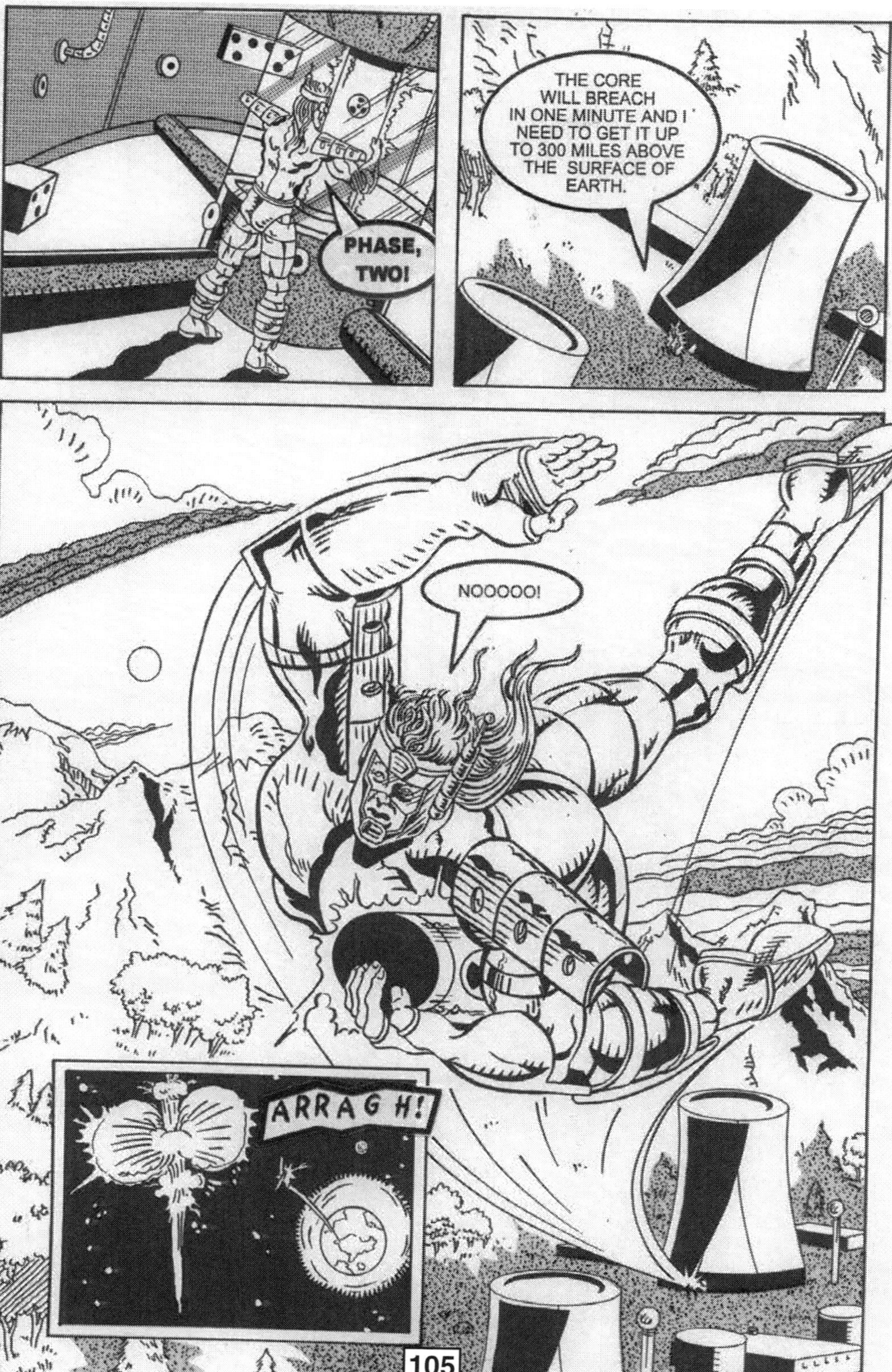
PHASE, TWO!
THE CORE WILL BREACH IN ONE MINUTE AND I NEED TO GET IT UP TO 300 MILES ABOVE THE SURFACE OF EARTH.
NOOOOO!
ARRAGH!

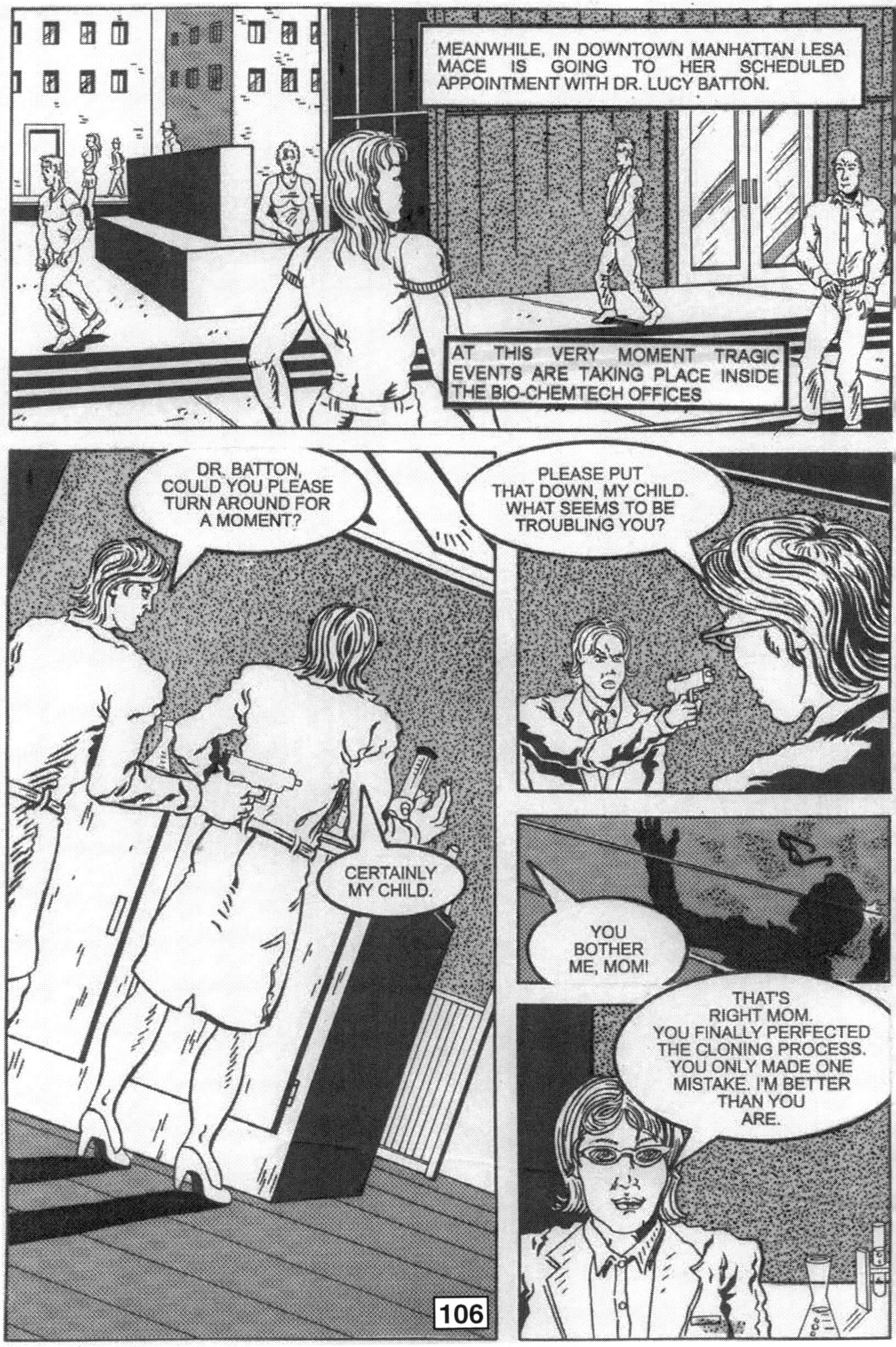
MEANWHILE, IN DOWNTOWN MANHATTAN LESA MACE IS GOING TO HER SCHEDULED APPOINTMENT WITH DR. LUCY BATTON.
AT THIS VERY MOMENT TRAGIC EVENTS ARE TAKING PLACE INSIDE THE BIO-CHEMTECH OFFICES
DR. BATTON, COULD YOU PLEASE TURN AROUND FOR A MOMENT?
CERTAINLY MY CHILD.
PLEASE PUT THAT DOWN, MY CHILD. WHAT SEEMS TO BE TROUBLING YOU?
YOU BOTHER ME, MOM!
THAT'S RIGHT MOM. YOU FINALLY PERFECTED THE CLONING PROCESS. YOU ONLY MADE ONE MISTAKE. I'M BETTER THAN YOU ARE.

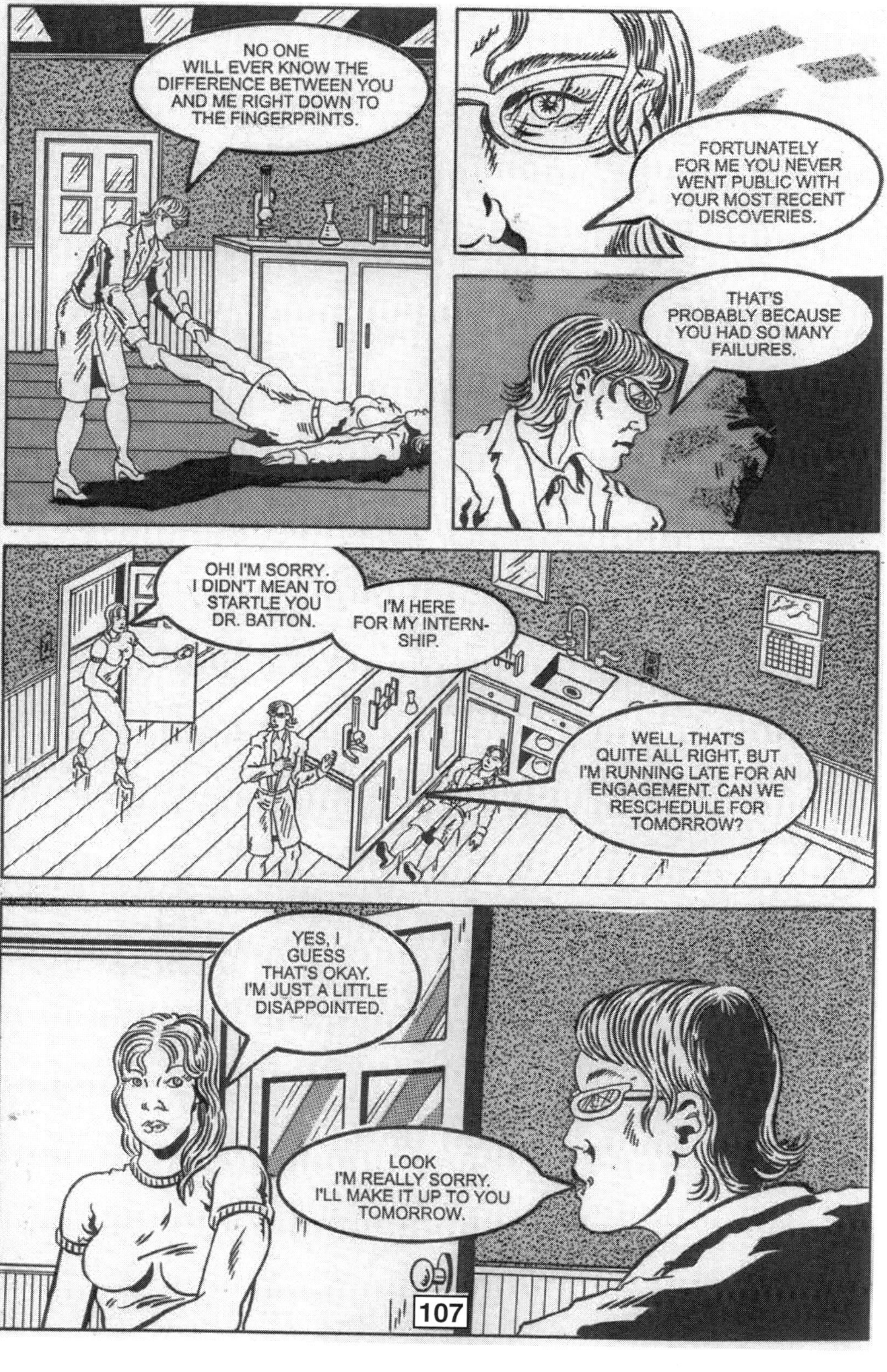
NO ONE WILL EVER KNOW THE DIFFERENCE BETWEEN YOU AND ME RIGHT DOWN TO THE FINGERPRINTS.
FORTUNATELY FOR ME YOU NEVER WENT PUBLIC WITH YOUR MOST RECENT DISCOVERIES.
THAT'S PROBABLY BECAUSE YOU HAD SO MANY FAILURES.
OH! I'M SORRY. I DIDN'T MEAN TO STARTLE YOU DR. BATTON.
I'M HERE FOR MY INTERN-SHIP.
WELL, THAT'S QUITE ALL RIGHT, BUT I'M RUNNING LATE FOR AN ENGAGEMENT. CAN WE RESCHEDULE FOR TOMORROW?
YES, I GUESS THAT'S OKAY. I'M JUST A LITTLE DISAPPOINTED.
LOOK I'M REALLY SORRY. I'LL MAKE IT UP TO YOU TOMORROW.

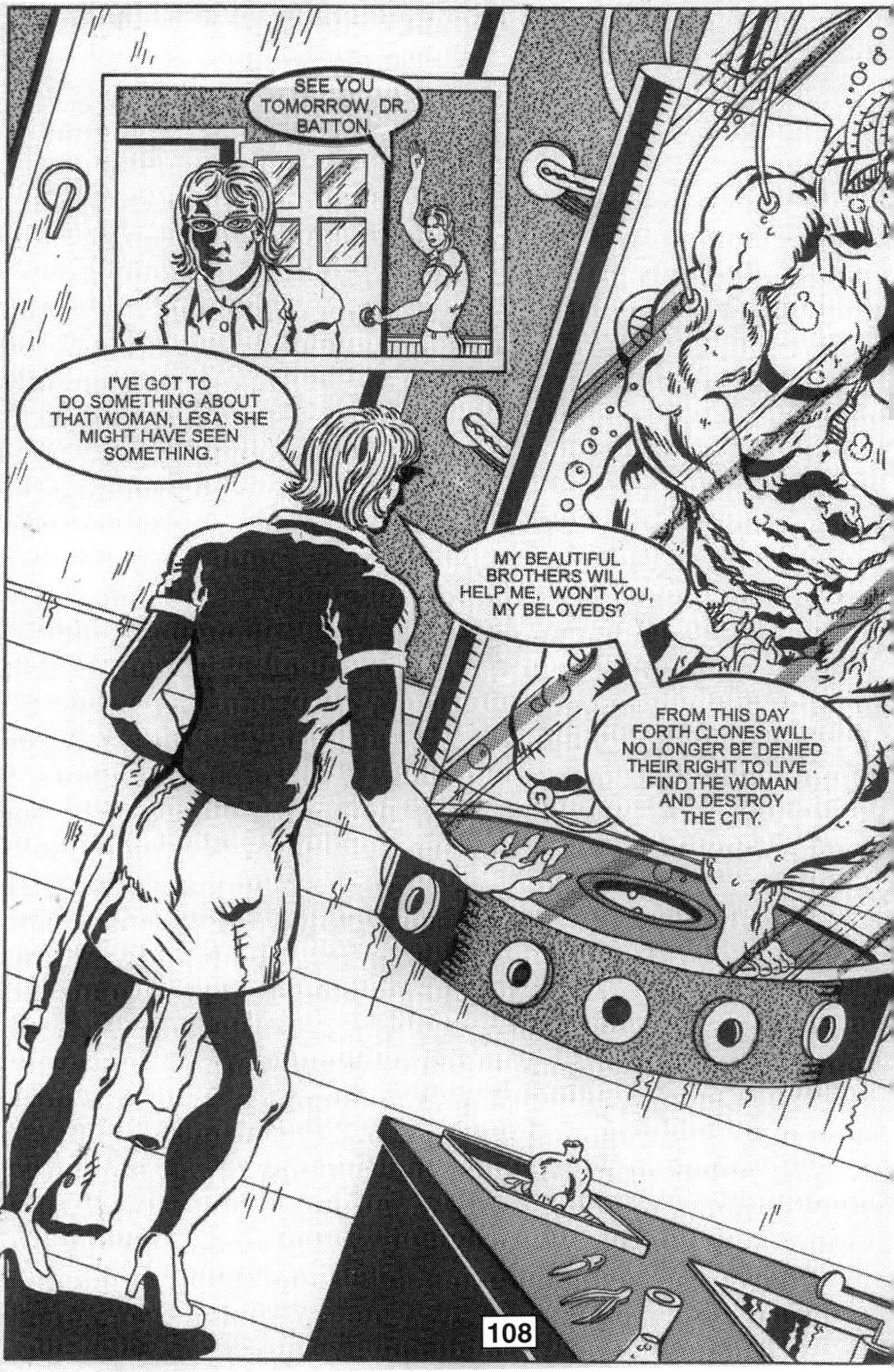
SEE YOU TOMORROW, DR. BATTON.
I'VE GOT TO DO SOMETHING ABOUT THAT WOMAN, LESA. SHE MIGHT HAVE SEEN SOMETHING.
MY BEAUTIFUL BROTHERS WILL HELP ME, WON'T YOU, MY BELOVEDS?
FROM THIS DAY FORTH CLONES WILL NO LONGER BE DENIED THEIR RIGHT TO LIVE . FIND THE WOMAN AND DESTROY THE CITY.

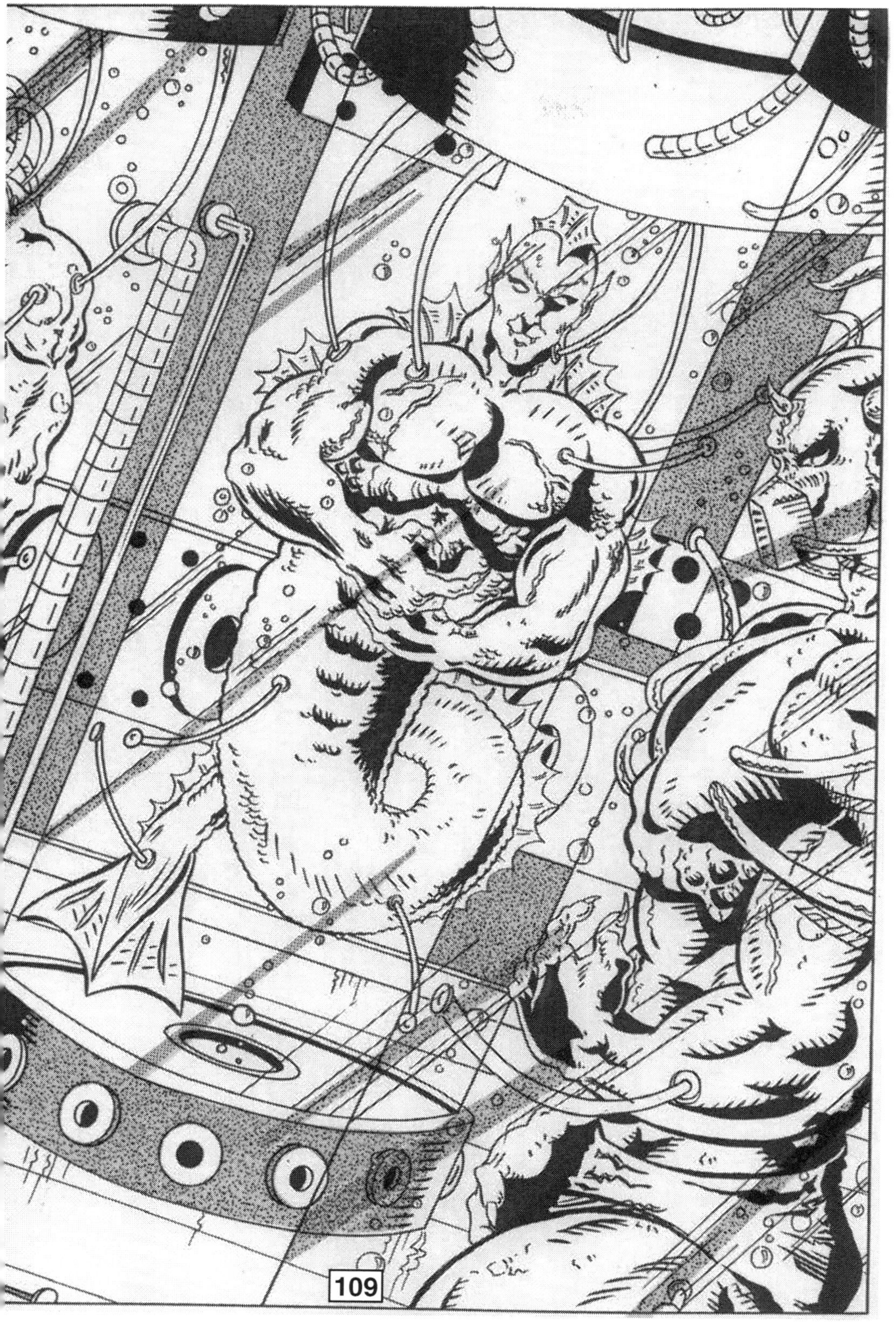

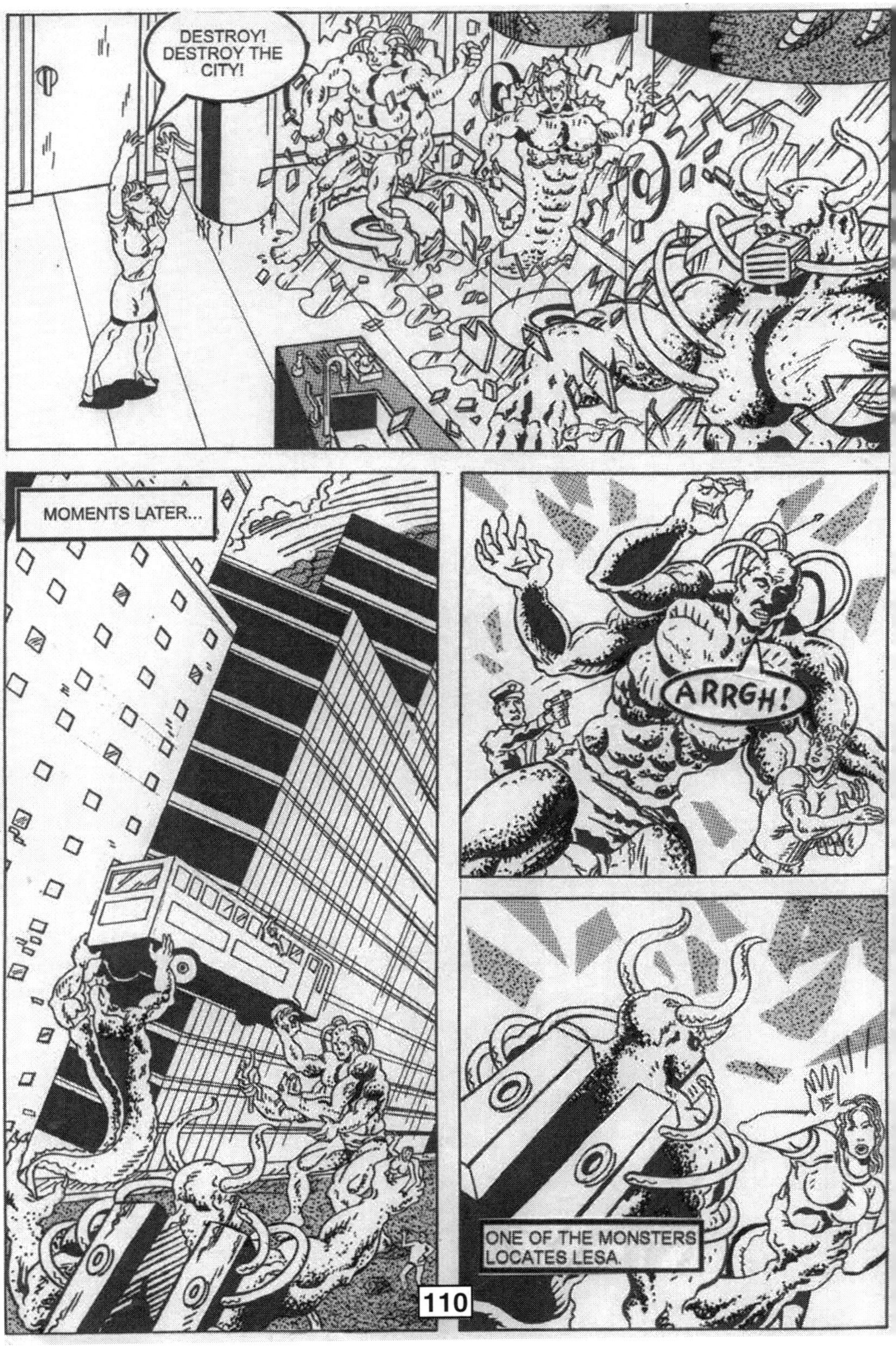
DESTROY! DESTROY THE CITY!
MOMENTS LATER...
ARRGH!
ONE OF THE MONSTERS LOCATES LESA.

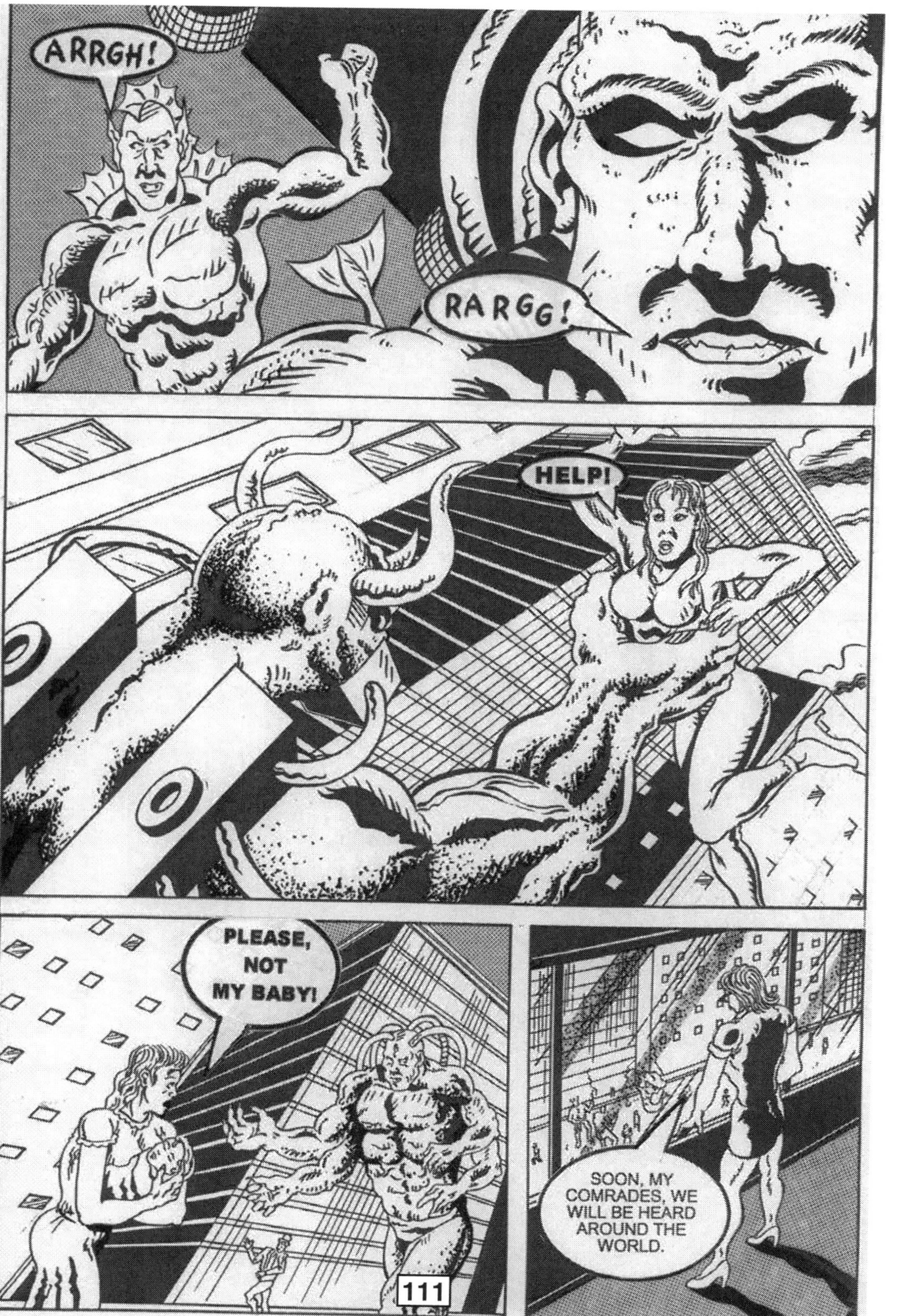
ARRGH!
RARGG!
HELP!
PLEASE, NOT MY BABY!
SOON, MY COMRADES, WE WILL BE HEARD AROUND THE WORLD.

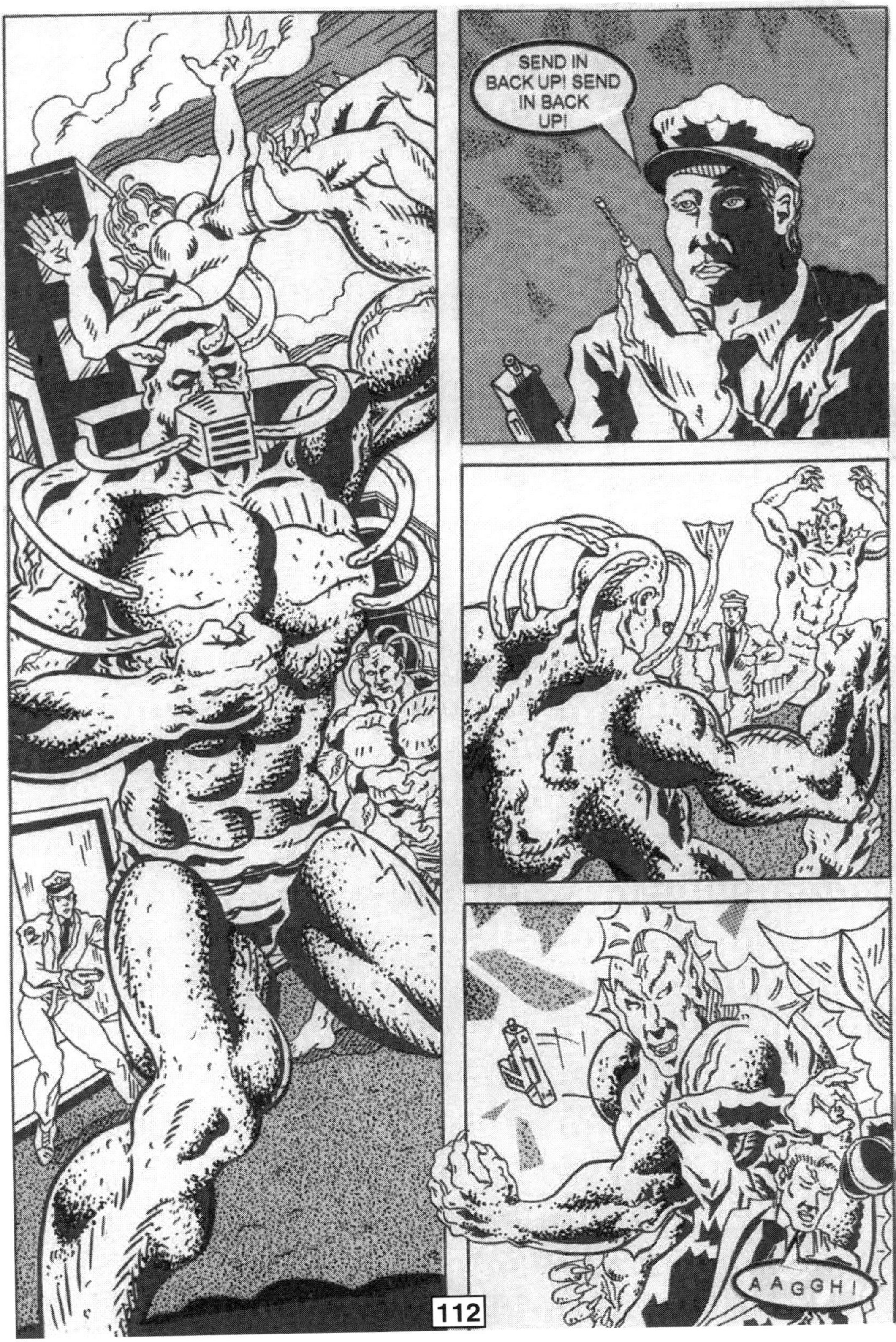
SEND IN BACK UP! SEND IN BACK UP!
AAGGH!

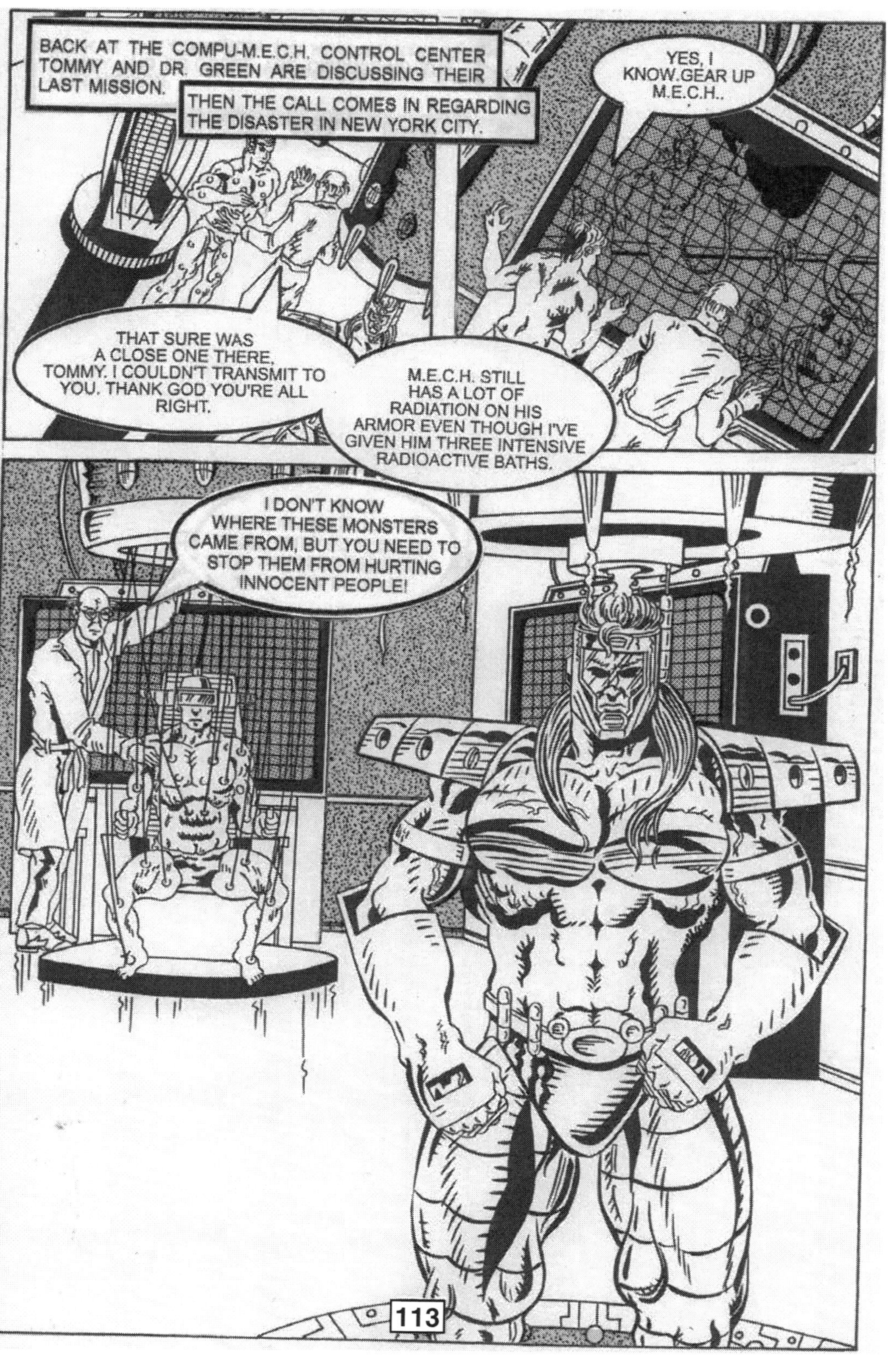
BACK AT THE COMPU-M.E.C.H. CONTROL CENTER TOMMY AND DR. GREEN ARE DISCUSSING THEIR LAST MISSION.
THEN THE CALL COMES IN REGARDING THE DISASTER IN NEW YORK CITY.
YES, I KNOW.GEAR UP M.E.C.H..
THAT SURE WAS A CLOSE ONE THERE, TOMMY. I COULDN'T TRANSMIT TO YOU. THANK GOD YOU'RE ALL RIGHT.
M.E.C.H. STILL HAS A LOT OF RADIATION ON HIS ARMOR EVEN THOUGH I'VE GIVEN HIM THREE INTENSIVE RADIOACTIVE BATHS.
I DON'T KNOW WHERE THESE MONSTERS CAME FROM, BUT YOU NEED TO STOP THEM FROM HURTING INNOCENT PEOPLE!

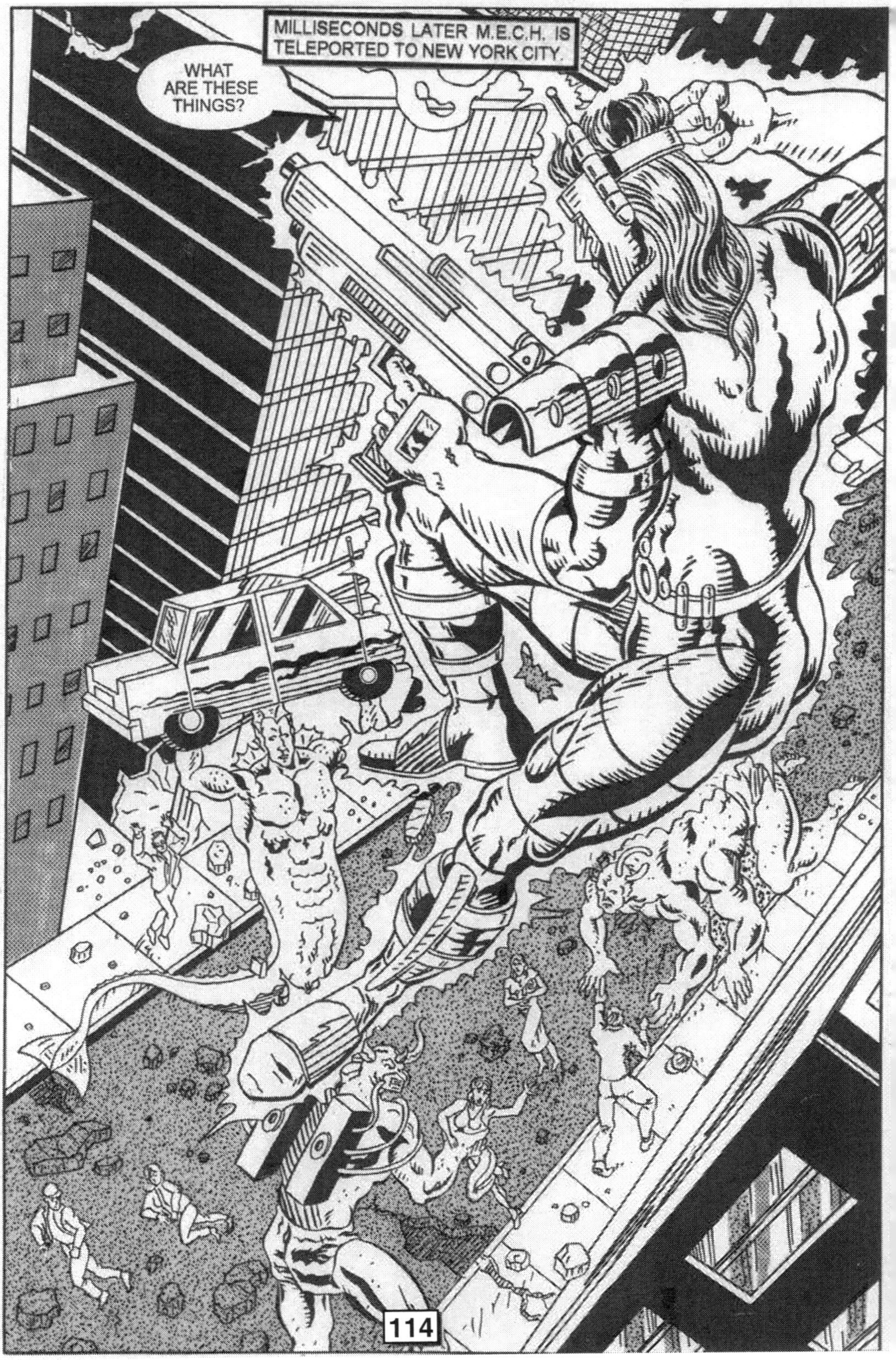
MILLISECONDS LATER M.E.C.H. IS TELEPORTED TO NEW YORK CITY.
WHAT ARE THESE THINGS?

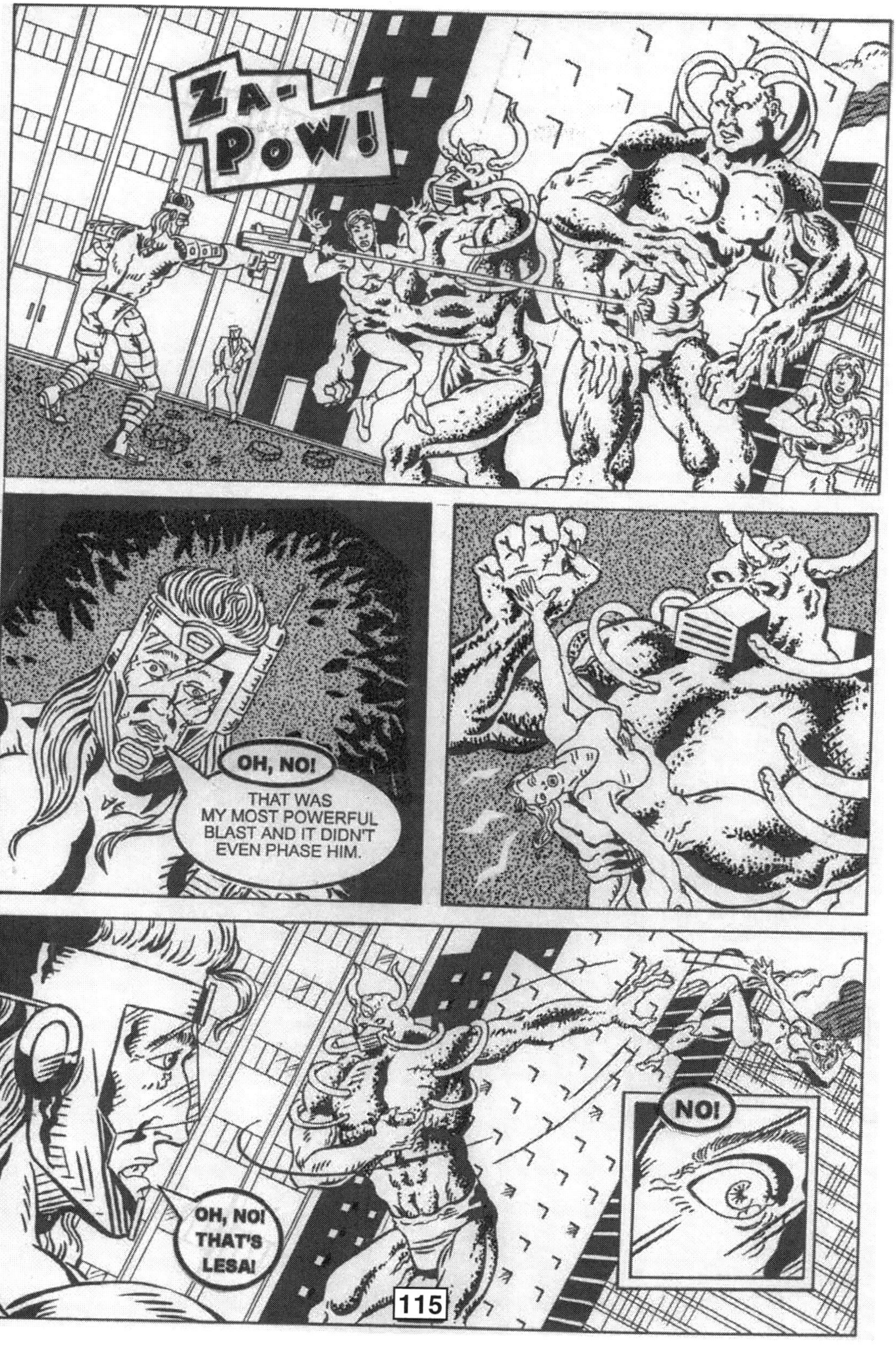
ZA-POW!
OH, NO!
THAT WAS MY MOST POWERFUL BLAST AND IT DIDN'T EVEN PHASE HIM.
OH, NO! THAT'S LESA!
NO!

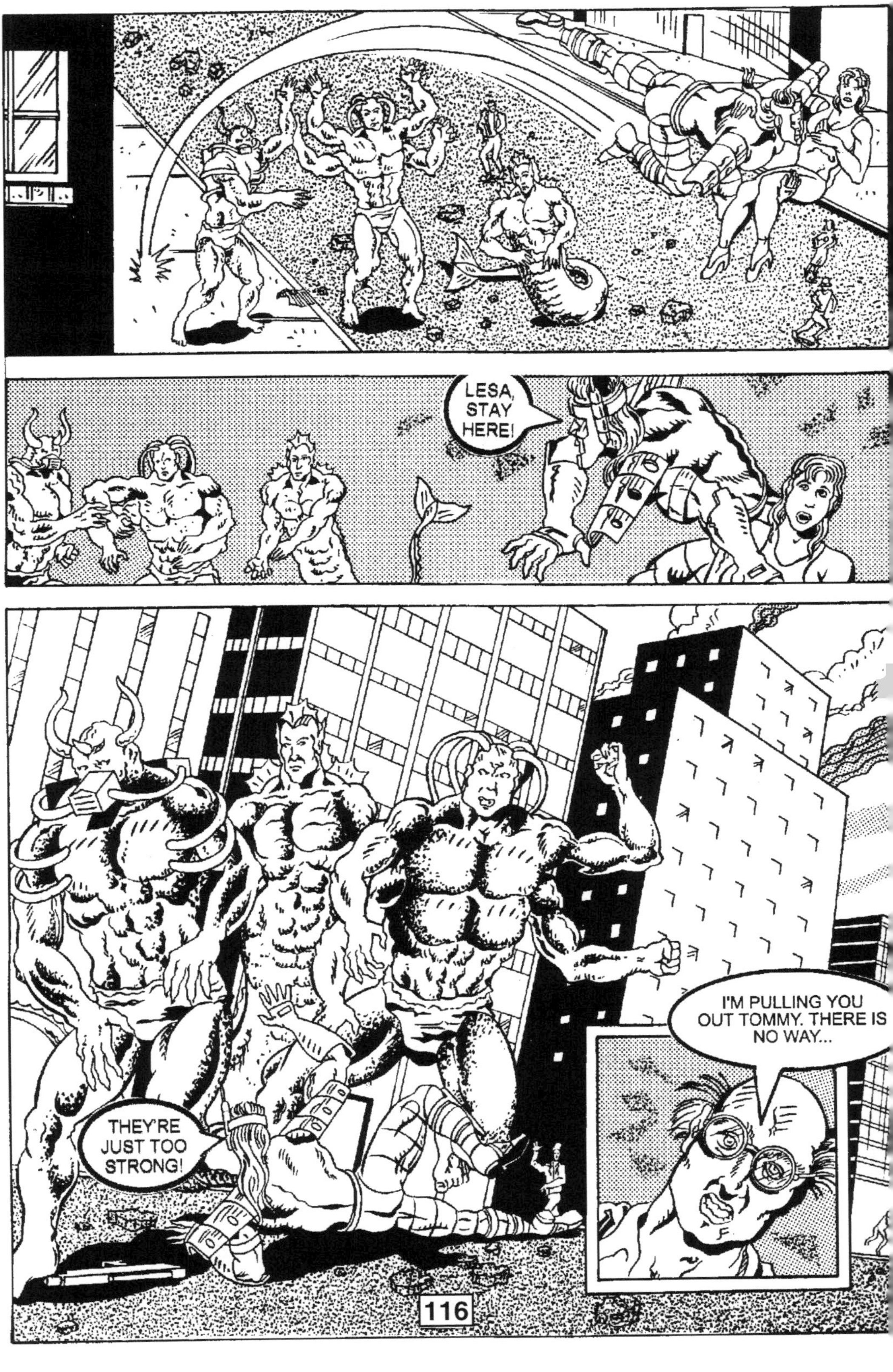
LESA, STAY HERE!
THEY'RE JUST TOO STRONG!
I'M PULLING YOU OUT TOMMY. THERE IS NO WAY...

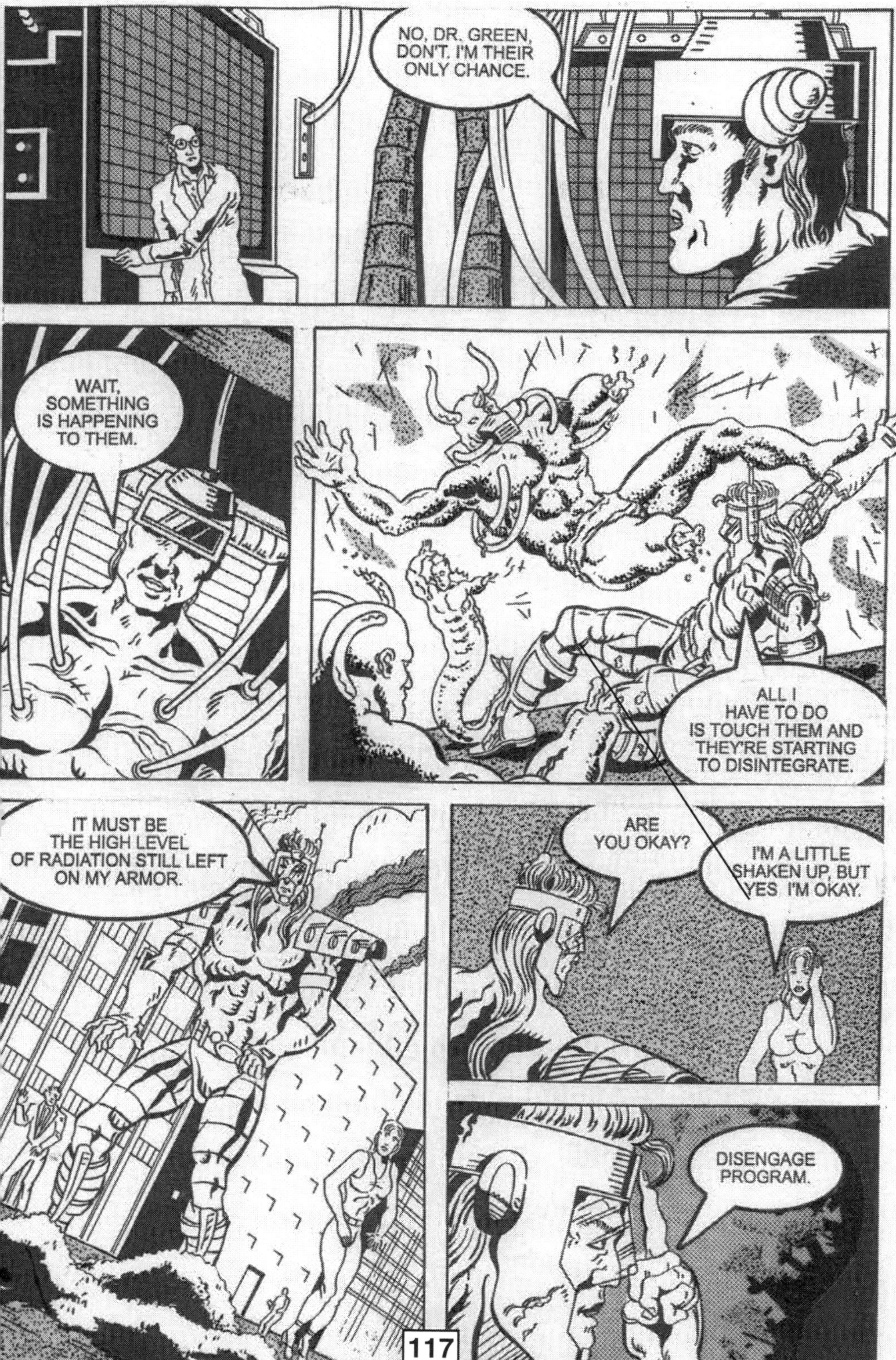
NO, DR. GREEN, DON'T. I'M THEIR ONLY CHANCE.
WAIT, SOMETHING IS HAPPENING TO THEM.
ALL I HAVE TO DO IS TOUCH THEM AND THEY'RE STARTING TO DISINTEGRATE.
IT MUST BE THE HIGH LEVEL OF RADIATION STILL LEFT ON MY ARMOR.
ARE YOU OKAY?
I'M A LITTLE SHAKEN UP, BUT YES. I'M OKAY.
DISENGAGE PROGRAM.

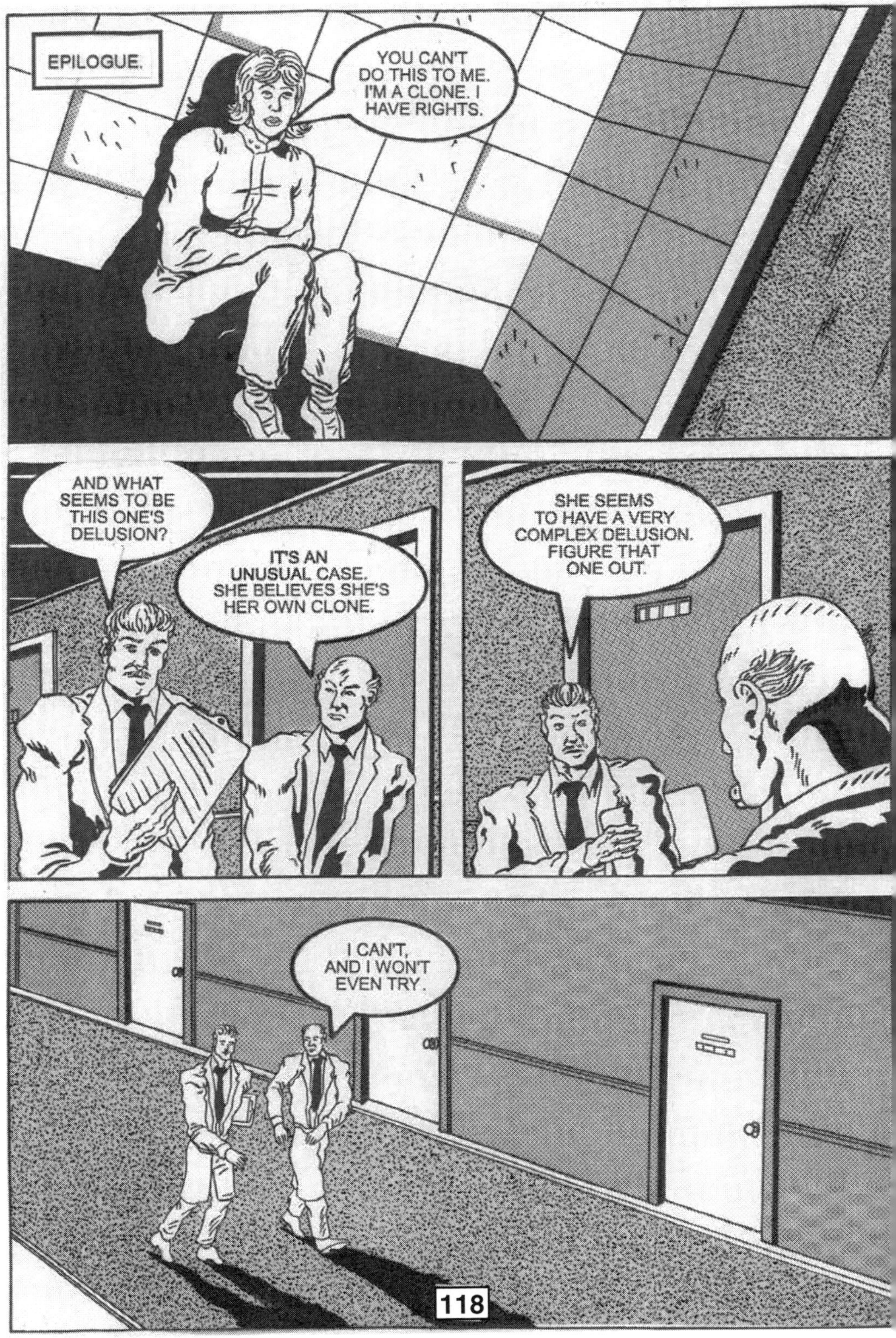
EPILOGUE.
YOU CAN'T DO THIS TO ME. I'M A CLONE. I HAVE RIGHTS.
AND WHAT SEEMS TO BE THIS ONE'S DELUSION?
IT'S AN UNUSUAL CASE. SHE BELIEVES SHE'S HER OWN CLONE.
SHE SEEMS TO HAVE A VERY COMPLEX DELUSION. FIGURE THAT ONE OUT.
I CAN'T, AND I WON'T EVEN TRY.

BACK UP ISSUE #4!

By Theodore Raymond Riddle

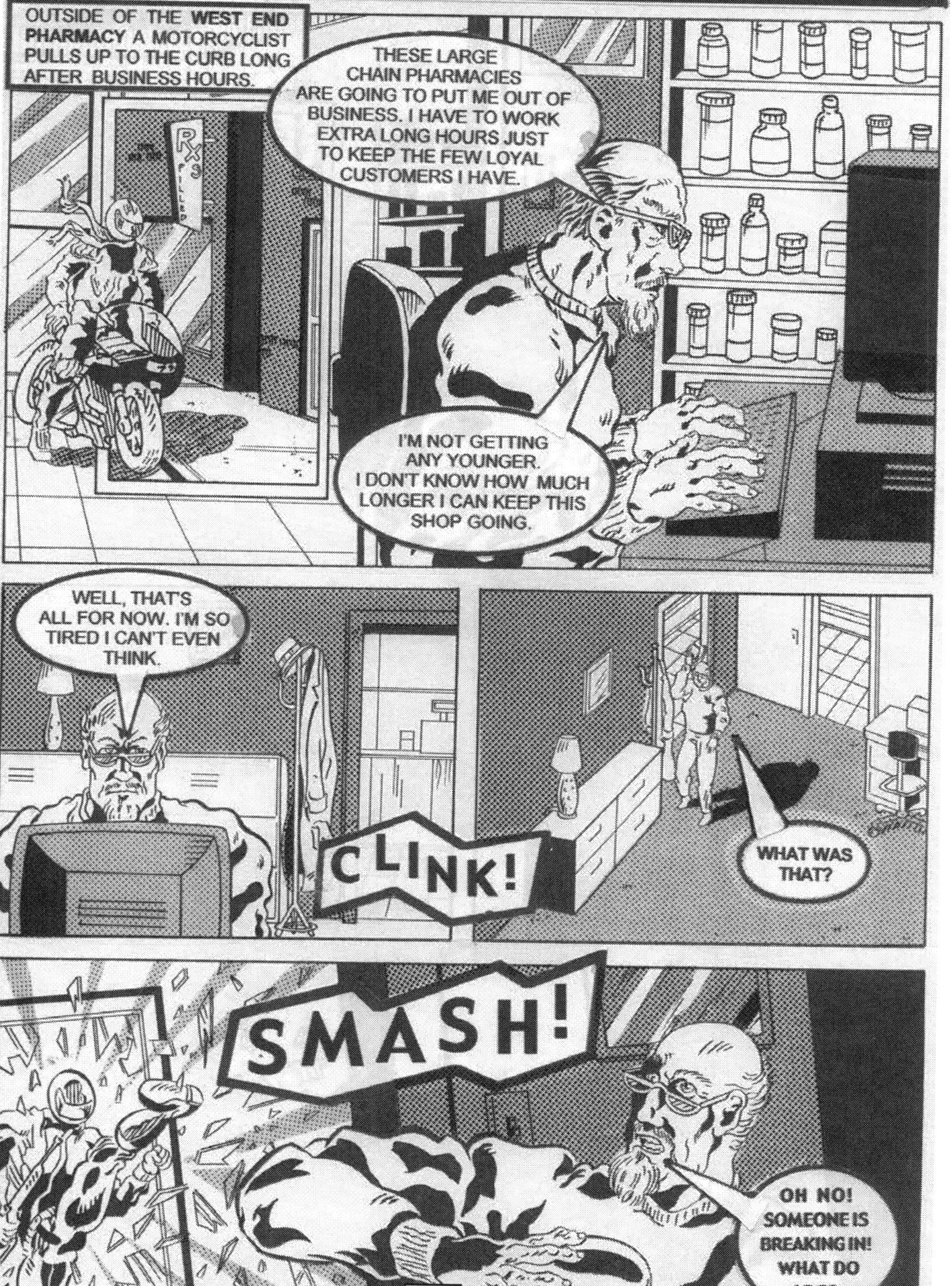

OUTSIDE OF THE **WEST END PHARMACY** A MOTORCYCLIST PULLS UP TO THE CURB LONG AFTER BUSINESS HOURS.
THESE LARGE CHAIN PHARMACIES ARE GOING TO PUT ME OUT OF BUSINESS. I HAVE TO WORK EXTRA LONG HOURS JUST TO KEEP THE FEW LOYAL CUSTOMERS I HAVE.
I'M NOT GETTING ANY YOUNGER. I DON'T KNOW HOW MUCH LONGER I CAN KEEP THIS SHOP GOING.
WELL, THAT'S ALL FOR NOW. I'M SO TIRED I CAN'T EVEN THINK.
CLINK!
WHAT WAS THAT?
SMASH!
OH NO! SOMEONE IS BREAKING IN! WHAT DO I DO?

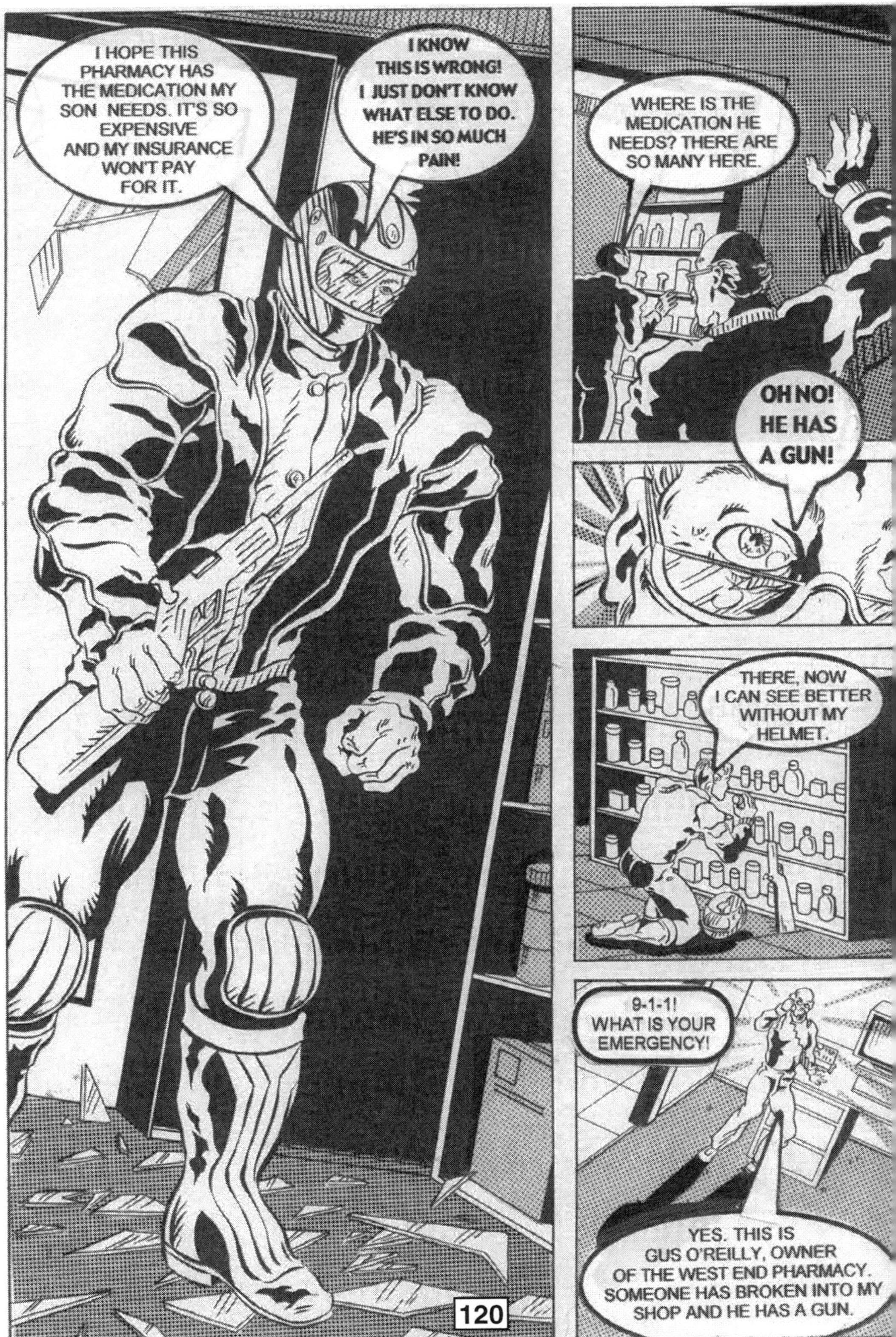
I HOPE THIS PHARMACY HAS THE MEDICATION MY SON NEEDS. IT'S SO EXPENSIVE AND MY INSURANCE WON'T PAY FOR IT.
I KNOW THIS IS WRONG! I JUST DON'T KNOW WHAT ELSE TO DO. HE'S IN SO MUCH PAIN!
WHERE IS THE MEDICATION HE NEEDS? THERE ARE SO MANY HERE.
OH NO! HE HAS A GUN!
THERE, NOW I CAN SEE BETTER WITHOUT MY HELMET.
9-1-1! WHAT IS YOUR EMERGENCY!
YES. THIS IS GUS O'REILLY, OWNER OF THE WEST END PHARMACY. SOMEONE HAS BROKEN INTO MY SHOP AND HE HAS A GUN.

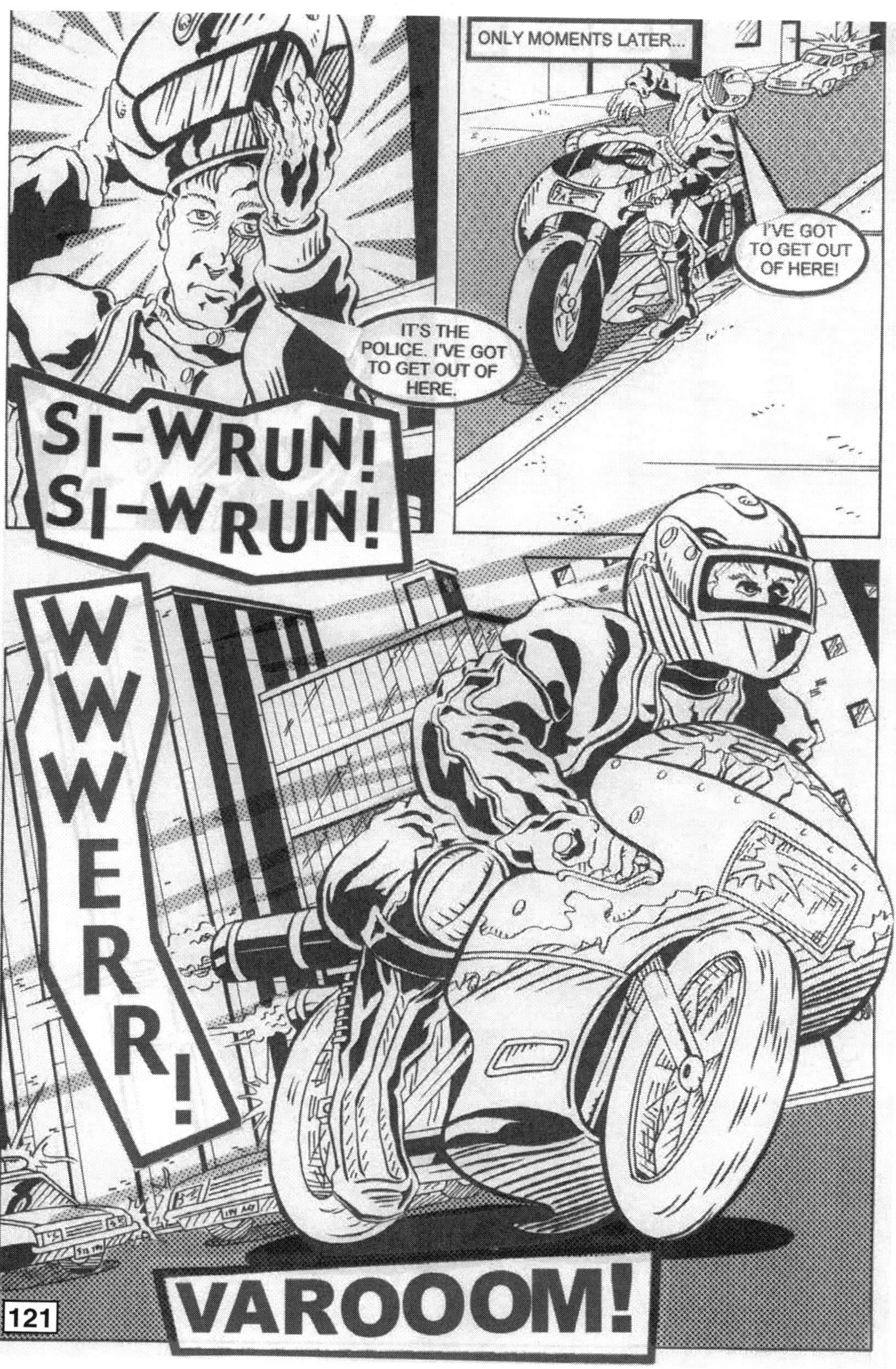

ONLY MOMENTS LATER...
I'VE GOT TO GET OUT OF HERE!
IT'S THE POLICE. I'VE GOT TO GET OUT OF HERE.
SI-WRUN! SI-WRUN!
WWWERR!
VAROOOM!

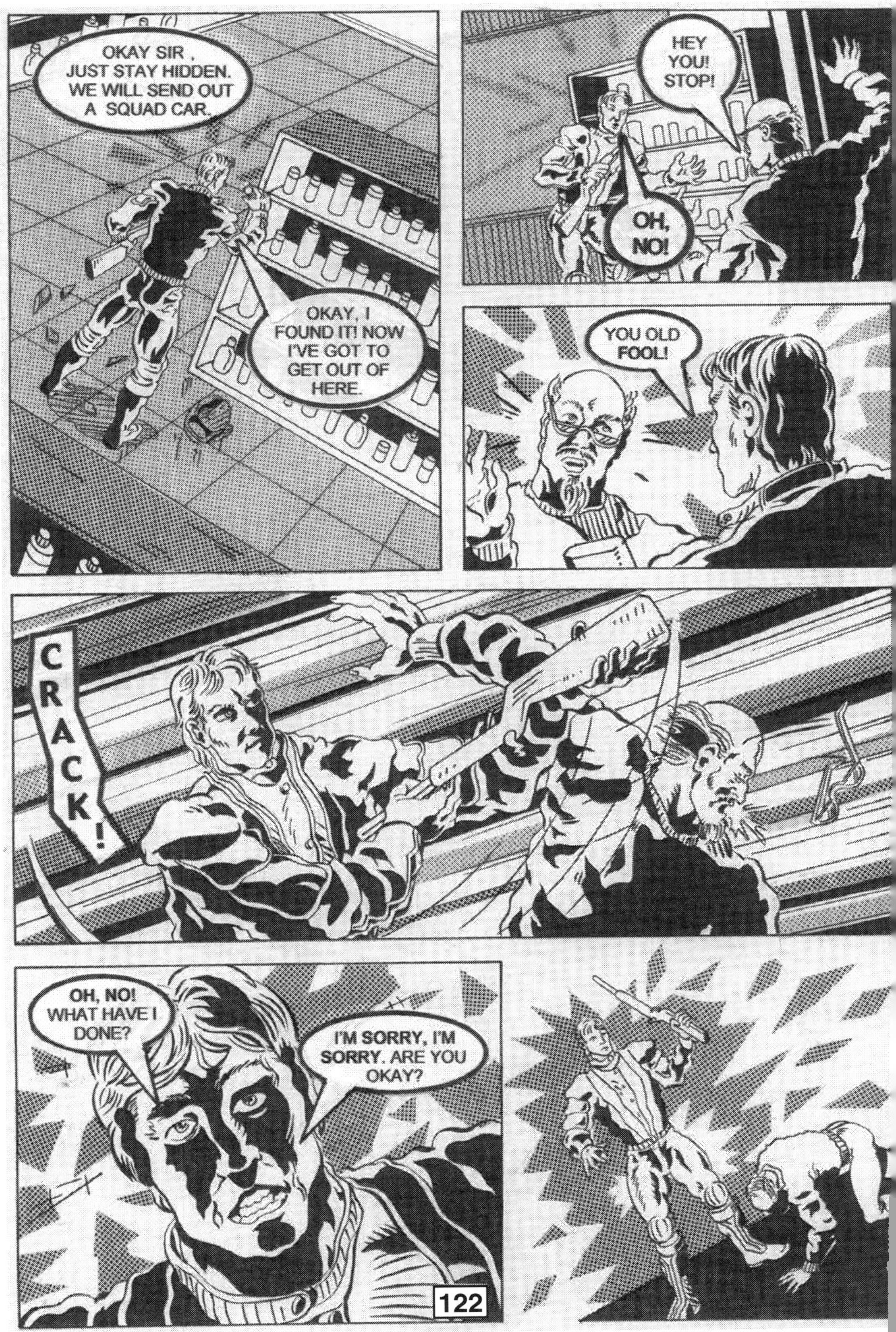
OKAY SIR , JUST STAY HIDDEN. WE WILL SEND OUT A SQUAD CAR.
OKAY, I FOUND IT! NOW I'VE GOT TO GET OUT OF HERE.
HEY YOU! STOP!
OH, NO!
YOU OLD FOOL!
CRACK!
OH, NO! WHAT HAVE I DONE?
I'M SORRY, I'M SORRY. ARE YOU OKAY?

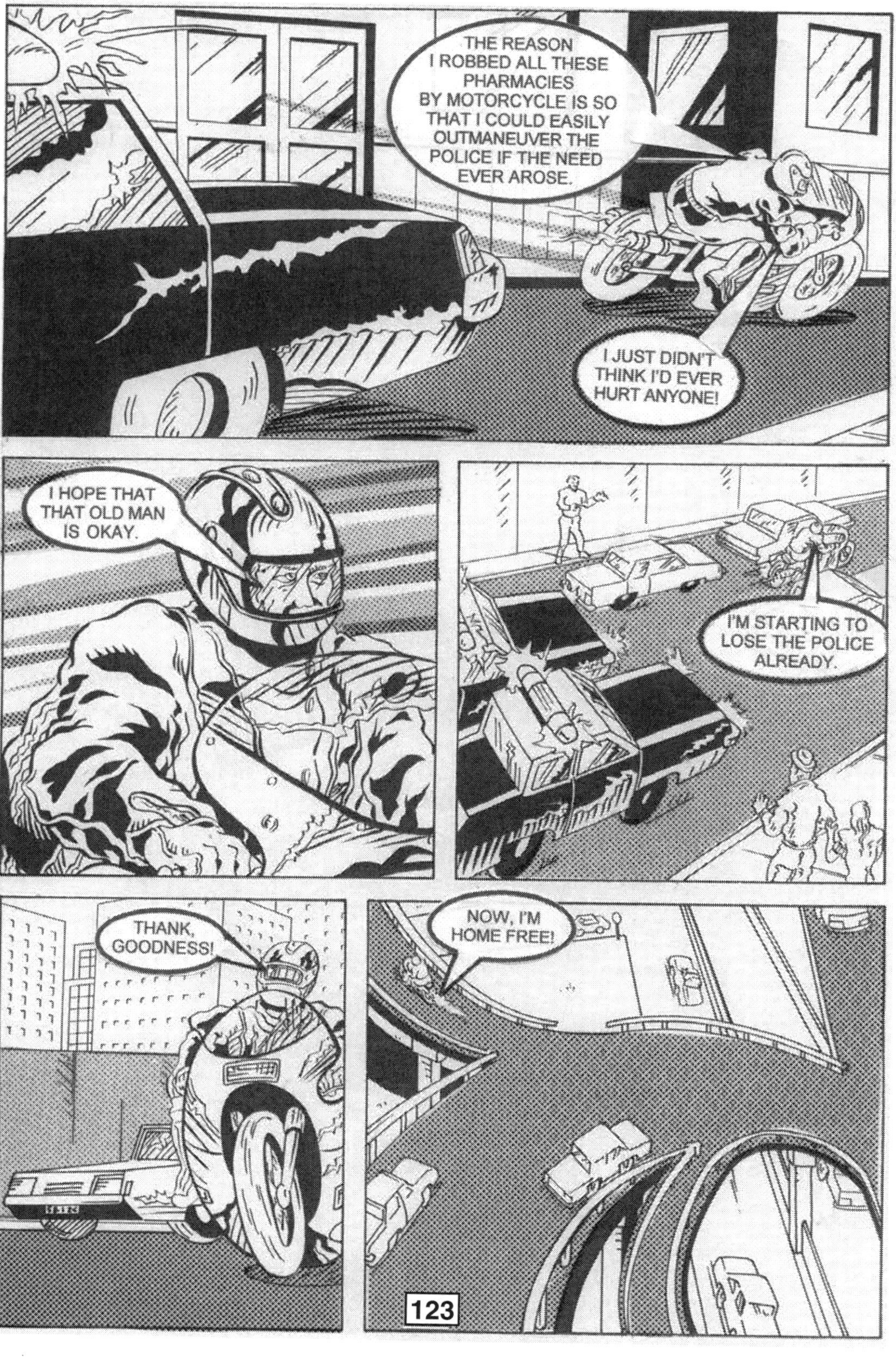
THE REASON I ROBBED ALL THESE PHARMACIES BY MOTORCYCLE IS SO THAT I COULD EASILY OUTMANEUVER THE POLICE IF THE NEED EVER AROSE.
I JUST DIDN'T THINK I'D EVER HURT ANYONE!
I HOPE THAT THAT OLD MAN IS OKAY.
I'M STARTING TO LOSE THE POLICE ALREADY.
THANK, GOODNESS!
NOW, I'M HOME FREE!

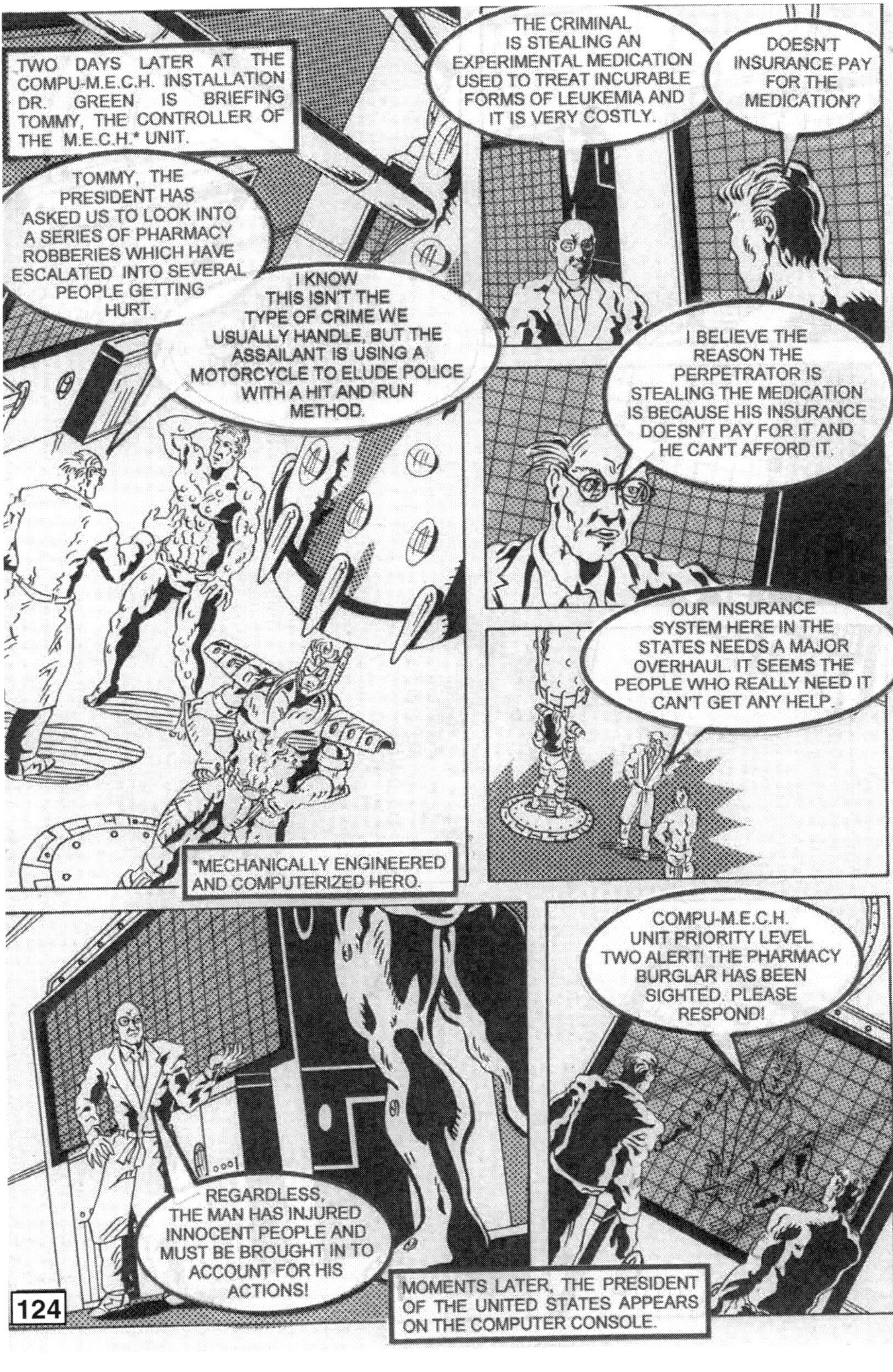

TWO DAYS LATER AT THE COMPU-M.E.C.H. INSTALLATION DR. GREEN IS BRIEFING TOMMY, THE CONTROLLER OF THE M.E.C.H.* UNIT.
TOMMY, THE PRESIDENT HAS ASKED US TO LOOK INTO A SERIES OF PHARMACY ROBBERIES WHICH HAVE ESCALATED INTO SEVERAL PEOPLE GETTING HURT.
I KNOW THIS ISN'T THE TYPE OF CRIME WE USUALLY HANDLE, BUT THE ASSAILANT IS USING A MOTORCYCLE TO ELUDE POLICE WITH A HIT AND RUN METHOD.
*MECHANICALLY ENGINEERED AND COMPUTERIZED HERO.
THE CRIMINAL IS STEALING AN EXPERIMENTAL MEDICATION USED TO TREAT INCURABLE FORMS OF LEUKEMIA AND IT IS VERY COSTLY.
DOESN'T INSURANCE PAY FOR THE MEDICATION?
I BELIEVE THE REASON THE PERPETRATOR IS STEALING THE MEDICATION IS BECAUSE HIS INSURANCE DOESN'T PAY FOR IT AND HE CAN'T AFFORD IT.
OUR INSURANCE SYSTEM HERE IN THE STATES NEEDS A MAJOR OVERHAUL. IT SEEMS THE PEOPLE WHO REALLY NEED IT CAN'T GET ANY HELP.
REGARDLESS, THE MAN HAS INJURED INNOCENT PEOPLE AND MUST BE BROUGHT IN TO ACCOUNT FOR HIS ACTIONS!
COMPU-M.E.C.H. UNIT PRIORITY LEVEL TWO ALERT! THE PHARMACY BURGLAR HAS BEEN SIGHTED. PLEASE RESPOND!
MOMENTS LATER, THE PRESIDENT OF THE UNITED STATES APPEARS ON THE COMPUTER CONSOLE.

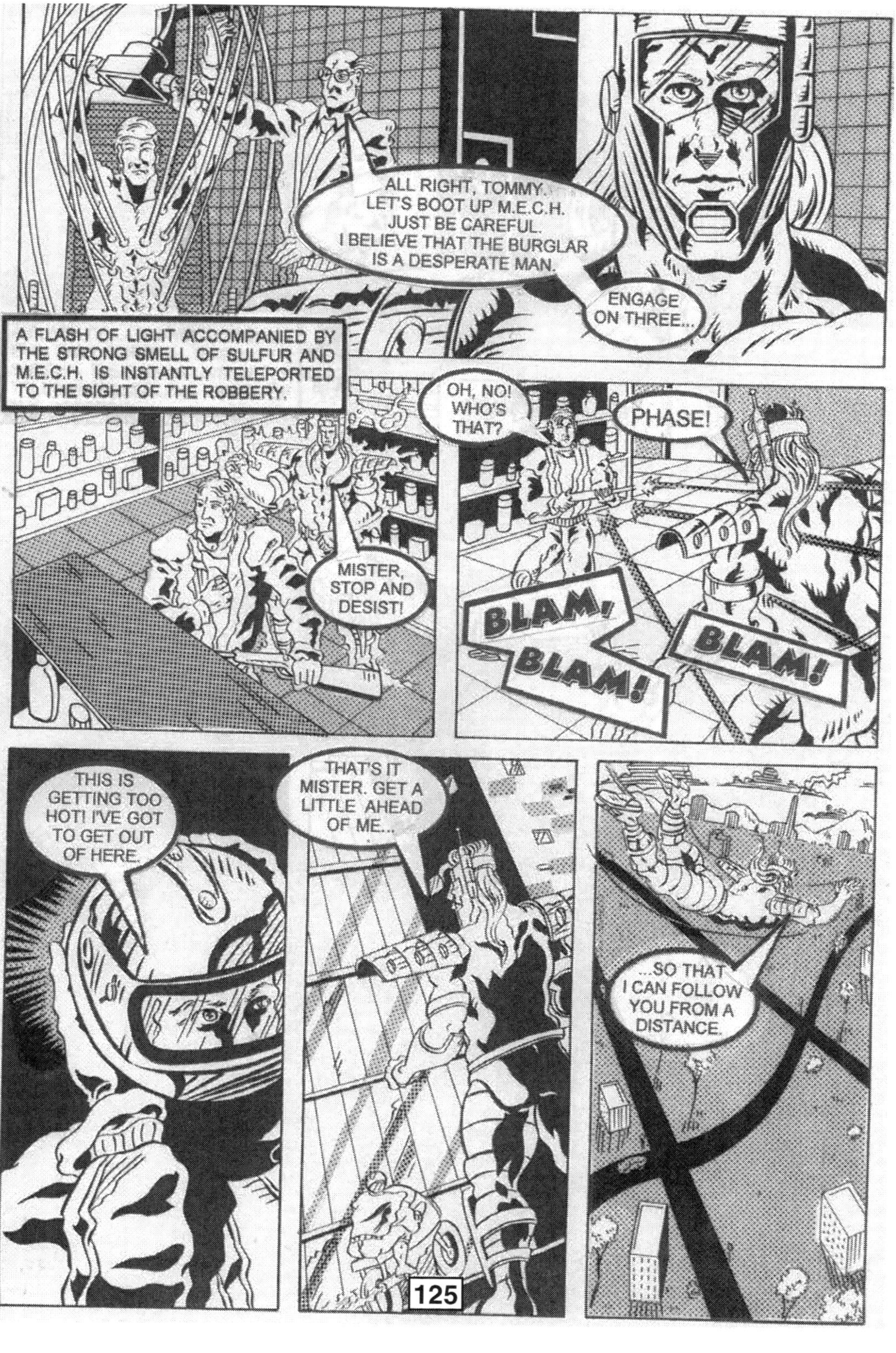
ALL RIGHT, TOMMY. LET'S BOOT UP M.E.C.H. JUST BE CAREFUL. I BELIEVE THAT THE BURGLAR IS A DESPERATE MAN.
ENGAGE ON THREE...
A FLASH OF LIGHT ACCOMPANIED BY THE STRONG SMELL OF SULFUR AND M.E.C.H. IS INSTANTLY TELEPORTED TO THE SIGHT OF THE ROBBERY.
MISTER, STOP AND DESIST!
OH, NO! WHO'S THAT?
PHASE!
BLAM,
BLAM!
BLAM!
THIS IS GETTING TOO HOT! I'VE GOT TO GET OUT OF HERE.
THAT'S IT MISTER. GET A LITTLE AHEAD OF ME...
...SO THAT I CAN FOLLOW YOU FROM A DISTANCE.

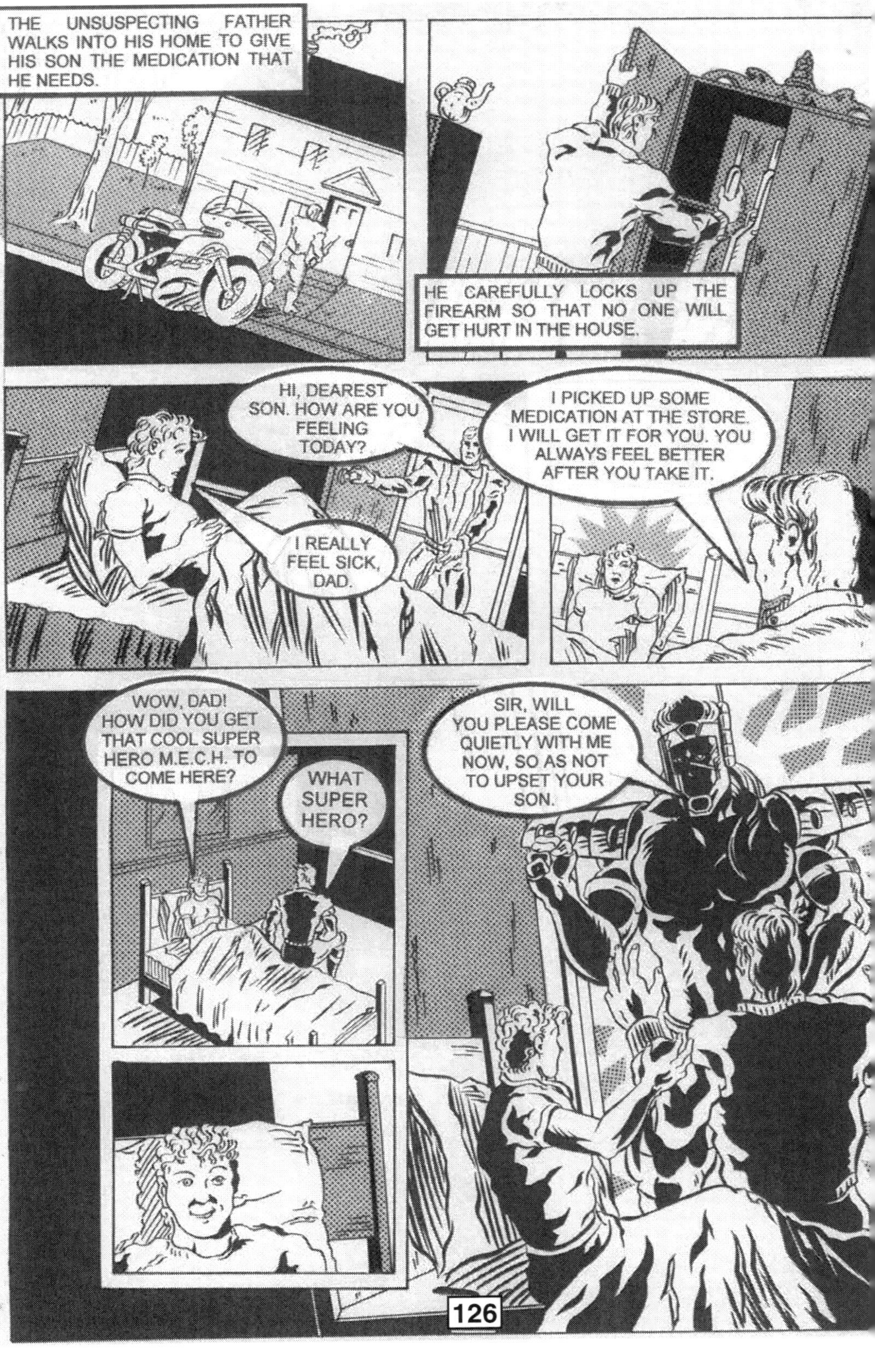
THE UNSUSPECTING FATHER WALKS INTO HIS HOME TO GIVE HIS SON THE MEDICATION THAT HE NEEDS.
HE CAREFULLY LOCKS UP THE FIREARM SO THAT NO ONE WILL GET HURT IN THE HOUSE.
HI, DEAREST SON. HOW ARE YOU FEELING TODAY?
I REALLY FEEL SICK, DAD.
I PICKED UP SOME MEDICATION AT THE STORE. I WILL GET IT FOR YOU. YOU ALWAYS FEEL BETTER AFTER YOU TAKE IT.
WOW, DAD! HOW DID YOU GET THAT COOL SUPER HERO M.E.C.H. TO COME HERE?
WHAT SUPER HERO?
SIR, WILL YOU PLEASE COME QUIETLY WITH ME NOW, SO AS NOT TO UPSET YOUR SON.

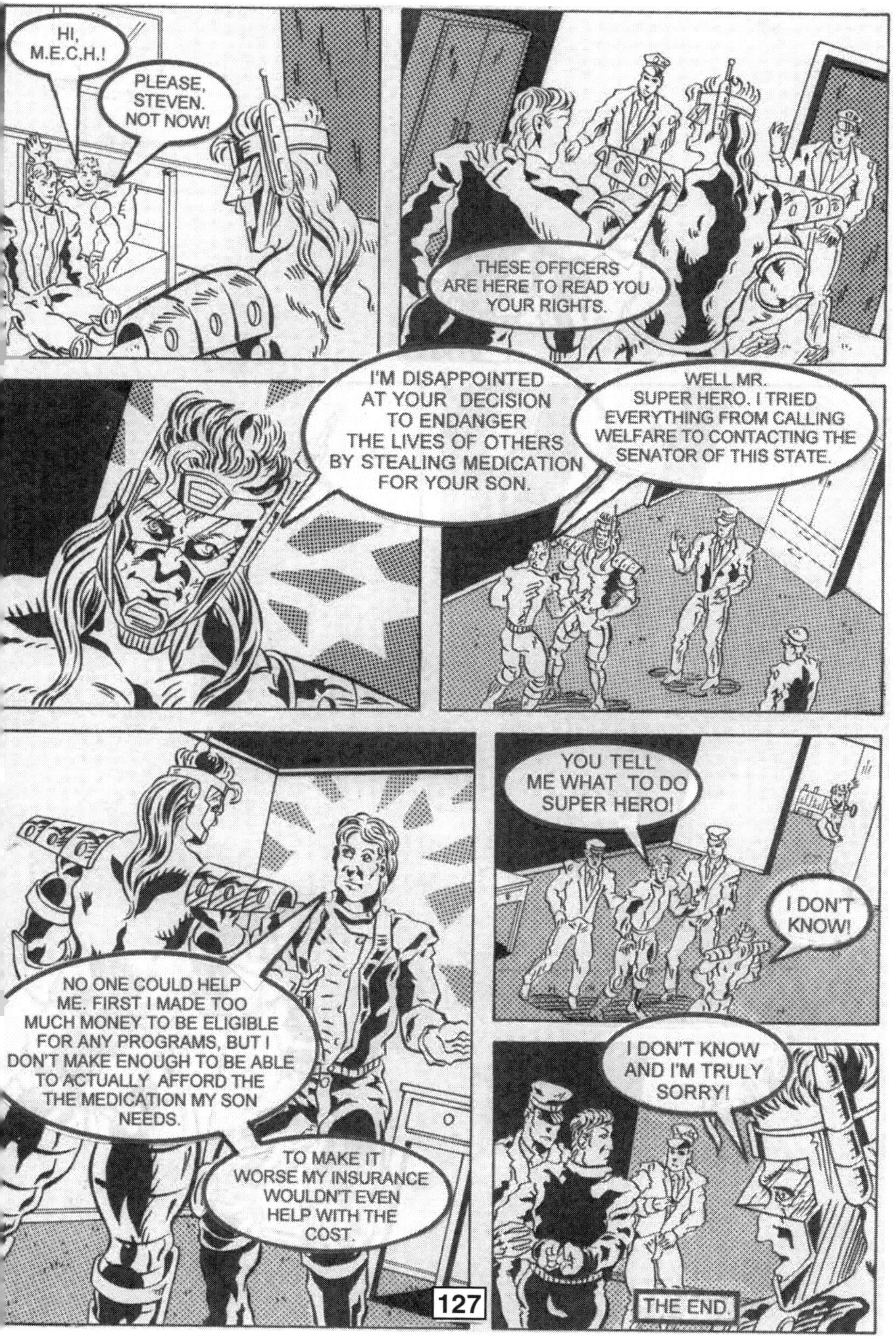
HI, M.E.C.H.!
PLEASE, STEVEN. NOT NOW!
THESE OFFICERS ARE HERE TO READ YOU YOUR RIGHTS.
I'M DISAPPOINTED AT YOUR DECISION TO ENDANGER THE LIVES OF OTHERS BY STEALING MEDICATION FOR YOUR SON.
WELL MR. SUPER HERO. I TRIED EVERYTHING FROM CALLING WELFARE TO CONTACTING THE SENATOR OF THIS STATE.
NO ONE COULD HELP ME. FIRST I MADE TOO MUCH MONEY TO BE ELIGIBLE FOR ANY PROGRAMS, BUT I DON'T MAKE ENOUGH TO BE ABLE TO ACTUALLY AFFORD THE THE MEDICATION MY SON NEEDS.
TO MAKE IT WORSE MY INSURANCE WOULDN'T EVEN HELP WITH THE COST.
YOU TELL ME WHAT TO DO SUPER HERO!
I DON'T KNOW!
I DON'T KNOW AND I'M TRULY SORRY!
THE END.

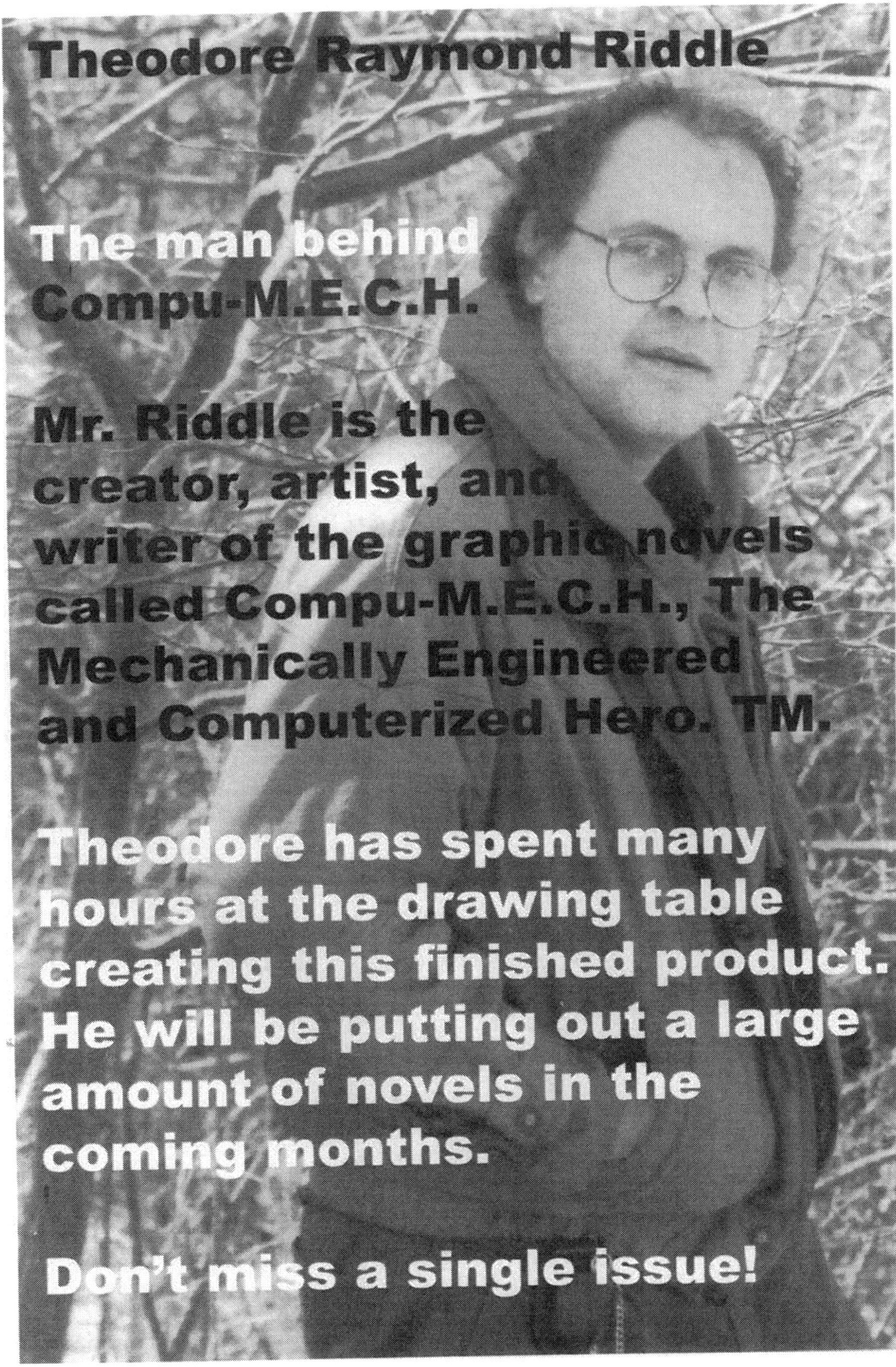
Theodore Raymond Riddle
The man behind
Compu-M.E.C.H.
Mr. Riddle is the
creator, artist, and
writer of the graphic novels
called Compu-M.E.C.H., The
Mechanically Engineered
and Computerized Hero. TM.
Theodore has spent many
hours at the drawing table
creating this finished product.
He will be putting out a large
amount of novels in the
coming months.
Don't miss a single issue!